Crystals Healing and Folklore

David Rankine

www.capallbann.co.uk

Crystals Healing and Folklore

©2002 David Rankine

ISBN 186163 200 2

Cover design by Paul Mason
Artwork by Sorita

Published by:

Capall Bann Publishing
Auton Farm
Milverton
Somerset
TA4 1NE

Dedication

To Anup,
Master of Secrets
Jackal-headed God
Walker between the Worlds
Your Priest offers eternal love and reverence

ACKNOWLEDGMENTS

For help with the text and material:

Sorita, Graham Jebbett, Phil & Tracy Bartlett, Lene Janzon, Caroline Wise, Aleq Grai, Chris Breen, Knoedel Kempers, Phil & Michelle Lightwood-Jones, Pandora Stevens, Richard Ward, David Goddard, Richard Andersen - Thank you.

Contents

Introduction

In this modern age, we seem to have rediscovered crystals. Everywhere you look nowadays people wear crystals and have them around their houses for ornamentation or use. Yet man's fascination with crystals stretches back to his very beginnings. Examine every culture and religion, somewhere you will find crystals being used symbolically, decoratively or practically.

As you will see, many crystals have been used since the dawn of man, and amulets made from crystals appear at least as far back as 3000 BCE, and form an important part of our heritage. Conversely some stones have only been discovered in the last century or two, and for this reason there is very little attributed to them in the way of myth or folklore, as we discover their uses through experience.

This book endeavours to cover the folklore and myths associated with crystals, as well as their symbolism and ways of working with them. Due to the universal use of crystals through different cultures and religions, you will find information concerning the use of crystals in many different spiritual systems contained within these pages.

What is a crystal? Dictionaries offer definitions like "A mineral formed in a definite geometric pattern", which whilst accurate do not give a feeling of what a crystal is. A crystal is an ordered collection of elements, forming (often) beautiful solid structures, which can be used very effectively to gather and to direct energy.

1

This is why ancient man used them for amulets and healing, and modern scientists use them for such precise functions as lasers (all the best ones use ruby as their focus), computers (the silicon chip), wirelesses (quartz to modulate the signal) and watches (tiny diamonds).

Crystals have become so much a part of our society that it is easy to overlook their importance in our lives, and our language. Even our speech is full of phrases mentioning crystals, like "Diamonds are a girl's best friend" and "Cast not your pearls before swine".

I hope that when you read this book, it will inspire you to appreciate anew the beauty and diversity of the mineral kingdom and man's enduring relationship with it.

David Rankine
September 2001

Crystals Since the Dawn of Time

Though crystals are considered by some people to be symbolic of the "New Age", they have been used since man could wield tools, and possibly even before. Here is a brief timeline BCE to give an indication of the extensive scale of crystal use by man.

75000 BCE   Rock crystal (quartz) decorative or possibly amuletic objects have been found in France, Spain and Switzerland dating to this period. Ivory, stone, bone and horn carved objects also found.

30000 BCE   Pyrite objects/amulets dating to this time found in caves in Europe.

25000 BCE   Amethyst and coral beads found in France used in decoration dating to this time.

20000 BCE   Agate objects found in France used in decoration or as amulets dating to this time.

7000 BCE   Carnelian and rock crystal (quartz) beads made in Mesopotamia (Iraq).

                     Copper being mined in Eastern Anatolia.

5300 BCE   Turquoise being mined for use in Mesopotamia

5000 BCE	Engraved cylinder seals made using crystals such as steatite and marble and used for identification of goods in Sumeria/Babylon. Gold, silver, copper and lead being used in pre-Dynastic Egypt.
4700 BCE	Faience (quartz grit covered with coloured glasslike substance) used in pendants and beads in Egypt.
4500 BCE	Emerald now being used in jewellery and amulets in Egypt.
4000 BCE	Harder stones like rock crystal now being used for seals. Malachite now being used in Egypt. Silver being used in jewellery in Chaldea.
3500 BCE	A pendant including beads of almandine garnet, amethyst, carnelian, shell and turquoise, with a turquoise ibex pendant has been found dating to this time.
3000 BCE	A belt decorated with agate, amazonite, carnelian (red), jade, lapis lazuli, steatite (green) dated to this time was found in Harappa (now in India).
	Quartz and smoky quartz being used in amulets in Egypt and Sumeria.
	Lapis lazuli mines in Afghanistan and turquoise mines on the Sinai Peninsula trading their gemstones in long distance trade as far afield as China and India.
2000 BCE	Diamonds now being mined and used in India, and rubys and sapphires in Burma.

1600 BCE	Glass now being used in some instances to imitate crystals in Egyptian artefacts.
1352 BCE	Tutankhamen buried, his mummy has 143 pieces of jewellery in the wrappings. Crystals used in the amulets were alabaster, amazonite, carnelian, jade, jasper, lapis lazuli, obsidian, quartz, turquoise, and of course there was a lot of gold.
700 BCE	Electrum - an amalgam of gold and silver, being used to make the first coins in Iraq - used to pay for tin from tin mines.
315 BCE	*On Stones* written by Theophrastus, the first major lapidary.

Communicating With Crystals

Whilst the idea of communicating with crystals might seem at first to be fantastic, let us consider the evidence for this idea. Certain crystals are pizoelectric, and as a result may be used in wireless sets, facilitating communication - every wireless set in the world having a quartz crystal in it.

Consider also the diamonds and other gems used in watches to help ensure accurate timekeeping; and of course the silicon chip (silicon being a primary component of silicon dioxide - quartz, glass, sand).

These facts alone are not necessarily conclusive, though they may easily be seen as indicative of a trend; however the question must be, how do you perceive awareness? And does that awareness extend to the mineral kingdom?

Some minerals are described as being "thirsty", "tired" or "working", terms which imply awareness, due to their behaviour, such as absorption of water. If we accept the premise that matter is constructed of energy, and extend this to say that everything on the earth that is material in form is energy manifest at different levels of consciousness, then we can coherently argue that crystals have an awareness and may be communicated with.

The trick is to try to put our awareness into a state where communication with something of a radically different awareness is possible. I include a meditation for contacting the essence or spirit of a crystal, in an attempt to determine the nature of the crystal and the most appropriate ways of working with it.

Let us consider the scientific evidence that crystals are sentient and possess awareness. In his book *A New Science of Life*, Rupert Sheldrake observes that crystals possess morphogenetic fields (energy bodies or auras) akin to those of animals and plants. He also points out that crystals also exhibit growth, and that improving conditions speeds up growth - if a small crystal (seed) is placed into a saturated solution of the same mineral, it will grow very quickly.

J T Fraser in *Time - The Familiar Stranger*, wrote "The idea that the earliest forms of life were crystal-like is not in itself new. It has been known that between the realms of the living and the non-living, crystals represent the highest degree of stable organisation. Inorganic matter is not able to create more ordered, stable systems than those found in crystals."

To conclude my presentation of scientific evidence I will quote from *The Body Electric* by Robert Becker and Gary Selden, who give a list of the essential conditions for an entity to be considered living: "A sort of crude consciousness and memory must be present from the first, an ability to sense damage and repair itself, and a form of cyclic activity must be present." They go on to observe "All these criteria are met by semi-conducting crystals."

The American Indians have long considered crystals to be sentient beings. Claude Kuwanituma, a Hopi spiritual leader, said "Man does not have the only memory. The earth remembers. The stones remember. If you know how to listen they will tell you many things."

For anyone who still holds to the mindset that crystals are not sentient, even if you question the possibility of communication, then you should accept that the meditation is likely to encourage communication with the unconscious mind which stores far more information than the conscious, and so is likely to produce images or ideas of worth and relevance regardless of belief.

Finally, if you do doubt the idea of communicating with crystals, have you ever had the experience of seeing a crystal you knew you wanted and had to have, and then subsequently told someone "It was telling me to buy it, I knew I had to get it!"

Contacting the Crystal Essence Meditation

From my experience I would have to say the most important thing to bring to working with a new crystal is an open mind free of preconceptions. Do not assume, for example, that the piece of magnetite you have just bought is to be used for work on the circulatory system because that's what magnetite is for. The uses of a crystal are like the contents of a good book, they unfold and become clear as you pay more attention to what is being said to you.

To this end, when you have a crystal you want to work with, the inevitable starting point is to contact the crystal essence and discover what it feels it can be used for. In doing this you may find you work with crystals for purposes not documented in material you may have read, if so this is great, do not feel it is invalid because you have not read it somewhere, trust your intuition and instincts, they won't lead you astray (whereas not listening to them will).

To contact the crystal essence, begin by making sure the crystal is clean (techniques for cleaning crystals are described at the end of this chapter). You may wish to prepare your environment (temple, own room, quiet outdoor spots are nice) with some incense or joss (a purifying scent such as frankincense or sandalwood is recommended).

Some form of centring exercise should then be practiced (the exercise in the chakra chapter is a good one). When you are feeling relaxed and centred, hold the crystal in your preferred hand and focus your attention on the crystal. If you prefer, you may hold the crystal to a part of your body that feels comfortable, such as to the third eye, heart or solar plexus (it is preferable if doing this to touch the crystal to bare skin, and not have intervening layers of clothing in the way to inhibit contact).

I have found that sitting cross-legged (half or full lotus if you can manage it) with both hands together around the crystal helps the body form a closed energy circuit, which enables better focus on the crystal. Lying down can also work but there is the risk of falling asleep! During the process keep your awareness on the crystal, if it starts to drift at any time or random thoughts enter your head, just gently push them away and do not chastise yourself, this often happens in meditation - the important consideration is to always gently return your awareness back to the crystal if you become distracted.

As your awareness of the crystal sharpens, you will feel the energy inherent in the crystal, and may have a sense of the matrix of energy that comprises the crystal. Silently call to the spirit of the crystal, its essence, to manifest itself in your mind's eye, so you can commune/communicate with it. This may take a little while, so do not become impatient.

The form the crystal essence takes in communication will be affected by your perceptions and by it. The actual form, which may be human, animal, mineral or other (e.g. I see the spirit of one of my crystals as a brightly coloured butterfly, another as a pixie on a mushroom, another as a Chinese sage, etc) is effectively the interface between you and the crystal, and will reflect the essence of your relationship with the crystal, so take careful note of as much of the detail of the form as possible - colours, textures, forms.

Ask the crystal essence if it has a name it would like to be called by, if you get a reply this can help greatly in subsequent work with the crystal (it may sound strange and not be in a recognised language, so don't be surprised if it tells you its name is something like Jurgle or Zwasgiok).

Having established the form the crystal essence will manifest itself to you in, and its name, you should then ask what uses the crystal would like to be put to, and see what it tells you. The crystal may communicate ideas to you in different ways - it could be words, images, feelings, etc. Do not expect it to give you written instructions or spoon feed you.

Remember that although you are attempting to interact with a very different type of energy to your own, courtesy and respect should be employed, they cost nothing and emphasise your desire to work with the crystal for positive means. Consider also that with practice comes familiarity, so be prepared to nurture your link with the crystal as you would a growing plant, to help it develop and flower so you can both work towards using your potential.

Repeating the exercise given here for contacting the crystal essence each time you work with the crystal when you start with a new crystal is both good practice and good manners.

Working with a crystal is similar in some respects to working with other entities such as elementals, nature spirits, angelic forces, etc. When we work with other (non-human) energies, magick works most effectively if the relationship is symbiotic, i.e. "power with" not "power over". The "power over" syndrome is by its nature parasitic, and it is still present in some aspects of occultism today. It is a remnant of the domination magicks practiced in previous centuries, and has no real place in spiritual growth, being more concerned with self-gratification of the ego than fulfilment of spiritual potential.

If you buy a crystal, and then do not clean it or attempt to communicate with it, then do not expect it to be particularly effective when used - remember courtesy costs nothing, and this applies to crystals, as well as to people.

Consecrating Your Crystal

Once you have purchased a crystal, you may wish to consecrate it, ready for use in ritual. A simple consecration ritual is given below as a guide, but do feel free to modify and adapt this to your own preferences. (See also Appendix 7) If you are working indoors, the altar should have some natural object or symbol of nature on it, such as a stone (particularly a hag stone, which represents the Earth Goddess), flowers, feathers, corn, etc. An outdoor altar needs very little, as nature is all around you.

Requirements

Sea salt (or a suitable consecrated crystal) & water (not tap) in small bowls
Candle (red is good, or beeswax)
Incense or joss (a strong purifying scent like frankincense or sandalwood is good) and censer
Suitable oil (depicting spirit)
Piece of silk or other bag for storage if crystal is not to be worn
These items should be set up on the altar ready.

Consecration

Start by having a ritual bath, allowing yourself to dry naturally (you may wish to use appropriate oils in the bath, as detailed in Appendix 6).

When you are ready ground yourself with an appropriate centring exercise (such as the chakra exercise in the chapter on Chakras).

Cast the circle in your preferred manner.

Call on the elements in turn at the appropriate quarter (starting with Air - East and moving round clockwise through Fire - South, Water - West to Earth - North) and ask for their blessings and energy.

Call on the Goddess and God in turn in whichever aspects you know them best (it is preferable if possible to call on aspects which match from the same pantheons, such as Isis and Osiris, Kali and Shiva, etc) and ask for their blessings and energy. If you work with other entities such as e.g. angels, power animals, spirit guide, call on them at this point and ask for their blessings, energy and guidance.

Pass the item through the incense smoke (if it is a large crystal you may move the censer around it and blow smoke over it as well as you do this), saying:

"I purify and consecrate you with the power of the element of Air."
As you do this visualize winds blowing over the crystal, removing any impurities or unwanted energies which may have accumulated around the crystal.

Pass the crystal through a candle flame, saying:

"I purify and consecrate you with the power of the element of Fire."
As you do this visualize fire caressing the crystal around its edges, burning away any impurities.

Sprinkle the crystal with water, saying:

14

"I purify and consecrate you with the power of the element of Water."
As you do this visualize water flowing over and around the crystal, washing away any impurities.

Sprinkle the crystal with salt, or touch the already consecrated crystal to it, saying:

"I purify and consecrate you with the power of the element of Earth."
As you do this visualize the crystal being surrounded by the earth, which absorbs any impurities.

Anoint the crystal with oil, saying:

"I purify and consecrate you with the power of the element of Spirit."
As you do this visualize the crystal being imbued with gold light.

Thank and say farewell to the God and Goddess, or whichever beings you called on.

Thank and say farewell to the elements (in reverse from North anti-clockwise through to East).

Open the circle.

Write up the ritual in your diary.

You may wish to wrap crystals which are not being left on an altar in silk, to preserve the charge on them.

Do not *allow anyone else to handle your magickal tools - the only exception being where they would be in physical contact if for example using a crystal for healing.*

Crystals in Daily Life for Health and Well-Being

Having raw chunks of crystals in rooms can noticeably enhance the energy of those rooms. Different crystals with their various qualities may be used to good advantage in different rooms around the house.

In the Bathroom keep pieces of coral and lapis lazuli to aid in relaxation when lazing in the bath.

For the Bedroom, pieces of haematite and jet kept near the bed, or under it, may help with back problems (though not under the mattress!). Amethyst and tourmaline are good stones for helping with insomnia, and also encouraging lucid dreaming. Never wear onyx to bed though, it has been considered to cause nightmares by many cultures for thousands of years.

In the Dining Room, I suggest orange calcite, which encourages digestion, being very sympathetic to the sacral chakra, and peridot, which is commonly used for digestive problems. Topaz as the stone for overcoming loss of appetite should perhaps also have a prominent place in the dining room!

The Living Room should contain stones which radiate serenity and an appreciation of beauty, as this is a room for relaxation, and so I strongly recommend chunks of rose quartz and jadeite.

The Toilet deserves crystals as much as any other room, and a piece of aquamarine to ease fluid problems, and jasper for bladder problems, are both worth considering.

If you have a Study, you might keep a piece of malachite in there, to encourage business matters, and magnetite to attract prosperity. Wealth magick has long been associated with magnetite, and it should be placed in the south (the place of wealth in Feng Shui).

In the Kitchen try Chrysocolla as a good inspirational stone to help you decide what to eat, and possibly pearl for patience when you have to do the cooking!

Finally, the Nursery. Obviously crystals in a nursery need to be kept very securely away from inquisitive hands and mouths. You might like to consider the following stones though. Both varieties of jade, i.e. jadeite and nephrite, are believed to encourage positive growth in children. Coral has been used for thousands of years by cultures all around the world as a protection for children from the evil eye (envy). Finally, sodalite and sunstone are both stones to promote general health and well-being.

It is worth consulting a book on Feng Shui to get some ideas as to the optimum places to position crystals (if you do not already have an interest in the subject). Obviously you would not put crystals where they can be reached by children or are likely to fall down the toilet, etc!

Weaɾiŋg Cɾɥstals

There are a number of ways you can wear crystals, you should decide what type of energy you wish to work with, and where it would be most appropriate to wear it. Be mindful of the nature of the crystals you are wearing, and strive to wear crystals of harmonious energies rather than discordant ones.

Remember they are there to enhance and focus your energies, crystals are not a crutch, although some people may work with them as such.

Also remember that crystals in contact with others, e.g. in rings or pockets, should be of a similar hardness or they will abrade. Crystals worn in pockets tend to affect the whole aura and body energy field.

Which finger a ring is worn on can make a difference to the effects received from the crystal or mineral. The correspondences for the fingers are given below:

Finger	Affects	Planet
Thumb*	Will, Intent	Will
Forefinger	Path, Direction, Action	Jupiter
Middle (big)	Inspiration, Intuition	Saturn
Ring finger	Creativity	Sun
Little	Change, Opportunity	Mercury

If we move from the fingertip to the hand, the three phalanges of the fingers correspond to the spirit, mind and body. Most rings will therefore be on the body part of the ring, where the change will be more concentrated on the physical level; rings worn on the second phalange would work more on the mental levels, and on the first phalange they would work more on the spiritual.

Some people believe wearing rings on the thumbs can have a constricting effect on the will, however if one accepted this belief, the effect could be avoided by using a stone which promotes strengthening of the will, and with an appropriate metal like gold or platinum. In days gone by it was believed that golden earrings would protect sailors from drowning (a belief which never passed the test, especially if the sailor couldn't swim).

Programming / Imprinting Crystals

I have often pondered why crystals of the same form should be usable for such divergent applications. The conclusion I have reached is that every type of crystal has a wide spectrum of possible uses, and when we interact with them, we are drawn to part of that spectrum (possibly the part we need to work with or to fill a gap in our healing repertoire) and the crystal becomes tuned to that part of the spectrum.

It follows from this perception that if we take an inventory of our strengths and weaknesses, we can see what areas we need to work on or with, and program crystals to work on these areas (also of course we can programme a crystal to help with a specific healing, particularly if it is a serious condition requiring frequent healing work - I strongly recommend a specifically programmed crystal for work purely on such a healing).

Obviously the intent of the programming is communicated to the crystal prior to performing the programming, to be sure it is in harmony with the crystal's preferences. By preference I recommend sticking to simple programs if you do use this technique, I use the analogy with computer programming - the simpler you keep things, the less can go wrong. If you start mixing large numbers of crystals with differing programming, energies can go astray and start to have unexpected and/or undesired results (though this is less likely to be a problem if a number of people are each using a programmed crystal of their own).

Thus to program a crystal, you might contact the crystal essence, gain it's approval, and then repeat a phrase as you stroke the crystal in a regular repeated motion, e.g. chanting "Help keep my visions clear" whilst making circular clockwise stroking motions on a quartz skrying ball.

A common example of programming used by many people today is having a piece of fluoride in water programmed to remove the fluorine.

To deprogram a crystal, burying it in the earth or keeping it immersed in a bowl of salt are the most common ways, as they both effectively erase the imprinted message whilst keeping the crystal in a positive environment.

Reflected in Crystal

Consider all the crystals you possess and know of. Which type of crystal do you feel most strongly attracted to, which one stands out as your "favourite". If none do, meditate individually with your crystals and see which one stands out.

When you decide which crystal is your favourite, analyse why? Is it a feeling you get from the crystal, does it alter your mood, does it have strong symbolic meanings for you, sentimental value, etc. Find out and record all you can about the crystal, and then consider how it relates to you. This is a process which requires very honest self-examination, but which can be very rewarding is a means of spiritual growth.

When you know why the crystal is your favourite, you will have more idea about yourself, your own perceptions and aspirations. Do not cop out by saying there are several you like equally, choose the one which resonates most strongly to you as your crystal.

If you have several other different crystals which you are particularly drawn to, it may be worth looking at them in light of the different aspects of your self such as the anima/animus, shadow, inner child, etc, or you may find for example that each one facilitates working with a different sub-personality; first, though, find the primary crystal.

Crystal Cave Meditation

If possible it is preferable to actually have a geode that you can hold whilst doing this meditation. You should have decided beforehand what type of crystal you want to be in the cave, this may be done by looking through the Gemmology or simply by using what you have.

If possible it is worth visiting any good accessible cave systems near you, to improve your connectedness to and appreciation of such caves, as well as bringing away with you images which help make it easier to hold the visualisation!

You may find this meditation easier to do if you tape it first (leaving appropriate pauses for yourself to experience events) so you can play it back and concentrate fully on the experience.

Create a sacred space in a manner you are comfortable with. Take a few minutes to still yourself and relax. Make sure you are sitting comfortably, and close your eyes. (An aura sealing exercise is a good idea to do at this point if you know one, the chakra sealing exercise in the chapter on Chakras is a good example).

Focus your awareness on your breathing, gently bringing it back if it wanders. In your mind's eye see the room (or space if outside) becoming filled with a white mist. It becomes thicker and thicker coalescing and blanking out everything around you until all around you is white mist, you are floating in a sea of white mist.

Then the white mist starts to disperse, thinning out, drawing back to reveal a cave around you. There is a hole in the roof or one side of the cave, letting in some moonlight which is reflected off the walls, the light bouncing from crystal to crystal as you look around, and realise the entire cave is lined with crystals. The floor is very smooth and polishes, like the face of a cut crystal, and there are facets of crystals all around.

Take time to explore and examine the crystals. Then sit in the middle of the cave and let your awareness expand to fill the cave. How does it feel? (You should remember this for later). Be aware of the energies flowing through the earth which you are now connecting to.

Expand your awareness further, feel the earth around you. What do you feel? You may continue expanding your awareness as much as you choose, so that e.g. you end up becoming the whole earth, or focusing inwards into the centre of the earth and becoming aware of the molten core of the earth.

After a while start to contract your awareness again, reducing it until you are back to the cave at the centre, and then looking around the cave, see the white mist start to fill the cave again, obscuring the walls and ceiling and floor. It completely blankets you so you are aware only of the sea of white mist around you. Now see it roll back and reveal the familiar surroundings of the room (or space) that you started in. If you do not feel fully earthed, stand up and stamp your feet a few times. Record your experiences in your magickal diary.

A variation on this theme worth trying is that when you have expanded your consciousness to that of the cave, you then become the universe, i.e. you become the first manifestation in the void.

Crystals as Magickal Weapons

Crystal knives are sometimes available in materials such as obsidian and flint. These items tend to have a surprisingly sharp edge, and may often resemble sacrificial knives somewhat (unsurprisingly).

Crystal knives direct energy remarkably well, and are very good for taking to outdoor sites, although care should of course be taken to protect the knife from chipping or breaking when carried. They are good for work where you might not want to work with metal, and for ancestor and atavistic work (and of course for working with systems where they were used, such as Egyptian, South American, etc).

The *ur-hekaut* knife used by the Egyptians for the ceremony of the Opening of the Ways (the beginning of the journey of the soul so important to the Egyptians in their quest through the Underworld to justification and union with the gods) was generally made of flint or obsidian, though the earliest of these were reputedly made from meteoric metal/crystal.

Knives made using softer minerals such as selenite carved from a large single piece of white/translucent crystal are starting to become available now as well, and are proving extremely popular with those who have tried using them. Such selenite knives must be treated even more carefully than flint and obsidian, being easier to chip and crack with their low hardness.

Crystal wands vary tremendously in size, from a few inches long and very thin, to a foot plus and a couple of inches across. The size of the wand may determine the type of work you use it for. Size:

Under 4" long and $^{1}/_{2}$"-1" wide can be used as healing wands, to focus on a specific area of the body and really concentrate the energy there, akin to putting a needle in a meridian or acupuncture point.

They can make good "pointers" and foci in crystal mandalas and spell webs. They may also be used to enhance lucid dreaming (see the section on dreamwork).

They can make very good cursing sticks, though this use is dangerous - unless you have a very good reason for doing it and know the universe is flowing with you when you do a curse, and can truly justify it, you are liable to suffer unpleasant backlash effects.

4"-9" long and up to 1" wide are ideal for healing wands for working with the chakras and areas of the subtle body. They are also a good size for general directing of energy, and may be used in place of a wand and/or an athame or dagger. Most of the wands in shops will fall into this category.

If you plan on using a crystal wand to replace other magickal tools, I would strongly suggest having a separate wand for healing work, and keeping the wand purely for your own circlework.

Over 9" long and 1"-3" wide are large wands, which may be used well in group work and particularly outdoors. These wands are very good for sending built-up energy at the climax of ritual. These wands are akin to a sword in that you probably would not work with them by yourself that often, as smaller wands may do the job just as well for solo work.

This is not to say that they don't have their uses - if you want a real good blast of energy and need to clear away some deadwood, work with a large wand and get to it!

Crystal chalices are becoming easier to obtain, though these tend to be in minerals such as alabaster, marble and onyx, which are not particularly watery in their attributions. Chalices used to be carved out of more precious stones in the past, in the Middle Ages amethyst chalices were particularly popular amongst the clergy and the rich as using one to drink from was thought to stop you getting drunk (due to the powers of the amethyst, see the entry in the Gemmology). Crystal chalices tend to be fragile around the stem, so if you are working outdoors you are probably better off with something a bit less delicate like wood or metal.

Crystal pentacles may be easily obtained, with polished slices of crystal cut with a diamond saw (known as potato slice) being sold in non-specialist shops as well as dedicated suppliers due to their popularity. They will often be of a material which has earthy symbolism, and so can replace a wooden or metal pentacle to good effect.

Potato slices tend to be cheap and come in a variety of colours and sizes, it is up to you to decide on the specification you desire, or see if your eye is taken by a particular crystal when you search. Potato slices (especially the agate ones) are often stained to look more eye-catching, so do check if it is a particularly stunning pink, blue or green for example.

Staining is a technique which has been practiced for at least two thousand years, there are records of crystals being stained in Roman times. Crystal slices can be used very effectively as good talismans as well.

Crystal offering bowls for salt, water and oil are also fairly common, and when cut from a single piece of a material such as moss agate are a delight to work with. Moss agate bowls are particularly good for use as offering bowls outdoors, they tend to have a good sympathy with outdoor sites.

If working by the sea I would recommend using shells rather than crystals for offering bowls, as these are more in harmony with the environment they came from, particularly if they have been found by you rather than bought. Offering bowls may also be used as receptacles for other crystals of sympathetic nature.

Crystal statuettes are sometimes available, and can be a beautiful enhancement to an altar or temple. These tend to be very expensive, but can serve as a good focus for the energy of a deity if you are doing a devotion to that deity. Small (and reasonably cheap) crystal animals are becoming increasingly common, and these can be good for work with totems, power animals, etc, or even to provide an object link with your familiar (if you have one).

It is also becoming easier to pick up other devotional objects such as Buddha's and Shiva lingams (holy phallus) in crystal form, which can enhance your personal devotional work.

Crystals may be added to fetishes and power objects with good effect. When combined with other natural objects such as bone, beads, feathers, wood, etc, they can produce objects with a very personalised energy appropriate to you and your work. The only limit is your imagination and the feeling of "rightness" that goes with something that works well and appropriately. So, for example you might set a crystal in a wand, or a headband, a scabbard, etc.

As Amulets and Talismans

Crystals have been used for thousands of years as amulets and talismans. Before we examine this useage, a distinction needs to be made between amulets and talismans.

An amulet is used for protection, be it from illness, diseases, specific dangers (such as protection from lightning, while travelling by sea, etc) "evil" (like the evil eye, evil spirits or people) or anything else.

A talisman is used to attract desired qualities or situations, such as fertility, wealth, luck, success (in business, litigation, hunting, fishing, etc), strength, etc.

A charm is generally an amulet, though the term is often used indiscriminately to describe both amulets and talismans.

Perhaps the greatest exponents of the use of crystals as amulets and talismans were the Ancient Egyptians. Carnelian was a particular favourite, being known as the "blood of Isis", and seemed to be viewed in the same way as rowan has been as a particularly potent protection from negative witchcraft and sorceries.

This protective talisman theme is also seen in ancient myths, such as Prometheus wearing a sapphire ring when he stole the fire from heaven, and Orpheus carrying a piece of agate as a protective talisman when he descended into the underworld.

Protective talismans were considered necessary for any dealings with spirits from the underworld - one Greek manuscript details a heart-shaped amulet of magnetite with the Underworld Goddess Hecate carved on it; reference is made to the amulet being "sweet smelling", suggesting the use of aromatic oils to anoint the talisman, possibly as part of an offering.

Egyptian amulets were usually small carved crystals of deities (who would protect from a particular ailment or condition) or (afflicted) parts of the body (such as hand, eye, foot, etc). This principle of sympathetic magick can be seen in early Europe through Celtic times right up until recently, with votive offerings (though usually wood, stone or metal) of afflicted body parts being thrown into rivers, lakes and holy wells and springs.

Other early cultures contemporary with the Egyptians also used amulets and talismans, so fine examples may be found amongst, e.g., the Sumerians, early Chinese culture, etc, and as time went by, the Greeks and Romans and other cultures continued this useage and maintained the tradition of crystal and mineral amulets and talismans.

Amulets have a long tradition of useage by sea-faring peoples, to provide protection from the fury that could be faced at sea. Many amulets and stones were used for this purpose (especially aquamarine, beryl and coral), and a Greek lapidary from 3-4th century CE details seven amulets to be made for differing forms of protection. The number seven might suggest the amulets were each used for a specific day of the week, though each amulet did provide a specialised form of protection.

The amulets were:

1. A carbuncle (garnet) and a chalcedony - to protect sailors from drowning.

2. Quartz or corundum - to protect from extreme weather.

3. Aquamarine - to banish fear.

4. Agate - to protect against the evil eye.

5. Coral, placed in strips of sealskin attached to the prow - to protect the ship from winds and waves.

6. Banded agate - to protect from the surging waves of the ocean.

7. Jet - providing major protection for any travelling by river or sea.

The Christian Church decided at an early date to declare its opposition to the use of amulets. At the Council of Laodicea in 355 CE Canon 34 decreed "Priests and clerks must be neither enchanters, mathematicians, nor astrologers, and that they must not make what are called amulets for these are fetters of the soul, and all who wear them shall be cast out of the church".

As the centuries passed this canon was used or ignored as was convenient by those in power in the church, as is witnessed by the talismanic use of gems by the rich and powerful, and indeed the use by the church of differing gems to depict rank and station.

```
ABRACADABRA
ABRACADABR
ABRACADAB
ABRACADA
ABRACAD
ABRACA
ABRAC
ABRA
ABR
AB
A
```

Abracadabra

As man entered the Middle Ages, more and more crystal usage became concerned with protection from ailments, particularly the plague. As will be seen in the Gemmology, many stones were thought to protect from plague, the most striking example being the Abraxas Stone (see Mythical Minerals chapter).

The Abraxas stones beautifully illustrate the thinking going into the amulet, being engraved on one side with the image of a deity (who is appealed to for assistance/protection) and on the other side with a magickal formula embodying the protective formula - Abracadabra being derived from the Chaldean phrase meaning "to perish like the word", reduces to an "A" and perishes like the word, so likewise by sympathetic magick any contagion or plague symptoms should also perish.

One of the most common themes found in Middle Eastern charms is protection from snake bites and scorpion stings, a fact of daily life in many countries.

Thabit Ibn Qurra (836 - 901 CE) recorded details of an interesting charm to rid a dwelling of scorpions. First an image of a scorpion was made out of either copper, tin, lead, silver or gold whilst Scorpio was in the ascendant in the heavens, and the glyph of Scorpio (♏)and appropriate astrological information engraved on the image. The scorpion charm was then buried under the place afflicted by scorpions, whilst reciting: "This is the burial of it and its species, that it may not come to that one and to that place."

It was considered more effective to make four charms and repeat this ritual, burying them at the four corners of the dwelling. This is a lovely example of sympathetic magick, using the image of the creature to be protected against, and the most propitious astrological times, to ensure success in the desired spell.

Protective charms are still in use in some parts of the world today, particularly the Mediterranean and the Middle East. Red coral charms shaped like a crescent moon, representing the protective hand gesture of index and little finger raised are still given to babies and worn through life as a protection against the "evil eye". Agate eye stones have been used in this manner for many centuries and their use continues still.

In India crystals were most prized in combination in amulets. The two famous amulets are the five gem Pancharatna, comprsiing amethyst, diamond, emerald, gold and pearl; and the nine gem Navaratna, comprising amethyst, cat's eye, coral, diamond, emerald, pearl, ruby, sapphire and topaz.

Crystals can be found to suit any attribution you may require for a talisman, and are easy to charge and carry - indeed simply carrying a crystal and playing with it while you are doing things will help it build up charge and also focus your unconscious mind on the energy of the talisman and help move you accordingly.

Shapes which work particularly well for protection are the sphere and egg. When casting a magick "circle" you are really casting a sphere, representing the universe, with you as the centre of the sphere (and of course we are all the centre of our own universe, so don't feel this is presumptuous).

Having a sphere as your focus can enable you to perceive the balance and uniformity of the sphere and the energies in it, and engender a more protective atmosphere about you.

The egg also tends to produce a very protective feeling, corresponding as it also does to the universe (as in many creation myths where the universe is formed from an egg), and to the spirit tatva (tatvas are elemental symbols representing the elements), particularly if the egg is black or purple as the spirit tatva is coloured.

Visualising yourself in the centre of the sphere or egg, with the sphere/egg being the centre of the sphere you have created can also produce a "double glazed" effect, increasing the protection around you.

Cut crystals were also used in the past as a badge of rank, though this may well have been due to the crystals being thought to be imbued with magickal properties, as with the lapis lazuli feather of Mayat (representing truth) worn by Egyptian judges set in gold and worn on a heavy gold chain. Chinese Mandarins also wore differing stones to denote their rank.

Amber is a very good general storer of charge and jet is hard to beat as a protective absorption talisman (though it needs regular cleaning, of course), which may explain the witches' traditional amber and jet necklace. These were also sometimes interspersed with bones, such as snake spine bones. The reasons for this are not clear, but there are a number of possibilities, such as passing on the enduring qualities of bone, drawing on qualities of the snake such as wisdom, regeneration, etc.

For specific examples of amulets in folklore and history, see also the entries on: Agate, Amethyst, Beryl, Carnelian, Chalcedony, Diamond, Garnet, Jasper, Jet, Magnetite, Malachite, Moonstone, Onyx, Peridot, Pyrite, Quartz, Sapphire, Serpentine, Topaz & Zircon.

Gem Tree Guardians

Another good shape for protective work, particularly for a property, is that of a tree. These may often be obtained from gift shops and jewellers as well as crystal shops, and come in many different varieties of crystal, and in varying sizes.

If you find a gem tree which does particularly appeal to you, purchase it without haggling. This old custom may seem antiquated, but there is a magickal reason - when you buy an object to work with it is (or should be unless secondhand) virgin, i.e. unused. You want the item to be unaffected by any energy other than your own, which means not beginning your work with it surrounded by an atmosphere of dispute to taint its energies.).

Take the gem tree home and clean it thoroughly (as described at the end of this section). Once the tree is clean, you may wish to try and see if it has a crystal essence to contact, but you may find it does not, being so many fragments brought together. If you find the tree has a crystal essence, check if it is happy to be used as a guardian. If it does not, you may wish to bless and consecrate it with the elements in a simple ritual (an example is given in the earlier chapter on consecrationof crystals.

When you have done this, take the gem tree and go to the outer boundaries of your property (front and back garden if you have them, hallway if in flats, etc) and hold the gem tree to each (obviously you will need to pick a time to do this when you are not going to be disturbed!), marking the boundaries.

Then take the tree and hold it to the corners of the house/apartment - to the four bottom and four top internal corners (cellars and attics should be included in this). Finally do the same with the room which you are going to keep the gem tree in. You have then set it up as a guardian to protect your property and those within it.

Salt Crystal Meditation

This meditation is for creating a safe sacred space for contemplation and inner peace and harmony. It is very simple and easy to perform, yet very rewarding, and is ideal as a precursor to other work to set the right mood.

Start the meditation as described in the crystal cave meditation, and as the mists disperse see yourself in a cuboid room. Visualise the room being as large as makes you comfortable. The walls are crystalline and translucent, all very solid and pure with no doors or entries.

You are inside a salt crystal. Nothing can enter the crystal unless you want it to. By concentrating you can, if you wish, change the colour of the walls, to black, or mirrored, or any colour. Scratch the surface of the wall and taste the salt on your finger.

Sit in the centre of the crystal and be aware, see how it makes you feel. Take time just to let the universe flow around you while you watch for a while from the untouchable space in the heart of a sacred salt crystal.

If you have problems with visualizing hard edges, and find the crystal becoming more cavelike, persevere with your perception of the crystalline shape, and it will come.

There is nothing inherently wrong with a cave/womblike shape, but that is not the purpose of the exercise. If the problems persist, you can always concentrate instead on using a sphere or egg as described earlier in this section.

The Chakras and the Subtle Energy Body

The Chakras are the energy centres in the subtle body which regulate the energy flows and interaction of the physical and subtle bodies (chakra means "wheel" or "disk").

There are seven main chakras, from the lowest at the base of the spine to the highest at the crown. Connecting these chakras and flowing through the body there are said to be seventy-two thousand nadis, tiny energy channels woven through the subtle body like "threads in a spider's web".

The chakras are depicted as lotuses, which are sacred flowers, as they grow up from the mud symbolising a path of development from the primitive to the divine. This mirrors the journey from the base chakra which roots us in the earth, to the crown chakra or thousand petalled lotus, which brings us cosmic consciousness.

Like lotuses the chakras can be opened and closed. Illness and fatigue can often result from chakras being too open, too closed or out of balance, the physical body reflecting the imbalance in the subtle. A balance needs to be reached, where in mundane daily life the chakras are partially open but not too much so, giving us awareness without excessive vulnerability to the inescapable stresses of our existence.

During magickal work we may open the chakras more to aid in altering our consciousness and expanding our awareness of the subtle (and subsequently closing them as much as we feel we need to after the magickal work is done).

In the information given below, the first bija-mantra (root sound) is the Sanskrit, the second is the Tibetan. Try working with the two systems and see which sounds produce better effects for you. If you find some from each system do, I would still recommend sticking to the one system rather than mixing and matching, as the combination of the sounds in a specific system can have effects beyond that you could achieve using part of a system of body sounds.

The Major Chakras

MULADHARA ("root") is located at the base of the spine and is known as the Base Chakra

Body:	Gonads and Adrenal Glands, Excretory System, solids such as bones, teeth, nails and hair.
Centre:	Instinct, Survival, Pleasure and Base Sexuality
Colour:	Red
Element:	Earth
Illnesses:	Obesity, haemorrhoids, constipation, anorexia, degenerative arthritis and frequent illness.
Inner State:	Stillness
Metal:	Lead
Oils:	Cedar, Musk, Patchouli, Sandalwood
Planets:	Earth, Saturn
Postures:	Balancing poses such as The Dancer, The Eagle, The Tree, and seated meditation poses such as The Lotus and The Thunderbolt.
Seed Sound:	LAM / RA
Sense:	Smell

SVADDISTHANA ("sweetness") is located at the level of the Sacrum, and known as the Sacral Chakra

Body:	Ovaries, Testicles, Spinal Column, Womb, Bladder, Kidneys
Centre:	Change, Creativity, Nurturing, Sexuality & Sensuality.
Colour:	Orange
Element:	Water
Illnesses:	Impotence, frigidity, uterine and bladder disorders.
Inner State:	Tears
Metal:	Tin
Oils:	Damiana, Gardenia, Orris, Rose
Planets:	Moon
Postures:	The Butterfly, Forward Bends, The Plough, The Shoulder Stand, The Triangle
Seed Sound:	VAM / MA
Sense:	Taste

MANIPURA ("lustrous jewel") is located at the Solar Plexus, and known as the Solar Plexus chakra.

Body:	Pancreas, Stomach, Liver, Gall Bladder and the Nervous System.
Centre:	Interaction with the Universe, the Digestive Process, and Emotions.
Colour:	Yellow
Element:	Fire
Illness:	Ulcers, diabetes and hypoglycaemia
Inner State:	Laughter, Joy, Anger
Metal:	Iron
Oils:	Calamus, Cardamon, Carnation, Cinnamon, Coriander, Ginger, Marigold, Orange
Planets:	Mars, Sun
Postures:	The Bow, The Cat, The Cobra, The Coil, The Twist.
Seed Sound:	RAM / DA
Sense:	Sight

41

ANAHATA ("unstruck") is located at the Heart and is known as the Heart chakra.

Body:	Thymus Gland, Heart, Blood, Vagus Nerve, and Circulatory System.
Centre:	Love, Being & Equilibrium, the source of Harmony
Colour:	Green
Element:	Air
Illness:	Asthma, respiratory problems, high blood pressure, heart conditions.
Inner State:	Compassion
Metal:	Copper
Oils:	Jasmine, Lavender, Marjoram, Meadowsweet, Orris Root
Planets:	Venus
Postures:	The Camel, The Cobra, The Fish, The Locust, Pranayama (Breath control)
Seed Sound:	YAM / SA
Sense:	Touch

VISHUDDHA ("purification") is located at the Throat and is known as the Throat chakra.

Body:	Thyroid Gland, Lungs, Alimentary Canal, and Hearing, Bronchial and Vocal Apparatus
Centre:	Active Magickal Power and of Dreaming
Colour:	Bright Blue
Element:	Aether / Sound
Illness:	Thyroid problems, throat and ear conditions.
Inner State:	Connection
Metal:	Mercury
Oils:	Benzoin, Frankincense
Planets:	Mercury, Neptune
Postures:	The Camel, The Fish, The Headstand, The Lion, The Plough, The Shoulderstand
Seed Sound:	HAM / SE
Sense:	Hearing

AJNA ("to perceive") is located on the brow above the nose, and is known as the Third Eye chakra.

Body:	Pituitary Gland, and represents Intuition, governing the Lower Brain, the Second (least dominant) Eye, Nose, and Nervous System.
Centre:	Spiritual Power, and of the passive magickal senses (such as Telepathy, Precognition, Clairvoyance, Clairaudience), and is the focus of Light
Colour:	Indigo
Element:	Light
Illness:	Blindness, headaches and nightmares.
Inner State:	Intuiting
Metal:	Silver
Oils:	Acacia, Aniseed, Mugwort, Saffron, Star Anise
Planets:	Jupiter
Postures:	The Corpse, The Shoulderstand, The Headstand, Alternative Nostril Breathing
Seed Sound:	AUM / SO
Sense:	Sixth

SAHASRARA ("Thousandfold") is located above the head at the Crown, and is known as the Crown chakra.

Body:	Pineal Gland, Upper Brain, Sorcerer's (First - more dominant) Eye.
Centre:	Evolution, residence of the Divine Spark, the focus of Thought
Colour:	Violet
Element:	Thought
Illness:	Depression, alienation and confusion
Inner State:	Bliss
Metal:	Gold
Oils:	Lotus, Rose
Planets:	Uranus
Postures:	The Headstand, The Lotus, All Meditation Poses.

Seed Sound: HUNG / GN
Sense: -

Chakra Sealing Exercise

This exercise is a simple but potent one which keeps the aura balanced and whole through regular (preferably daily) practice, and can also be used for energising and ensuring clear boundaries before other work:-

Visualise the base chakra as a disk (or sphere if you find it easier) of spinning red light (the colour of light it responds to), and when you see it clearly, inscribe a pentagram of gold light on the disk, vibrating (either silently or aloud) the seed sound for the chakra (Ra). Then move to the second chakra and visualise it as a disk (or sphere) of spinning orange light, and when it is clear, inscribe a gold pentagram on it, vibrating the seed sound (Ma). Move up through the chakras repeating this process, moving through the colours of the rainbow up to violet light for the crown chakra, inscribing a gold pentagram on each and vibrating the appropriate mantra. As you do this, you should feel the energy moving up the spine.

After having inscribed the pentagram on the crown chakra, imagine each pentagram was a seed, and visualise that seed bursting forth gold light, surrounding the body and filling the aura.

When you can feel the gold light surrounding your body, concentrate the energy on any areas of the body which are in pain or feel weaker. I recommend this exercise be done every day, irrespective of any other magickal work which you may be doing. If it is built in to the daily routine, it will greatly strengthen the aura. I would strongly recommend doing the exercise before going to bed at night.

If you work in an environment which is unpleasant or distasteful to you in some manner, try adding an extra piece onto the end of the exercise, where you visualise the outside of your aura like a mirror, reflecting anything negative back to its source.

If you are going to be moving on to healing work from this exercise, add the following to the end.

When you have filled your aura with gold light and done whatever redeployment of energy you feel is required by your body, concentrate on the chakras in your feet. Vibrate the mantra HUM and feel the feet chakras drawing up energy as gold light (to symbolise the liquid molten core of the earth) from the earth beneath you with each in-breath, rising up your legs and through the base, sacral and solar plexus chakras up to the heart chakra.

Then concentrate on your crown chakra, and feeling the energy of the heavens above, draw this down as silver light into your crown chakra with each out-breath, bringing it down through the third eye and throat to the heart chakra.

See the gold and silver energies swirling together and blending at your heart chakra, and continue to draw up earth energy as gold light on the in-breath, and draw down stellar energy as silver light on the out-breath, until you feel full of healing vitality which you can then use for the healing.

With practice you should find that it becomes easy to continue this visualisation whilst healing, this is particularly valuable in a situation where you need a lot of energy, and also ensures you do not make the mistake of draining yourself through using your own energy.

For Skrying and Divination

The classic divination image is probably the woman with quartz crystal ball, and indeed in the past skrying balls were most often made of quartz, as well as beryl and obsidian.

It is worth noting the suggestion made by Kunz in *The Curious Lore of Precious Stones* that the quartz ball in the sceptre and beryl ball in the mace of the Scottish crown jewels may originally have been used for divination, and that they were known as "Stones of Power", reputedly being traceable back to the druids.

Cost now means people are more likely to work with a ball made from lead crystal or a coloured glass fishing float, but divination can be practised with any natural crystal (though I would not recommend using synthetic crystals, so check when purchasing crystals such as zircon).

Although any crystal can be used for divination, my experience agrees with the historical perspective suggesting obsidian is one of the best, both as a sphere and mirror, along with the quartz family and the beryls. It may be worth starting with a coloured glass ball or even a bowl of water to determine if you have the patience and aptitude to skry, and move onto a more expensive lead crystal or quartz ball when your skills have developed a bit.

To skry successfully takes a lot of time and practice. It is a skill which really has to be worked at to develop any real

46

ability in (unless you are exceptionally lucky and have a natural talent for it).

To start, one should practice in a darkened room, with no or minimal disturbing sounds, and just a candle for light. First focus the mind through a technique you are comfortable with, such as breath control or meditation.

Then concentrate the attention on the sphere, keeping it focused on the centre of the sphere. If your attention wanders away at any time, just gently return it to the centre of the sphere, do not get angry or allow your attention to follow the distractions. If you see any clouding in the sphere, make a note of the colour.

Spend about ten to fifteen minutes doing this. Repeat this every day. After a while you may find the clouds disperse and images start to form (this does not happen for everybody, some people only ever see clouds or get feelings off the crystal ball). If or when this happens, make a note of the images and attempt to decipher them later, do not try to work them out there and then, as this may disperse your concentration and result in you losing other images which may have been following as part of a sequence.

You may find it valuable to get a book about symbolism to help work out the meanings of images, as they tend to be symbolic and somewhat obtuse rather than specific images of people and situations you know which can be immediately understood. Below are listed the meanings generally associated with the cloud colours which people tend to see.

Colour	Meaning
White	Good fortune
Silver	Great good fortune, possibly after difficulties
Gold	Happiness and prosperity
Grey-Black	Ill fortune, the darker the worse
Red	Danger, take care; alternatively sexual passion
Orange	Emotional difficulties ahead
Yellow	Difficulties ahead
Green	Happiness in emotional life
Blue	Promotion or business success

Agate eyestones are also good for skrying, particularly trying to locate missing objects. Meditating for a while lying down, and concentrating on the breath, with an eyestone placed on the third eye to which the awareness is shifted after a few minutes of breath meditation, works well.

Images from the pre-conscious mind of places around your dwelling place or situations you have been in may well fill your mind. These may give you some insight into where the missing item is, but if not, it could be your mind wandering. As with skrying, if the attention wanders, gently bring it back into focus without any self-recrimination or anger (it is a common occurrence when meditating or focusing the mind).

The name of the Mayan God, Tezcatlipoca, translates as "mirror that smokes", indicating the smoking or misting of the obsidian mirror used by the Mayan magicians (whose patron he was as God of Magicians) before the images started to form. Mirrors (not necessarily magick ones) were also made in the ancient world from substances such as pyrites and copper which produce a highly reflective surface on polishing.

If one wanted to make a crystal magick mirror perhaps the easiest way would be to buy a flat slice of crystal and set it into a frame which you have made or found. A fluid accumulator made from a combination of essential oils corresponding to all of the planets and the elements in equal measure will help empower the mirror and also provide a good fluid "back" which is sympathetic with the skrying function of the mirror (this could be further empowered, such as with a few drops of your own blood, if intended for personal use). This back for the mirror should be convex.

The orphic poem Lithica describes a magick sphere made of stone. The material is called sideritis and ophitis, and is described as black, round and heavy.

The Trojan soothsayer Helenus was said to have used this sphere to foretell the downfall of Troy. There is an intriguing description given which is clearly of the consecration of the mirror - how he fasted for twenty-one days, wrapped the sphere in soft garments, like an infant, and offered sacrifices to it until by the magick of his prayers "a living soul warmed the precious substance".

In ancient times a bowl of mercury was used to skry in, but this practice is not really recommended due to both the expense and unavailability of mercury, and its poisonous nature when inhaled. Lead was also used for skrying, with molten lead being poured into a bowl of water, and divination done from the shapes made by the rapidly cooled globules of lead.

In the Bible we find reference to divination using a silver chalice amongst the Hebrews, in Genesis xliv 1-5, Joseph having sent Benjamin away with the chalice hidden in a sack of grain, sends messengers to catch up with him and ask for its return with the words "Is not this it in which my lord drinketh, and whereby indeed he divineth?"

A curious technique used by the Persian magi is worth recounting. They used a golden ball set with a sapphire and encrusted with celestial symbols; this would be attached to a strip of bullhide and swung around, whilst the magi chanted spells and incantations. After a time the magi would fall into a trance, when he could read the future or discover things happening far away. Kunz hypothesised that by fixing his gaze on the fast moving and shiny sphere the magi would induce the appropriate altered state to achieve the desired visions.

A pre-medieval technique of divination which is still used today is that of dactylomancy - divination with a ring. A gold wedding ring is suspended by a thread over a table with the letters of the alphabet and numbers 0-9 on it, and its motions spell out words and messages, like a planchette (ouija board).

According to Ammianus Marcellinus this technique was used to determine Valen's successor, giving the correct answer by naming Theodosius. Another version of dactylomancy is to suspend a wedding ring by a hair over a glass and ask questions. If the ring bangs the side once the answer is "Yes", and twice is "No".

Although it seems to go against the teachings of the church, there can be no doubt that a degree of "white" magick was practiced by priests and people in power without fear of reprisal or denouncement. Skrying was definitely one of the techniques which came into this category.

An illustration of this comes from a sixteenth century manuscript where the remark is made "the crystal should be laid on the altar on the side that the gospel is read on" . The manuscript continues that "these angels being once appeared will not depart the glasse or stone until the Sonne be sett except you licence them".

Clearly a licence to depart is the realm of the ritual magician, even in the case of angels. In one of the books attributed to Faust there was given information about preparation of crystals and mirrors, which continued the theme of using magick within a Christian context.

As an aid to skrying, drinking a cup of mugwort tea has been used for many centuries, and you may find this of assistance in improving skrying abilities. To prepare place two tablespoons of mugwort in one cup of boiling water, leave to steep for fifteen minutes, strain and drink.

Crystal Ball

As Astral Doorways

Rose quartz is a good stone to start with, and carnelian has been used in this manner for many centuries, holding it in front of a candle and focusing on it until you are ready to project through it. If you have a stone which feels right, then start by using it.

Any crystals may be used in this manner, and it can be most rewarding experiencing different types of landscape as you try out different crystals as doorways.

One should project through the crystal in the same way you would with a tarot card or mandala. Carrying the crystal around bodily for a period of time prior to using it as a doorway makes projection a lot easier for many people as their link with the crystal has been strengthened by the period of attunement.

If you are going through a lot of stress in your life, or having therapy to deal with major traumas, you may find that the imagery in the landscapes becomes disturbing or unpleasant. If this occurs it is up to you whether you wish to continue, the imagery may be of value, but may also be more than you want to deal with at a given time, so choose with your own well-being in mind.

Foɾ Dɾeamwork

Crystals and dreams have a long intertwined history. They have been used to aid in dreaming, and seeing different crystals in dreams is believed to have symbolic importance.

There are two techniques I would suggest using crystals that can aid lucid dreaming.

For the first method I would recommend using a quartz point, which should be able to fit in your clenched hand comfortably and be fully enclosed by your hand, no more than 2" long say.

The quartz should be held in your dominant hand during sleep, and stored in silk under your pillow during your absence. If the quartz is used for a period of time, and kept well charged, you will soon find it aids lucid dreaming greatly.

When you see your quartz in the dreamstate you know you are progressing, the next stage is to focus on it as it will help you maintain lucidity once gained.

An alternative to this is to have several thin quartz wands (three or four) and wear a glove on your preferred hand, with one of the wands down each finger of the glove held tight to the finger. This can produce a strong sensation of having a claw, which may be encouraged to build up power animal linking.

It also gives you a focus for shifting to animal form easily when you are dreaming (women may find this particularly noticeable and useable during their bleeding, a time when

53

dream research suggests up to 70% of dreams may be animal related).

This claw/glove technique may or may not work for you, it is up to you to go with what feels right - if it is uncomfortable or makes you feel silly, you don't have to do it!

Another technique is to bind a stone into your navel. For this an appropriate stone needs to be found, a cabochon cut stone works very well, and should not be so large as to be uncomfortable, nor so small as to disappear into your navel.

A material such as silk (the tie for a kimono or dressing gown is ideal) should be used for the belt, it should be something that is not going to make you uncomfortable, and preferably a natural material. Suggested stones to work with in this way are labradorite, moonstone, opal, tourmaline and the beryls.

It is worth sticking with one stone until you have reached a good degree of lucidity before shifting to others to experiment. Working in this manner may produce feelings of greatly increased solidity and "reality" in your lucid dreams, be aware that the dreamworlds can be every bit as real as the mundane waking state - and magick works in them more effectively than in the waking state as the mundane constraints do not apply.

The Symbolism of Crystals in Dreams

Considering how long crystals have been used by man, it will perhaps be no surprise that there are attributions for what seeing different crystals in dreams are supposed to mean. Indeed, these attributions are centuries old, and I list here all the attributions I have been able to find.

Stone	Dream Meaning
Agate	A journey by sea.
Alexandrite	A coming time of need.
Amber	A voyage.
Amethyst	Next venture will be successful, and/or freedom from harm.
Aquamarine	New friends.
Beryl	Happiness in store.
Bloodstone	Distressing news or long life!
Carnelian	Impending misfortune.
Cat's Eye	Treachery ahead.
Chalcedony	Friends rejoined.
Coral	Recovery from illness.

Diamond	Victory over enemies.
Emerald	A positive future and contact with old friends, and/or much to look forward to.
Garnet	The solution to a problem or mystery is at hand, and/or the acquisition of wisdom.
Jasper	Love returned.
Jet	Sorrow.
Lapis Lazuli	Successful affairs of the heart, and fidelity.
Magnetite	Subtle dealings and contentions.
Moonstone	Light, bright colour - Travel and good health Dark colour - Impending danger.
Moss Agate	An unsuccessful journey.
Opal	Great possessions
Pearl	Faithful friends.
Peridot	A need for necessary caution.
Quartz	Freedom from enemies.
Ruby	Unexpected guests.
Sapphire	Escape from danger
Topaz	No harm will befall the dreamer.
Tourmaline	An accident will happen.
Turquoise	Coming prosperity.
Zircon	Success or a heavy storm.

Crystals and Their Use in Healing

Much has been written on the subject of healing with crystals, which is not surprising as it is one of the most effective ways to work with crystals. There are various ways to work with crystals for healing, including placing crystals on the chakras, using a crystal wand as a focus, placing crystals around the body, etc, or a combination of these techniques.

Before discussing healing techniques, I would stress elements worth incorporating in the pre-healing routine:

> 1. Cleanliness - both yours and the person being healed, is to be encouraged. Obviously there may be circumstances where this is unfeasible, such as camping out in the wilds, but even then you as the healer should wash your hands.

> 2. Permission - assuming the person has already given you permission to heal them (by asking), you should agree the parameters you are working within, i.e. establish clear boundaries. When you heal someone they are trusting you and allowing you a degree of power over them, this must not be abused.

> 3. To help keep clear boundaries you should establish such parameters as:- is touch involved, and if so on what parts of the body; is the person comfortable removing items of clothing or would they be happier if they kept everything on (any negligible reduction in

energy you may feel is caused by healing through clothes is more than offset by keeping the person relaxed and not having to heal someone who is tense and resistant to the healing you offer).

4. If you are doing absent healing, you should offer the healing to the person's higher self (or in the case of animals it can be offered to the totemic spirit of the animal, such as Cat or Dog, etc), as people are not always open to healing and may not want it. **Never** try to force someone to accept healing, there may be valid reasons why they do not accept healing (including not believing in it for a start), and it is bad practice and negative magick to try and impose your will on others.

5. Clarity - having determined the mechanics of the healing, see if the person wishes to join in, and if so describe the visualisations you use so they can see it and reinforce their own healing (e.g. "I am directing the healing through the quartz wand as a ray of gold light which is passing into your aura and forming a corona around your heart chakra to strengthen and reinforce it).

6. Responsibility - you have a responsibility to yourself as well as to anyone you heal, so do not use your own energy when healing. Before you start, use an energising exercise, such as the chakra exercise given in the chapter on Chakras, and include the drawing energy from the earth beneath and heavens above. If you drain off your own energy into healing someone, not only do you become more prone to illness, but you are also likely to catch whatever the person you were healing had.

7. If you are close to the person you are healing it can be difficult to remain objective, but it is vital to channel energy when you heal, never use your own. Also, for

obvious reasons, you should not heal other people when you are ill, under the influence of drugs which knock you off balance, or heavily pregnant.

8. Balance - even if the problem is around one area, you should always work in a balanced way, as illness tends to stem from imbalance. This means if you are giving healing to an area on the left side of the body, you do the same on the right side of the body; the same is true with the chakras, even if working on a problem with one or two of them, you should still balance this by working with the other main chakras.

Having prepared thoroughly, you then have a choice as to which technique of healing to is most appropriate to the condition you are treating.

Using a crystal wand and working up the chakras in turn, vibrating the mantra for each a set number of times as you focus on directing the healing energies to balance the chakras and close them down if too open. The energy is focused at the heart chakra and directed as gold energy along the energy channels in the arms to the healing chakras in the hands, and then through the wand to the chakra.

Depending on how you feel at the time you may wish to work with the wand a few inches above the body, or actually touching the skin. If the tip of the wand does touch the skin the energy will be felt to resonate in the body of the person being healed more strongly. This technique works well on problems with the subtle body and emotional/mental problems.

Remember also that you should always balance up when working with healing energies - if you work on the right side of the body, repeat the same on the left side.

Placing an appropriate crystal on each of the chakras of the person to be healed, and directing your energy into the crystals as described above (with or without a wand as a focus) with appropriate chakra-mantras can work very well if the person has a condition that is more physical rather than emotional or mental.

This technique tends to work well to alleviate rather than cure if the condition is serious, and needs frequent repetition. It should be remembered that even if you wish to concentrate on one chakra, you should still work on all of them to ensure the balance of the energy body.

Though the combination of crystals should be determined through experience, looking at the A-Z section after this chapter may offer some ideas, and I include a combination I have found to work very well over the years for general healing work:

Quartz	for	Crown
Amethyst	for	Third Eye
Tourmaline	for	Throat
Emerald	for	Heart
Amber	for	Solar Plexus
Aquamarine	for	Sacral
Carnelian	for	Base
Moss Agate	for	Feet

I have included an attribution of crystals for the feet as although not one of the major seven chakras, they are of similar importance - our feet are the link which connects us to the earth.

The chakras in the feet respond to the vibration of the mantra HUM, so this may be used if working with chakra-mantras. For visualisation I visualise the feet chakras as responding to white light, which then splits prismatically to form the rainbow through the seven major chakras. If you find this does not work well for you, try basic earthy colours such as brown or black until you find what works best for you.

An energy web formed around the body, as described in the section below, with the focus crystal placed on the afflicted area of the body and combined with the use of essential oil rubbed on the area and the crystal works well for healing requiring a lot of energy, particularly if other people are involved in the healing and providing energy to empower the web which you can then focus.

Remember that when more than one person is healing, for maximum effectiveness you should have agreed beforehand on details of technique (like what colour you are visualising the healing energy, if one person is acting as the focus of the other participant(s) energy or all are focusing directly on the person being healed, etc).

Rubbing a crystal over the afflicted part of the body whilst concentrating your energy appropriately (through mantra, visualisation, breath control, etc) can work well, particularly if combined with massage and/or knowledge of the meridians and/or subtle body. Spheres are particularly good for this, rolling over the body, although any crystal which is smoothed and has no rough or sharp edges may be used if deemed appropriate for the condition being treated.

Absent Healing may be performed on people or animals who are not in the same location as you.

Wearing crystals to help alleviate a condition is another technique, preferably (though often not feasibly) so the crystal is resting on the afflicted area, or an area which connects directly to the area in terms of energies. The most common example of this technique is the copper rheumatism bracelets so many people wear. Rings, bracelets, pendants, ear-rings, etc are all examples of this, though I emphasise that at least part of the crystal should be in direct contact with the skin for maximum effectiveness.

The technique for binding a crystal into the navel for during the night given in the earlier Dreamwork section can work very well for problems with internal organs. If the crystal is appropriately selected and programmed to help with whatever sort of healing is required, it can act whilst you are asleep and do the most good by working at the level of your unconscious without any of the conscious mind's censor mechanisms to inhibit its effects.

The quartz family are generally used as healing foci - stones such as quartz, rose quartz, citrine, amethyst and smoky quartz, though all stones have some value for dealing with differing complaints. Jet is a very good absorber of negative charge, but it must be cleaned regularly otherwise it will end up having a negative effect on the recipient/bearer.

The A-Z of Illnesses / Requirements which follows covers many different ailments and conditions, as well as magickal uses, and suggested stones to work with them.

A-Z of Illnesses/ Requirements & Crystals to Work With

Abdominal Problems	Smoky Quartz
Abundance	Citrine Quartz
Addiction (overcoming)	Amethyst, Kunzite, Rhodocrosite, Rose Quartz, Spinel Ruby, Topaz
Adrenal Glands	Peridot
Amnesia	Amber, Dinosaur Bone
Amplifier	Ametrine, Diamond, Opal, Quartz
Analysis	Peridot
Anger (release)	Lepidolite, Ruby, Spinel
Anxiety	Azurite
Apathy (overcoming)	Onyx
Appetite (lack of)	Topaz
Appreciation of Beauty	Jadeite, Nephrite, Rhodocrosite, Rose Quartz, Turquoise
Arthritis	Chrysocolla
Asthma	Amber

Astral Body (strengthening)	Rhodocrosite
Astral Doorway	Agate, Beryl, Carnelian, Opal
Astral Projection	Carnelian, Moldavite, Moonstone, Opal, Tektite
Astral/Psychic Vision	Amethyst, Beryl, Iceland Spar, Malachite, Sapphire, Tiger's Eye
Aura Healing	Labradorite
Aura Strengthening	Hematite, Labradorite, Rhodonite, Tiger's Eye
Back Problems	Hematite, Jet (lower back)
Balancing (emotions)	Chrysocolla, Diamond, Emerald, Moonstone, Peridot, Ruby, Zoisite
Balancing (energies)	Aqua Aurora, Aventurine, Diamond, Hematite, Onyx, Rose Quartz, Staurolite
Balancing (giving form)	Agate
Base Chakra (unblocking)	Carnelian
Benevolence	Chalcedony, Topaz
Bladder	Jasper
Blockages (clearing)	Garnet, Malachite, Smoky Quartz, Spinel
Blood[1]	Carnelian, Emerald, Garnet, Heliotrope, Hematite, Magnetite, Pyrites, Ruby, Spinel

[1] Note the ancient Mexican word for blood is chalchiuhatl which translates as 'water of precious stones'.

Blood Poisoning	Heliotrope
Blood Pressure (reducing high)	Rhodonite
Bones	Coral, Fluorite, Lapis Lazuli, Pearl
Bone Marrow	Heliotrope, Onyx
Boundaries (maintaining)	Fortification Agate
Brain Disorders	Diamond
Breathing Problems	Amber
Bronchitis	Rutile Quartz
Business (enhancing)	Malachite
Calming (atmosphere)	Agate
Calming (emotions)	Agate, Chalcedony, Rhodonite, Turquoise
Cardiovascular System	Kunzite
Cervix	Zoisite
Chakras (rapid closing of)	Rhodonite
Circulatory System	Agate, Garnet, Magnetite, Malachite, Onyx, Rhodocrosite, Ruby, Spinel
Clairvoyance	Amethyst, Aquamarine, Tiger's Eye
Clarity	Alexandrite, Cat's Eye, Emerald, Fluorite, Jadeite, Nephrite, Peridot, Sapphire
Colon	Agate, Citrine Quartz
Communication (improving - to others)	Calcite (Blue), Opal

Communication (improving - to self)	Aquamarine, Labradorite
Concentration	Smoky Quartz
Connecting with the Earth	Moss Agate
Counselling (as recipient)	Smoky Quartz
Courage (physical)	Amber, Hematite
Courage (to speak)	Carnelian
Crown Chakra (unblocking)	Diamond, Herkimer Diamond, Quartz
Cycle Completion	Garnet
Deception (guarding against)	Heliotrope
Depression (overcoming)	Chrysoprase, Fluorite, Kunzite, Labradorite, Smoky Quartz, Zircon
Digestive Organs	Citrine Quartz, Peridot, Tiger's Eye
Digestive Problems	Calcite (Orange), Chrysocolla, Peridot, Pyrite
Directing Energy	Ametrine, Aqua Aura, Obsidian, Quartz, Rhodocrosite, Ruby
Discrimination	Cats Eye, Emerald
Divination	Agate, Moonstone
Dreaming	Amethyst, Ammonite, Aquamarine, Azurite, Beryl, Labradorite, Moonstone, Opal, Quartz, Rose Quartz, Topaz, Tourmaline
Ears	Onyx

Earthing	Agate, Heliotrope, Hematite, Jadeite, Jasper, Marble, Nephrite, Onyx, Pyrite, Sapphire
Earth Energies	Ammonite, Chrysocolla, Jadeite, Nephrite, Staurolite
Earth Healing	Ammonite, Chrysocolla, Jadeite, Nephrite, Staurolite
Eclipse Magicks	Black Sunstone
Eczema	Aventurine, Gypsum, Jasper
Emotional Problems (dealing with)	Aquamarine, Coral, Fluorite, Heliotrope, Jet, Malachite, Moonstone, Peridot, Rhodocrosite, Rutile, Rutile Quartz, Smoky Quartz, Zircon, Zoisite
Emotional Stability & Strength	Calcite (Orange), Citrine Quartz, Coral, Fluorite, Marble, Rhodocrosite
Endocrine System	Amber, Amethyst, Rutile Quartz
Endurance	Hematite
Energy (restoring)	Amber, Garnet, Rhodonite, Spinel, Tiger's Eye, Tourmaline, Zircon
Epilepsy	Aquamarine, Moonstone
Evil Eye	Agate (eyestone), Coral (red)
Exorcism	Agate

Eyes	Alexandrite, Beryl, Cat's Eye, Emerald, Iceland Spar, Jadeite, Lapis Lazuli, Nephrite, Opal, Ruby (esp. Star), Sapphire (esp. Star), Tiger's Eye, Topaz
Faerie Magicks	Hagstones, Silver, Staurolite
Fasting	Aventurine
Fear (banishing/releasing)	Chalcedony, Chrysocolla, Citrine Quartz, Ruby, Sapphire, Spinel, Zoisite
Fertility	Carnelian, Coral, Gypsum, Moonstone
Finances (improving)	Chrysoprase, Magnetite
Fluid Retention	Amethyst, Aquamarine, Moonstone, Prase
Frustration	Chrysoprase
Gallbladder	Carnelian, Citrine Quartz, Jasper
Gallstones	Chalcedony
Gambling	Aventurine, Jadeite
Gardening	Moonstone
Growth (all combined)	Jadeite, Nephrite
Growth (emotional)	Zircon, Zoisite
Growth (physical)	Coral
Growth (spiritual)	Amethyst, Labradorite, Moldavite, Obsidian, Sunstone (black), Tektite, Topaz, Tourmaline

Hair Disorders	Pearl
Happiness	Rose Quartz
Headaches	Amethyst
Healing (emotional)	Azurite, Citrine, Emerald, Quartz, Rose Quartz
Healing (physical)	Agate, Emerald, Onyx, Quartz
Healing (mental)	Amethyst
Health (general)	Sodalite, Sunstone
Heart Chakra (unblocking)	Amber, Emerald, Fluorite, Garnet, Sunstone
Heart Problems	Amber, Citrine Quartz, Emerald, Garnet, Heliotrope, Jadeite, Lapis Lazuli, Nephrite, Onyx, Rhodocrosite, Sapphire, Sunstone, Zircon
Higher Self (working with)	Labradorite, Moldavite, Ruby (star), Sapphire (star), Tektite
Hope	Chrysoprase
Hormonal Problems	Garnet (almandine & pyrope)
Humour (restoring sense of)	Tiger's Eye
Hypnosis	Azurite
Hypochondria (overcoming)	Cat's Eye Tiger's Eye
Hysteria (coping with)	Malachite
Ideas (giving form)	Ametrine, Coral, Tiger's Eye
Identity (loss of)	Fortification Agate

Illusions (dispelling)	Staurolite
Immune System	Amethyst, Emerald, Jadeite, Ruby, Topaz
Impotence	Alexandrite, Carnelian
Indecision (overcoming)	Amber, Zircon
Inertia (overcoming)	Heliotrope
Inflammation	Hematite
Inner Beauty	Opal
Inner Peace	Sapphire
Inner Work (e.g. guide, sub-personality)	Rutile Quartz, Smoky Quartz
Insight	Alexandrite, Chrysoprase, Tiger's Eye
Insomnia	Amethyst, Lapis Lazuli, Malachite, Zircon
Inspiration	Amethyst, Ametrine, Chrysocolla
Instinct (developing/attuning)	Citrine Quartz, Obsidian
Integrating Energies	Rhodocrosite, Ruby, Sapphire (star)
Intestines	Obsidian
Intuition	Amethyst, Chalcedony, Opal
Irritability (reducing)	Chalcedony
Kidneys	Carnelian, Citrine Quartz, Emerald, Jadeite, Jasper, Nephrite, Onyx, Rhodocrosite, Smoky Quartz
Knowledge (gaining)	Zircon

Kundalini (blockages)	Carnelian, Serpentine, Smoky Quartz
Labour (easing pain)	Ametrine, Moonstone
Legal Matters	Hematite
Leg Problems	Spinel Ruby
Lies (detecting)	Emerald
Liver	Aquamarine, Carnelian, Citrine Quartz, Emerald, Jasper, Obsidian, Ruby, Zircon
Love	Beryl, Emerald, Fluorite, Opal, Rose Quartz
Loyalty	Kyanite
Luck	Aventurine, Gypsum, Opal, Staurolite
Lunar Magicks	Moonstone
Lung Disorders	Calcite, Carnelian, Chrysocolla, Citrine Quartz, Opal
Lymphatic system	Agate, Rhodonite
Magnetism (Personal)	Hematite, Magnetite
Mania (soothing)	Kunzite
Manifesting Ideas	Carnelian, Coral
Massage	Agate
Meditation	Aquamarine, Lapis Lazuli, Zircon
Memory (improving recall)	Amber, Ammonite, Dinosaur Bone, Emerald, Rhodocrosite, Serpentine

Mental Discipline	Sapphire
Mental Growth	Opal, Rhodocrosite, Zircon
Mental Problems (inc. illness)	Aquamarine, Emerald, Labradorite, Sapphire, Tourmaline
Menstruation Difficulties	Chrysocolla, Coral, Jet, Malachite
Migraine	Amethyst
Miscarriage (preventing)	Ruby
Nails (finger/toe)	Onyx
Nerves	Aquamarine
Nervous System	Alexandrite, Amber
Neurological Problems	Emerald
New Ventures	Amazonite
Nightmares (protection from/ relief)	Coral, Jet, Lepidolite, Malachite, Rhodocrosite, Tourmaline
Pancreas	Agate, Alexandrite, Carnelian, Malachite, Smoky Quartz
Panic Attacks	Aquamarine, Chalcedony, Sapphire
Passion	Ruby, Spinel
Past Life Work	Amber, Ammonite, Dinosaur Bone, Beryl, Jet, Opal, Zircon
Patience (improving)	Pearl
Perception (improving)	Aventurine

Perseverance	Amazonite
Physical Stamina (increasing)	Heliotrope
Pineal Gland	Amethyst, Diamond, Opal, Zircon
Pituitary Gland	Amethyst, Diamond, Lapis Lazuli, Opal, Sapphire, Zircon
Pollution (protection from)	Obsidian, Turquoise
Pragmatism	Kyanite
Precognition/Prophecy	Opal
Pregnancy (easing)	Moonstone
Protection (emotional)	Garnet, Jet, Malachite, Obsidian, Rose Quartz, Smoky Quartz, Tourmaline, Turquoise
Protection (spiritual/psychic)	Amethyst, Ammonite, Chalcedony, Garnet, Ivory, Jadeite, Jet, Labradorite, Moldavite, Nephrite, Obsidian, Onyx, Ruby, Smoky Quartz, Tektite, Tiger's Eye
Protection (home)	Peridot, Ruby
Protection (travelling)	Agate, Aquamarine (over water), Jet, Serpentine, Turquoise
Psychism (developing)	Aquamarine, Azurite, Cat's Eye, Citrine Quartz, Iceland Spar, Jet, Lapis Lazuli, Moldavite, Moonstone, Obsidian, Sapphire, Tektite

Psychism (problems)	Moonstone
Psychosomatic problems (dealing with)	Aventurine
Purification (body)	Aventurine, Diamond, Emerald, Jet, Spinel Ruby
Purification (emotional)	Aquamarine, Chalcedony, Diamond, Emerald, Jet, Rose Quartz
Purification (mental)	Chalcedony, Diamond, Emerald, Jet
Purification (spiritual)	Amethyst, Diamond, Emerald, Halite, Jet, Rose Quartz, Sapphire
Purity (of love)	Emerald
Purity (of will)	Topaz
Rashes	Aventurine, Gypsum
Regeneration	Topaz
Relationships (recovering from)	Rhodocrosite
Relaxation	Citrine Quartz, Coral, Kunzite, Lapis Lazuli, Rose Quartz, Smoky Quartz, Topaz
Reliability (improve)	Kyanite
Resolve	Garnet
Rheumatism	Copper (bracelets)
Riding (staying on the horse!)	Turquoise
Sacral Chakra (unblocking)	Amazonite, Aquamarine
Sea Magicks	Aquamarine, Coral

Seasonal Affectiveness Disorder (relief)	Aqua Aura
Self-Confidence	Emerald, Rhodonite, Rose Quartz
Self-Discipline	Kunzite, Sapphire
Self-Esteem (improve)	Alexandrite, Citrine Quartz, Kunzite, Pearl, Pyrites, Rose Quartz
Self-Evaluation (honest)	Pyrites, Tiger's Eye
Selflessness	Topaz
Senses (improving)	Jasper
Sensitivity (enhancing)	Tourmaline
Serenity	Chrysocolla, Rose Quartz, Topaz (blue)
Sexual Blocks or Problems	Alexandrite, Carnelian, Chrysoprase, Opal, Serpentine
Sex Drive (increasing if low)	Garnet (almandine & pyrope)
Sexual Organs (problems)	Smoky Quartz
Shyness (overcoming)	Aventurine, Carnelian
Skin Disorders	Gypsum, Jasper
Sight (astral)	Agate (eyestone), Amethyst, Iceland Spar
Sight (physical)	Iceland Spar
Skrying	Agate (eyestone), Beryl, Moldavite, Obsidian, Tektite
Solar Magicks	Amber, Gold, Sunstone

Solar Plexus Chakra (unblocking)	Amber
Spleen	Alexandrite, Amber, Heliotrope, Lapis Lazuli, Malachite, Nephrite, Pearl, Rhodocrosite
Spine (lower)	Carnelian
Stability	Hematite
Stellar Magicks	Labradorite, Lapis Lazuli, Moldavite, Tektites
Stillness (body)	Aventurine
Stillness (mind)	Aventurine
Stomach	Obsidian, Pearl, Sapphire
Storing Charged Objects	Alabaster
Storing Energy	Amber, Aqua Aurora, Aventurine, Chrysocolla
Strength (physical)	Diamond
Strength (spiritual)	Diamond, Ruby, Spinel
Stress	Alexandrite, Amazonite, Aqua Aura, Aquamarine, Azurite, Gypsum, Lepidolite, Onyx, Rhodocrosite, Topaz, Turquoise
Sunburn	Aventurine
Swelling (reducing)	Jadeite, Nephrite
Talismans	Amber, Carnelian, Tiger's Eye
Teething	Coral (esp. red)

Third Eye (unblocking)	Agate (eyestone), Amethyst, Azurite, Sapphire (esp. Star)
Throat Problems	Kyanite, Lapis Lazuli, Tourmaline
Throat Chakra (unblocking)	Tourmaline
Thymus Gland	Amber, Jadeite, Opal
Thyroid Gland	Chrysocolla, Jadeite, Kunzite, Lapis Lazuli
Tolerance (improve)	Kunzite
Toothache	Aquamarine
Toxins (help elimination)	Citrine Quartz
Tranquillity	Lace Agate, Rose Quartz
Transformation (energies)	Lepidolite, Smoky Quartz
Trauma (overcoming)	Alexandrite, Zoisite
Truthfulness	Kyanite, Lapis Lazuli
UFO Encounters (understanding/integrating)	Moldavite
Ulcers	Chrysocolla, Hematite, Pearl
Urine Problems	Prase
Virtue	Jadeite, Nephrite
Visualisation (blocks)	Malachite
Visualisation (improving)	Tiger's Eye
Vitality (increase)	Opal, Ruby, Zircon
Voice Work	Calcite, Kyanite, Lapis Lazuli
Warrior (inner)	Obsidian

Water Levels	Aquamarine, Prase
Wealth (attracting)	Jadeite, Magnetite, Nephrite, Pyrites, Staurolite
Willpower (improving)	Garnet (almandine & pyrope), Gypsum, Heliotrope, Ruby (star), Sapphire (esp. star), Sunstone (black), Topaz
Wisdom	Lapis Lazuli, Topaz
Womb (problems)	Moonstone

As A Spirit Trap

Although not given much attention in our modern "civilized" age, crystals have long been used as spirit traps. Some famous examples which spring to mind are the trapped spirits said in the Orient to reside in star stones (see the entries on Ruby and Sapphire in the Gemmology) and the trapped angel in the zircon at Mecca (see the entry on Zircon in the Gemmology).

"Demons", or "astral garbage" or whatever one calls the many forms of negative energies (well, negative to humans anyway) may be compelled or tricked into crystals, or if the entity is physically detectable, a crystal may be plunged into its form to contain it (though not using your hand as you do not want physical contact with the entity).

I consider amethyst and quartz are the best stones for this purpose, and shapewise, spherical (or egg) stones are the best to work with as spirit traps, not having any corners or edges for an entity to manifest in.

Once the entity has been trapped in the stone, the crystal should be stored in salt until you decide what to do with it. You must decide whether to transmute it, destroy it, leave it in the crystal and forget about it or send it back where it came from - it becomes your karmic responsibility (I see karma as being primarily about cause and effect, action and responsibility).

As A Personal Focus

To disperse or focus energies in times of extreme emotional duress or for concentration is a very important way of working with crystals - a sort of crystal "worry-bead" which becomes charged with your energy. I must stress here that I use the term "disperse" to describe translating the energy from you to the crystal for storage in a form useable later, when required, and do not mean waste.

The type of crystal used depends entirely on the individual preference, though a stone which reflects you best is recommended. This crystal should never be touched by anyone else, as you want to keep your link to it pure.

Acrostics & the Magickal Name / Aspects of the Magickal Personality

Magickal name can have a great deal of power in them. A technique which developed in 17th and 18th Century England and France was acrostics, the setting in to rings, brooches and bracelets of combinations of crystals, the first letters of whose names would express a sentiment. This technique can easily be adapted to create a crystal form of a magickal name set into an appropriate piece of jewellery.

Below are some examples of acrostics, with expensive and cheaper varieties of stones:

Hyacinth	or	Hematite
Opal		Onyx
Pearl		Peridot
Emerald		Essonite

Cat's Eye	or	Carbuncle (Garnet)
Hyacinth (Zircon)		Hematite
Aquamarine		Amethyst
Ruby		Rutile
Iolite		Idocrase
Topaz		Tourmaline
Yu (Jade)		Yu

There are a couple of "fudges" with this technique which become clear on looking at some of the names. One is that other names of stones are used e.g. hyacinth for zircon and yu for jade are common substitutions. Another is that cheaper minerals whose properties are not clearly known are used in place of precious or semi-precious gemstones. The former substitution is fine, but I would not recommend the latter, it is far better to stick with stones you know, and strive for a balance between size and cost of what you desire.

If we now take a couple of names which might be used as magickal names for examples, we can demonstrate the point further. For a lot of the letters there may be more than one stone e.g.

Hematite	could equally be Heliotrope
Emerald	could equally be Enstatite
Lapis Lazuli	could equally be Labradorite, Lepidolite, etc
Ivory	could equally be Iolite
Opal	could equally be Obsidian or Onyx
Sapphire	could equally be Smoky Quartz, Sodalite, Sunstone, etc

If there is a choice of stones you can obviously go with preference or availability depending on your temperament, the choice of stones does allow for a good degree of flexibility on a lot of the letters, enabling you to choose stones which you work better with and feel more resonance for. Thus we can have two very different sets of energies making up a name, e.g.

Moonstone	Malachite
Obsidian	Onyx
Ruby	Rhodocrosite
Garnet	Gypsum

Amber	Amethyst
Nephrite	Nephrite
Aventurine	Agate

It should be observed that this technique could not be used with private magickal names in company if the jewellery is clearly visible, as it would be divulging a part of oneself which should be kept hidden.

This working with of crystals to emphasise the magickal name can be seen as part of the work of developing the magickal personality. The primary crystal (and others you feel a link to) as mentioned in the earlier section Reflected in Crystal may be incorporated into your magickal personality as part of the development and reinforcement process.

The following excerpt from Dion Fortune's *Moon Magic* is a good example of someone using jewellery to help develop their magickal personality:

It would require Huysmans to do justice to the ear-rings I have possessed - jade, amber, coral, lapis, malachite for day; and for the night I have great jewels...I wear my own fashions, and they come from the "soft furnishings" as often as not, for there is a richness in the great breadths of the draperies that one does not find in the dress materials...I like rings, too, so big that I can hardly get my gloves on over them; and bracelets like fetters on my wrists.

If you have magickal jewellery, use it as such. Magickal jewellery should generally be worn when doing magick, not all the time in an effort to impress or look glamourous. There is an important distinction here between using tools to create a glamour which develops into the magickal personality you want (a process of development), and just striving to look glamourous (a process of ego flattery/self-gratification).

83

If you do wear an item all the times, e.g. a magickal ring, subtle changes can still be used to emphasise the difference between the magickal personality and the mundane personality in action, such as switching the ring over so it is on the same finger on the other hand when assuming the magickal personality.

As An Energy Web

Spell Webs

Creating a particular shape appropriate to the nature of a spell you wish to perform, a sort of crystal mandala, and making that shape with appropriate crystals, with the focus crystal coated with a layer of a sympathetic essential oil works well. The oil acts as an accumulator and the energy built up and directed into the crystal web is collected in the oil. The oil may then be used as desired, to anoint oneself or an object as required.

Spell Circuits

A circuit can also be created in this manner which is used as a regular "battery". Crystals to represent each of the planetary and elemental energies should be included in this, and a special "key" stone used corresponding to spirit.

The shape of the glyph should be given some consideration (as should the positioning of the individual planetary and elemental stones) and be in harmony with your magickal direction, e.g. if you are working on stellar magicks you might decide to work with a Nuit star, for earth magicks you might work with the earth symbol of an equal-armed cross in a circle.

The spirit stone should not be included in the circuit glyph, this comes in later. As each stone is placed vibrate a mantra which goes with that element/planet, this might be a divine name or associated creature, emotion, etc. When they are all in place, touch the spirit stone to each crystal in turn, visualising a line of (appropriately coloured) energy joining the stones and forming the circuit. From here there are two different possibilities.

Firstly, you can replace the stone of the planet or element you wish to work with for the spell or ritual with the spirit stone, and hold the planetary/elemental stone you have removed as the focus for your energies and the energies which build up in the crystal circuit.

Do not remove the planetary/elemental stone appropriate to the nature of the spell/ritual, but instead lightly cover it with a layer of an appropriate essential oil (correspondences are given in Appendix 6). Hold the spirit stone as your focus, and with it direct the energy you generate into the spell circuit so it accumulates into the oil which acts as an accumulator for the energies.

When you have finished raising energy and it is time direct the energy and to bind the spell, the oil may be used to anoint yourself and seal energy in, anoint an object to empower it, stored for later use, etc.

Room Enhancement/ Protection

To enhance the energy of a room such as a temple, crystals may be located at the corners or vertices of the room, and then charged to act as a web to enhance the energy of that space. As a protection for a temple or living space this is a technique which can work very well.

This technique works especially well with the quartzes, particularly amethyst, but you might like to experiment with appropriate Elemental crystals in the corners of a room or such like. Spheres are suggested as being the optimum shape for this, not only do they hold energy very well, but their shape is ideal as it has no corners (see the entry on spirit traps)

A Salt and Water Purification

Salt and water are both often used for purification. In Wicca the circle is often sprinkled with blessed salt water before it is cast. The technique I give here is a very simple one which is a good precursor to ritual when working in a group.

A (large) bowl of water and a bowl of salt are passed around the circle. The first person takes as long as they need to state the baggage they are carrying with them and that they have brought to the ritual. As s/he does this they sprinkle a bit of salt into the water and stir it in with their preferred hand.

When the first person has finished s/he passes it to the next person in the circle anti-clockwise from them (as this is a process of banishing negativity, and banishing is generally down anti-clockwise, as opposed to the sunwise or clockwise of invoking). The second person repeats this process, and passes the salt and water on. This continues until the bowl has gone all around the circle. Everybody else should remain silent and contemplate either their own baggage (before purifying) or centring themselves (after purifying).

If anyone feels the need, the bowls should be passed around a second time, etc. Although this process can take some time, it is a worthwhile investment of time, as it ensures everyone has let go of the stresses and baggage's of mundane living and can get on with the magickal work in a relaxed atmosphere of trust.

Crystals and the Environment

Before you buy a crystal from a shop or a stall, please remember to always ask where the crystal comes from and how it was mined. Unfortunately a lot of crystals are now strip mined, which is very harmful to the land. Crystals which have been strip mined usually have a feeling of being psychically fractured or distressed about them.

Open cast or strip mining excavates large chunks of land to extract precious minerals without needing to tunnel below the surface. It can cause short and long term environmental damage through accelerated soil erosion and through acid water damage. The exposure of exposed fragmented rocks to water can also create acids such as sulphuric acid which also degrade the environment.

As strip mining eliminates the soil and overlying rock above a mineral deposit, this means that even with replanting after the mining is completed, it will still take many years for vegetation and animals to return to the land.

Another material which you may wish to check the origins of before purchase is coral. These ancient ecosystems are under threat from a variety of causes. The threats include dynamiting, cyanide poisoning and fine mesh nets (both for fishing), sewage and sedimentation pollution.

It is shocking to realise that coral reefs in every major tropical region of the world bleached white from pollution during the

1980's. This bleaching depresses coral growth rates and in some cases results in mass coral mortality and enormous aquatic population loss, and can even contribute to potential species extinctions.

The other material I would ask you to check before buying is ivory. Obviously the trade in ivory and resulting murder of elephants is to be abhorred and not supported. The way to do this is either (a) not buy ivory, or (b) only buy antique ivory. Ivory that is old (i.e. decades or more) goes a yellow colour and eventually to a yellowy-brown. If ivory is white or cream coloured, you know the elephant has been killed recently.

These disgusting trades and abuses of our environment are obviously not things you would wish to support, so please make your voice heard and counted by checking out these little details before buying that beautiful crystal or piece of coral or ivory.

Caring For Your Crystals

There are certain "rules" which hold true for all crystals. Contact with chemicals should be avoided (this can include substances such as hair sprays and perfumes which may contain a lot of chemicals), as should excessive exposure to light and extremes of temperature (severe heat or cold may damage the crystals).

Do not store crystals in air-tight bags, especially polythene and modern plastics, as such a sterile environment may have negative effects on the crystal, and in some cases cause fading.

If not being stored in e.g. a geode, they should be wrapped in silk, that great insulator of magickal charge, when not being used, or salt is also fine for non-programmed crystals (as it has a tendency to erase any programming and leave them blank).

Crystals should be washed under flowing water (not too hot or cold - avoid exposing your crystals to any sort of excesses of temperature) after usage to keep them clean.

I would not recommend using tap water, I work with water from sacred wells poured over the crystal (so it flows) to cleanse mine. "Moonraked" or "sunraked" water may be used for appropriate lunar or solar crystals.

Blessed salt water may also be used. If you do not have easy access to a sacred well or spring, still mineral water may be blessed and used in its place.

In Medieval Europe gemstones were placed in honey as it was believed to improve the lustre and make them more brilliant.

If you keep crystals in a pouch, be careful to check the hardness as you may find softer crystals being scratched by friction with harder ones. If you are keeping crystals of differing hardnesses together, it may be worth investing in some little pouches or silk to keep them individually wrapped.

It hopefully goes without saying that personal crystals should not be touched by anybody other than yourself (except in the case of healing). Crystals worn as necklaces, anklets, etc, should be cleaned regularly. If not, you may well find they develop the annoying habit of breaking and scattering crystals everywhere.

Some crystals have special cleaning requirements, detailed below and re-mentioned in the entries in *The Gemmology.*

Amber - Amber is easily scratched, and should be stored in a soft material (something like velvet, silk or felt would be ideal). For cleaning a mild soap with lukewarm water should be used, and a soft cloth then used to polish it dry. If a piece of amber has lost its lustre, rubbing with a soft cloth soaked in virgin olive oil can help restore the lustre.

Opal - Opals can contain up to 10% water, and must not be kept near a heat source such as a radiator, as this can cause them to dry out and crack. If left in a dry environment opals can lose their colour, ideally they should be stored in a small container of water. For cleaning, opals should be held in the hand and have cold (appropriate) water poured over them.

Pearl - Pearls contain around 2% water and as with opals must not be kept near a heat source such as a radiator, as this can cause them to dry out and crack. Pearls should not be exposed to acidic liquids such as vinegar or red wine, as this will cause them to dissolve. To clean pearls (including the strings) they should be gently agitated in potato floor so they get covered, and then the flour cleaned off. Do not use soap or detergents near pearls, it can affect them and cause them to lose their lustre.

Moonraking

A technique which may be used with a metal bowl (ideally silver or silver plate, but copper may also be used) or a crystal bowl is "moonraking". The bowl should be half filled with water and left in a place where the full moon's rays can shine down onto it.

The moon's rays may be "raked" into the water in the bowl with appropriate gestures of the hands or with a suitable crystal wand. The silvery light of the moon should be visualised filling and charging the water during this process, and you may wish to chant or use mantra.

When you feel the "moonwater" is sufficiently charged, it may be used to skry in. You may also wish to keep this water to use for cleaning crystals.

The same technique could be extended to "sunraking", although a gold plated or brass bowl would then be used, and gold light from the sun visualised filling the water rather than silver.

You might also like to try putting a piece of bloodstone in the water to see if you can foretell a coming eclipse (see entry on Heliotrope).

A Healing Rainbow

From ancient times through the Middle Ages and into recent thought, a belief has existed that the colour of a stone determined the kind of healing it could be used for.

Hence we see attributions like these:

Red   Haemorrhages, stopping bleeding, blood problems.

Orange   Energy and vitality problems.

Yellow   Jaundice, nervous conditions.

Green   Eye problems.

Blue   Calming the mind, cooling fever, antiseptic and pain relief.

Indigo   Sleep problems.

Violet   Spiritual problems, purity, chastity.

So, for example, any red stone would be considered able to stop haemorrhages. This attribution of properties by colour and/or shape to crystals, plants and other objects was known as the Doctrine of Signatures. This Doctrine states the magickal principle that some things resonate better together through their similarities (e.g. colour and/or shape) and may be used to affect others more effectively through virtue of this association. Many examples of this will be found in *The Gemmology* under the individual entries for crystals.

Artificial and Created Crystals

With the passing of time have come more and more techniques to imitate gems and pass them off to unsuspecting buyers. In recent times these developments in techniques have also led to crystals being manufactured which are almost indistinguishable from those found in nature, and in some cases new crystals created by forming new combinations. Examples of these developments and techniques are detailed below.

Created Crystals

There are several created crystals now available on the market, the only one of which I have covered in this book is aqua aura, which is quartz with gold bonded to the surface giving it a very attractive transparent blue colour.

The others are aqua aurora, which is quartz with titanium boned to the surface, and opal aura, which is quartz with platinum bonded to the surface. Aqua aurora has a metallic sheen, with a play of rainbow colours on the metallic surface. I find this stone to have a strange feel to it which makes me disinclined to try to work with it, (as if the bonding has imprisoned the quartz in a metallic coating,) but do not be put off by my experience as this may not be the case for other people.

Opal aura has a white surface with an opalescent play of colours on it, I cannot comment on the feel of this stone as I have only seen it in pictures. Ruby aura is quartz with ruby bonded to the surface, which has a curious feel to it.

Composites

A technique that has become more common in recent years is the production of composite gems, known as doublets or triplets. There are several different ways of doing this depending on the gem being used.

The most common way to make a doublet is to put a top sliver of the material being imitated onto a cheaper base, such as with a diamond top slice on a colourless sapphire or spinel base; this technique is used with an appropriately coloured glass base added to the gem top, such as red glass under garnet for ruby, or green glass under beryl for emerald.

Using glass of the same or similar colour means the whole piece is flooded with the colour, making it harder to detect. Triplets work on the same principle, but with three layers (the third usually being a thin coloured glass layer), only one of which is the actual stone offered for sale.

Doublets and triplets are usually mounted in jewellery, so the join is not easily visible, and the gem part of the composite is the exposed piece, fooling people to believe they have an expensive stone.

The most common example of this counterfeiting of fine gems with composites is with opals, where a layer of curved quartz over the top of the opal enhances the brilliance of the softer opal whilst also protecting it.

To determine if a stone is a composite, using a low to medium magnification lens will often reveal the joins, and a layer of air bubbles may also sometimes be revealed between the layers by such an examination.

Copies

At a glance some gems closely resemble other gems. In fact you will find mineralogists will not tend to commit themselves to an identification without tests in a laboratory, unless the identity of the stone is absolutely certain already.

The most common example in this day and age is probably colourless zircons and sapphires being passed off as diamonds. Another common example is red garnet and red spinel being used for ruby - the Black Prince's Ruby and the Timur Ruby in the British crown jewels are both red spinels.

Many of the stones claimed to be rubies in old items of jewellery are likely to be other stones, large good quality rubies are exceptionally rare, and have at times in history sold for up to eight times the price of diamonds. There are a number of instances of stones being passed off as other stones, the most significant are perhaps green tourmaline being passed off as emerald and citrine quartz as topaz.

There is also a historical phenomenon of gems being called the name of another gem, for reasons which are now unclear (if ever they were clear!). Some notable examples of this are lapis lazuli being referred to as sapphire - the inclusion in descriptions of the gold flecks in sapphires giving away the true identity of the stone; and also peridot being referred to as emerald.

Dying

Another common trick when selling crystals is to dye the crystal, either to improve the colour or to make the colour more even. Necklaces of stones where all the crystals are exactly the same colour are likely to have been dyed.

Usually it is the more porous stones that are dyed, so among the most commonly dyed stones we find agate, jade, rose quartz and turquoise. Agate has been dyed since Roman times, and "potato slices" are frequently dyed, if they are particularly vividly coloured (pink, for example) they should be examined carefully for signs of dye.

Thomas Nicols, writing in the 17th century, wrote in protest about dyed jasper that: "It is ascribed by way of Glory to the King of Egypt that the first adulteration of jasper by tincture was from him, but the glory of this praise, if I be not mistaken, doth even become his shame."

Fakes

Objects have been found from 4700 BCE Egypt such as beads and pendants that were made of faience (a core of quartz grit surrounded by a glass-like coloured glaze).

By 3100 BCE the Egyptians were using fake crystals in artifacts, in the form of soapstone glazed blue and green as a substitute for turquoise. Whether this was a result of a need for a cheaper substitute, or if supply was not meeting demand, this does demonstrate how long man has been imitating the natural beauty of crystals.

Around 1600 BCE glass itself was introduced and used as a substitute for gems, being easily colourable and workable and cheap.

The use of glass to imitate crystals has continued through to the present day, and we have an Italian glassmaker to thank for the name of the stone "aventurine", as he was working on a speckled green glass and the colour he produced was "by chance" ("aventurra") similar to the sparkling colour of aventurine, and the name was given to that variety of stone.

In the last century or so a shiny black glass has been passed off to the unknowing as "French Jet", which it is not.

99

Heat-Treatment

Heat-treating of crystals to improve their appearance is a very common phenomena. There is some acceptance of heat-treating to improve the colour of stones - the majority of certain stones are heat treated to obtain their finest colour.

Stones which are commonly heat treated to improve the colour include aquamarine (to intensify colour or bring out the blue), diamond (some green and yellow) and zircon (all blue and colourless have been treated).

There are also stones which change their name with their colour, when low quality amethyst with uneven purplish colour is heated it changes to a more even golden brown, becoming citrine quartz.

Manufactured

The scientific developments in the last century have led to processes enabling the production of flawless gems which have many commercial uses, e.g. large flawless rubies can be used in scientific lasers. The gems such as diamond, emerald, ruby and sapphire cannot yet be produced in the sort of size required for jewellery, though research is still ongoing into new techniques and refinements.

There is still a massive prejudice against manufactured or "synthetic" gems, and natural gems will sell for up to five hundred times the cost of their synthetic counterpart even though they are more likely to be flawed or irregular.

Reconstituted Crystals

There are several stones sold which are sometimes marketed in a reconstituted form. These reconstituted forms are generally different in some respect(s) from a natural example of the crystal. The stones which have been reconstituted to turn small fragments into more commercially valuable gems are amber, beryl, ruby and sunstone.

Amber is one of the most successfully reconstituted stones. Fragments of amber may be combined into a larger whole using a hydraulic press at high pressure, in the absence of air at a temperature of around 180^{0}C (358^{0}F). The amber fragments are pressed together and flow into a larger whole, which has the appearance of untreated amber, and is known as ambroid.

Attempts to reconstitute beryls (including emerald) did not produce the expected results. The cooled result of the heating retained the beryl colour, but formed a glass with a beryl composition. This glass had different physical properties to beryl, such as lower hardness, density, refractive index, etc, making it easy to detect as a treated substance and not the genuine article.

In the early 1880's an unknown Swissman produced reconstituted rubies by heating them together at 180^{0}C (3272^{0}F), and adding chromic oxide. The rubies lost their colour when heated, and the chromic oxide restored the ruby colour. When the reconstituted nature of the "Geneva Rubies" became known, interest waned and the bottom fell out of the market, halting their commercial production.

Sunstone is frequently reconstituted, and it is very difficult to determine whether a stone is reconstituted or not apart from by the name - reconstituted sunstone is often sold under the name of goldstone.

CRystal ARtefacts

The High PRiest's BReastplate

I shall devote some attention to detailing the High Priest's Breastplate, as it is a significant artefact in a number of ways, not least of which is that it may be the original source of zodiacal attributions for gems.

Several hundred years before Christ, Aaron, the first High Priest of Jerusalem, was the first bearer of the High Priest's Breastplate. This breastplate bore twelve stones, each with the name of one of the twelve tribes on it. The stones are listed in the description given in the Bible in Exodus 28:15-20, though it must be borne in mind that names given to stones have sometimes changed. The description from Exodus (Authorised Version) and a list of the twelve stones recorded in the original Hebrew, and subsequent versions is given below:

And thou shalt make the breastplate of judgement with cunning work; after the work of the ephod thou shalt make it; of gold, of blue, and of purple, and of scarlet, and of fine twined linen shalt thou make it.

Foursquare it shall be being doubled; a span shall be the length thereof, and a span shall be the breadth thereof.

And thou shalt set in it settings of stones, even four rows of stones: the first row shall be a sardius, a topaz and a carbuncle: this shall be the first row.

And the second row shall be an emerald, a sapphire, and a diamond.

And the third row a ligure, an agate. and an amethyst.

And the fourth row a beryl, and an onyx, and a jasper; they shall be set in gold in their enclosings.

And the stones shall be with the names of the children of Israel, twelve, according to their names, like the engravings of a signet; every one with his name shall they be according to the twelve tribes.

And thou shalt make upon the breastplate chains at the ends of wreathen work of pure gold.

And thou shalt make upon the breastplate two rings of gold, and shalt put the two rings on the two ends of the breastplate.

And thou shalt put the two wreathen chains of gold in the two rings which are on the ends of the breastplate.

And the other two ends of the two wreathen chains thou shalt fasten in the two pouches, and put them on the shoulder-pieces of the ephod before it.

And thou shalt make two rings of gold, and thou shalt put them upon the two ends of the breastplate in the border thereof, which is in the side of the ephod inward.

And two other rings of gold thou shalt make, and shalt put them on the two sides of the ephod underneath, toward the forepart thereof, over against the other coupling thereof, above the curious girdle of the ephod.

And Aaron shall bear the names of the children of Israel in the breastplate of judgement upon his heart, when he goeth in *unto the holy place, for a memorial before the Lord continually.*

And thou shalt put in the breastplate of Judgement the Urim and the Thummim; and they shall be upon Aaron's heart, when he goeth in before the Lord: and Aaron shall bear the judgement of the children of Israel upon his heart before the Lord continually.

Considering the dimensions of the breastplate, a span being around 8" - 9" (20cm - 221/2cm), this would suggest the gems themselves might have been up to 21/2" (6^1/$_4$cm).

The original breastplate (assuming it was real) was lost during the Babylonian captivity of the Jews. Around 500 BCE a second breastplate was made, it has been suggested that the inscriptions on this breastplate may have been Chaldean or Syro-Chaldean rather than Hebrew.

This second breastplate was taken by the Romans when Titus sacked Jerusalem in 70 CE, and then taken to Rome and processed triumphantly through the streets and into the Temple Of Concord. After 455 CE with the fall of Rome the location of the second breastplate becomes speculation, and though lost the breastplate was not forgotten, with the legends about its power growing.

The second breastplate may have had different stones in it to the first, the original breastplate would have used stones known to the Egyptians and others in the area around 1400 - 1300 BCE. In the eight hundred years or more in-between other crystals came into common usage, and the ability to cut harder crystals improved.

Accounts of the powers of the breastplate were usually biased in one way or another. The Jewish historian Josephus (37-95 CE) gave an eyewitness account of the breastplate, and how it signalled the presence of God at the sacrifice, and could predict victory in battle.

Four hundred years later the Bishop of Constantia attributed oracular powers to the gem, elaborating the earlier statements and hence developing the legend of its powers. The Bishop stated that the stones could change colour to a dusky hue to indicate the approach of death by disease, or the colour of blood signifying death by violence; however if the gems shone clearly this indicated that people had not sinned.

The Kalpa Tree

The Kalpa Tree in Indian myth is described as being made entirely of gems. It was a symbolic offering to the Gods, described as a glowing mass of precious stones, and makes a very good place to visit (via pathworking/meditation) for serenity and repose when you need a tranquil place to go. We can see the fruits being rubies is consistent with the belief that colourless sapphires were unripe rubies, which could ripen like fruit into red rubies.

The tree was described as being made up of the following stones:

* The uppermost section of the trunk was made of cat's eye.
* The middle section of the trunk was made of topaz.
* The bottom section of the trunk was made of diamond.
* The roots were made of sapphire.
* The shoots were made of emerald.
* The fresh young leaves were made of coral.

* The rest of the foliage was made of green zircon.
* The fruits were rubies.

CRystal Skulls

Of all crystals, perhaps the one which holds the attention of the public more than any other is the "Skull of Doom", the stunning carved quartz skull found earlier this century.

No	Tribe	Hebrew Stone Name	Greek Septuagint c. 250 BCE	Greek Josephus c. 90 CE	Latin Vulgate c. 400 CE	Authorised Bible 1611 CE	Modern - Probable Stone
1	Reuben	Odem	Sardion	Sardonyx	Sardius	Sardius	Carnelian
2	Simeon	Pitdah	Topazion	Topazion	Topazius	Topaz	Peridot[1]
3	Levi	Bareketh	Smaragdos	Smaragdos	Smaragdus	Carbuncle	Emerald
4	Judah	Nophek	Anthrax	Anthrax	Carbunculus	Emerald	Garnet
5	Issachar	Sappir	Sappheiros	Iaspis	Sapphirius	Sapphire	Lapis Lazuli[2]
6	Zebulon	Yahalom	Iaspis	Sappheiros	Jaspis	Diamond	Quartz
7	Joseph	Leshem	Ligurion	Liguros	Ligurius	Ligure	Zircon
8	Benjamin	Shebo	Achates	Amethystos	Achates	Agate	Agate
9	Dan	Ahlamah	Amethystos	Achates	Amethystus	Amethyst	Amethyst
10	Naphtali	Tarshish	Chrysolithos	Chrysolithos	Chrysolithus	Beryl	Citrine
11	Gad	Shoham	Beryllion	Onyx	Onychinus	Onyx	Onyx
12	Asher	Yashpheh	Onychion	Beryllos	Beryllus	Jasper	Jasper

There has been much speculation about the possible uses of crystal skulls, and suggestions they may have been crystal "computer banks" or psychic foci.

The fact that the shape is that of the skull indicates to me a connection to the ancient belief that the head (and specifically the skull) was the seat of the soul. When we start to examine

---

[1] Though the third stone is referred to as topaz, it is considered unlikely this was the actual stone.

[2] Though the fifth stone is called sapphire, we know from the contemporary refences that this term was used generically at the time to describe lapis lazuli.

crystal skulls with this in mind, there can be no doubt that these items are powerful artefacts of change.

Working with crystal skulls, you may find very quickly that they unlock memories from deep in your past, in vivid detail. This makes them very valuable as aids to work dealing with childhood traumas such as abuse, deaths of kith and kin and other events which may have left deep scars and hold up a lot of energy in blockages.

Even small crystal skulls, which are now quite easily available, can be very beneficial for work on self-integration - I possess a small rose quartz skull given to me by friends which has been very useful at times of integrating released energy from the psyche.

Sacred Treasures

Crystals are often considered to be amongst the most sacred of items in various cultures. In Shinto, four of the ten sacred treasures were jewels. These were the Life-Inspiring Jewel, the Jewel of Perfect Health and Strength, the Jewel of Resuscitating the Dead and the Jewel of Warding off Evil from Roads. In Chinese Buddhism, three of the eight sacred things (or emblems of good luck) were also crystals/minerals, being lapis lazuli, pearl and shell.

Crystals and Fabulous Places

There is a long tradition of describing fabulous places, such as dwelling places of deities or great holy men in terms of crystal. Below are given the best known of these.

The Islamic Heavens

Six of the seven heavens are said to be made of precious gems and metals:

The 1st Heaven is of pure silver, filled with all the stars and their Angel warders, and the dwelling place of Adam and Eve.

The 2nd Heaven is of pure gold, and the dwelling place of John the Baptist and Jesus.

The 3rd Heaven is of pearl, the dwelling place of Joseph, and presided over by Azrael (the Angel of Death) who ceaselessly writes the names of the new-born and blots out the names of the newly deceased in his book.

The 4th Heaven is of white gold, the dwelling place of Enoch, presided over by the Angel of Tears, who sheds tears endlessly for all the sins committed by mankind.

The 5th Heaven in of silver, dwelling place of Aaron, and presided over by the Avenging Angel, who rules over elemental fire.

The 6th Heaven is of ruby and garnet, the dwelling place of Moses, presided over by the Guardian Angel of Heaven and Earth, who is half snow and half fire.

The 7th Heaven is of divine light beyond description, the dwelling place of Abraham.

It is quite possible the expression "In Seventh Heaven" is derived from this source.

Mount Meru

Mount Meru is a sacred Indian site, dwelling place of the Gods. The four faces of Mount Meru are made of precious stones and metals. The North face is golden, the East is of silver, the South is of Cat's Eye, and the West is of Ruby. Mount Meru was surrounded by a ring of iron mountains.

The High Priest's Breastplate, from "*Vesitus Sacerdotum Hebraicorum*" (1680)

New Jerusalem

New Jerusalem is described in Revelations 21:18-21, as follows:

The walls are of Jasper. The 12 gates are each made of a giant Pearl. The streets are of Gold described as being like translucent glass.

The 1st Foundation is of Jasper.

The 2nd Foundation is of Lapis Lazuli.

The 3rd Foundation is of Chalcedony.

The 4th Foundation is of Emerald.

The 5th Foundation is of Sardonyx.

The 6th Foundation is of Carnelian.

The 7th Foundation is of Peridot.

The 8th Foundation is of Beryl.

The 9th Foundation is of Topaz.

The 10th Foundation is of Chrysoprase.

The 11th Foundation is of Zircon.

The 12th Foundation is of Amethyst.

Prester John's Palace

The gates of Prester John's palace were said to be made of sardonyx with the powdered horns of horned serpents set in them, both materials working to prevent anyone bringing poison into the palace. A judicial courtyard for trial by combat had onyx tiles, to bolster the courage of the combatants. Prester John's bed was said to be made of a huge sapphire, which ensured his continuing chastity.

Curious Customs

Blood Offerings to Crystals

It has been recorded (by Kunz among others) that among the Cherokee Indians quartz was considered a powerful divinatory and hunting talisman, and there were instances of the fetish lump of quartz being rubbed with the blood of the prey and treated as a live creature joining in the consuming of the prey.

The Burmese Bghai tribe had stone fetishes in each house, and these were placated with periodic blood offerings to the indwelling spirits of the stones. Both these instances indicate a more animistic view of a vital world which takes magick for granted, a view largely dismissed by today's exoteric society.

The use of blood, a source of great magickal power, with crystals, which are great foci of power, can obviously generate a great deal of energy, but I leave it to the reader to consult with their crystals and decide if they wish to explore this area, with the emphatic caveats of being aware this type of magick can be more wild and unpredictable if not worked extremely rigorously, and that it is obviously wise to use sterilised needles or blades if you are taking blood to offer (unless it is menstrual when collecting it will not be a problem).

Burning Crystals

The burial mounds of the Mississippi Valley have revealed large quantities of burned pearls which appear to have been offered during the funerary rites for important persons. The Spaniard Francisco Lopez de Gomara recorded the Indians of New Granada making offerings by burning gold and emeralds before images of the sun and moon, which they considered the highest deities. Beyond the idea of demonstrating devotion and piety through sacrifice of what is most precious, we can only speculate on the significance of these actions.

There are also examples of burning with a specific aim in mind, like the Roman uses of jet, to drive off serpents, or when cast on a red-hot axe, to make a wish. In the Orient amber used to be burned as a disinfectant prior to the practice of medicine.

The "Chuninga"

The Australian aborigines have a custom of preparing a chuninga, which is made from a flat piece of either wood or stone, when a baby is due. The chuninga is stored in a sacred cave until initiation (usually at puberty) when the child and chuninga are (re-)united. This power object is then only used for ceremonies such as healing, especially for circumcision and subincision (of ultunga stones), and for giving courage and power, being stored in the cave at all other times.

In some Old Stone Age caves there have been found inscribed stones which strongly resemble chuningas. When holed and a string put through it, the chuninga can also be used as a bullroarer. In an age where rites of passage have become trivialised or non-existent, this concept is one with a great deal of appeal, and an interesting way to subtly bring power objects and magick into a child's life without imposing on his/her will.

113

Crystal Cosmetics

The ancient Egyptians used both powdered lapis lazuli and malachite in eyeshadow. It has been suggested that these uses were of ritual significance, to provide the bearer with clear vision and insight, which considering the relative cost of the stones does seem a likely possibility.

Rose quartz was used by the Romans, and believed to help get rid of wrinkles. In 17th-18th century France powdered pearl was used in cosmetic powders to improve the texture and lustre of the skin.

Crystal Gender & Reproduction

It was a common belief, recorded by the authors of antiquity, such as Theophrastus (writing 315 BCE) and Pliny the Elder, right through to the nineteenth century, that stones have two forms, a male and a female, which may have different qualities ascribed to them.

Browning wrote "And the tent shook, for mighty Saul shuddered - and sparkles 'gan dart, from the jewels that woke in his turban, at once with a start - all its lordly male-sapphires, and rubies courageous at heart." (Saul, VIII). Readers will not be surprised (considering the contemporary social structures) to discover that the male stones were usually considered to be the more powerful in terms of their properties. The different colours of a stone explained the genders - lighter stones were usually female and darker male.

An extension of this belief was that crystals could reproduce, and would do so if buried in the ground, a notion which continued until at least the sixteenth century in Europe, and still does in some parts of the world such as Borneo (see the entry on Pearl in The Gemmology).

Crystal Scents

Another curious medieval belief was that crystals had a scent, and that crushing crystals for medicinal use would release this scent. There is a record of this in Olaus Barrichius, (tome iv, p338, 1757), where the experiment of grinding precious stones for several weeks in a glass pestle and mortar is detailed, and the resulting smell from the ground gemstones was described as being like March Violets.

Heraldry and Crystals

The system of attributions found in heraldry developed mainly in the 13th century. Among the colours, furs and designs was a system of distinguishing royalty and peerage, known as "Blazoning by planets and precious stones". The attributions were developed as shown below:

Name of Tincture	Colour	Planet	Crystal
Or	Gold	Sun	Topaz
Argent	Silver	Moon	Pearl
Sable	Black	Saturn	Diamond
Azure	Blue	Jupiter	Sapphire
Gules	Red	Mars	Ruby
Vert	Green	Venus	Emerald
Pupure	Purple	Mercury	Amethyst
Tenny		Caput Draconis	Zircon
Sanguine		Cauda Draconis	Sardonyx

Imbedding Crystals

The imbedding under the skin of quartz pebbles (known as *ultunga* stones) by aborigines for power, and of rubies under the skin for protection in battle and to stop bleeding both indicate a belief in the ability of the power of crystals to be more effective for the body if the crystal has become "part" of the body.

This practice is one that can be equally achieved by less drastic means such as in jewellery, particularly being mindful of the current vogue for piercings - a ring with a crystal on it can be attached to ears, nose, nipples, navel, etc.

If the idea of imbedding a crystal under your skin appeals to you, consider this - how will this crystal affect the integrity of your subtle body, i.e. have you considered all the implications of this act? There may be some relevance in doing this when there is a cultural tradition which gives power to this action in itself, but "copy cat" imbedding is in my view perhaps more of a self-mutilation than a spiritual act.

The Language of Angels (Enochian) and Crystals

In the Enochian language skryed by John Dee (also known as the language of Angels), there are several minerals referred to. Interestingly all the references are in the 8th, 9th and 10th calls, of the 30 calls (or keys) to the Angels which Dee recorded. The minerals referred to are diamonds, salt, sulphur and zircon (hyacinth).

Call	Enochian Word	English Translation
8	Avabh	Hyacinth (Zircon)
9	Achildao	Diamonds
9	Balye	Salt
9	Limlal	Treasure
10	Salbrox	Live sulphur

Flint Arrowheads and Axes

The word flint comes from the Greek *plinthos* meaning "a brick". Flint has been used by man since his earliest days, for weapons and tools. Flint items have been regarded as having magickal properties for thousands of years, it was only in more recent times that flint items were correctly recognised as being what they are rather than the result of magickal occurrences.

Flint was also written as flend, flent, flynd, flynt, flynte, and vlint. Flint is now classed amongst the varieties of chalcedony and has a variety of colours - grey, greyish white, black, brown, red and yellow.

Flint Arrowhead

Flint arrowheads (also known as glossopetrae) were believed in the Middle Ages to be the fossilised tongues of serpents. Another creation belief was that the arrowheads were the

117

teeth of bloodsucking witches and vampires, who preyed on children.

When mounted in silver they were thought to be an effective charm to protect cattle from fairy and elf bewitchments, this continued until recent times in Ireland, where the silver mounted arrowheads are known as saigead. Silver mounted arrowheads were also thought to protect the house they were kept in from lightning, being regarded as the solid manifestation of lightning flashes. It was also believed that glossopetrae fell from the heavens in the waning of the moon, and for this reason they were prized for use in Lunar magicks by medieval magicians.

In Ireland in the Middle Ages if a woman found a flint arrowhead she would be elevated to the position of village medical counsellor, due to the ascribed properties of the arrowhead. The arrowhead would be soaked in water, and the water given to the afflicted person to drink. This water was also thought to heal cows and horses which had been wounded by "elf shot" or "elf darts".

Around Europe arrowheads were placed in outbuildings to protect cattle from diseases. Shepherds carried flints to protect sheep during lambing and from foot-rot, and they were also placed in stys to protect pigs from swine fever. Horse-breakers carried them to protect their horses from evil.

They were also put in fruit trees to ensure the crop did not fail. In Italy flint arrowheads were worn by children around the neck to protect them from illness and the evil eye.

In France flint arrowheads were kept inside or placed in the foundations or walls of houses and even churches to protect the buildings from fire and lightning. In Switzerland, flint arrowheads anointed with butter and whirled on a thong round the head three times and thrown at the door of a dwelling when a storm was approaching was believed to protect it from lightning strikes.

Flint axes and hammerheads were known as "thunderstones", and were collected by the Romans who highly valued their protective magickal properties, and they also thought they prevented the return of the dead. Collections of thunderstones have been found in Roman temples in Britain testifying to this belief.

The Romans also set pieces of flint with coral into dog collars to prevent the dogs going mad. Flint arrowheads were set in gold and carried to bring good fortune in ancient Greece. Flints were carried by gypsies for luck, and protection from the "Devil's Imps". Poachers carried them for luck and to avoid detection.

In Norse myth thunderstones were thought to have been thrown at misbehaving trolls by Thor to keep them in order. Nordic folklore tells of large quantities of ale being poured over thunderstones and then given to the expectant mother to drink to aid the birth (in France they were thought to ease childbirth as well, though without the beer!). In Sweden thunderstones were believed to protect the bearer from elves.

In India flint arrowheads were known as "Thunderbolts of Vishnu", and were considered a sacred symbol of that deity in parts of Southern India. In Burma the arrowheads were also believed to be thunderbolts, and were used to determine the truth of a matter. An arrowhead would be placed in water, and anyone taking an oath would drink the water first before saying the words. The belief was that anyone who lied after drinking the water would be punished by the spirits. They were also used by the Burmese to cure and prevent appendicitis.

In Indonesia and Sumatra flints were considered very lucky, and were used to sharpen the kris, (a wavy bladed knife made of meteoric iron) itself a very magickal item. In Japan flint was used to cure boils and ulcers.

A Slavic belief was that flint could cure warts on man or beast, and that during Passion Week they would reveal hidden treasure. In Brazil pieces of flint were used as divining stones to locate gold, treasure and water.

Among the Pueblo Indians there were Flint Societies which were concerned with the weather and witchcraft, both areas which flint has been widely associated with.

From all these examples it can be seen that the use of flint arrowheads was widespread and amuletic, with protective qualities to people, places and beasts.

A corpse was found at Duggleby Howe (Britain) of a seventy year old man holding a polished semi-transparent piece of flint to his face, which may have been a skrying stone (the polishing and positioning of these tone both suggesting this).

The Ancient Egyptians used special flint knives to make the first incision in the dead body prior to embalming. They also believed that scarabs carved from flint worn over the heart would protect the heart and ensure long life.

The "Ethiopian Arrows" recorded by Herodotus were subsequently discovered to be flint arrowheads. A curious more recent belief in America (North Carolina and Alabama) was that placing flint in the fire would keep hawks away from the chickens.

There is also much South American folklore about flint, as it was one of the few stones commonly available, and its properties made it very useful and valuable, indeed it was deified as the "fire-maker".

One Aztec myth tells of how the Goddess Citlalicue ("She of the Star Skirt") gave birth to flint and hurled it to the earth. The flint landed in Chicomoetec, producing 1,600 gods.

It has also been suggested that Itztlacoliuhqui-Ixquimilli, the God of Castigation, may be personified flint. He is frequently sohwn with an open gnawing mouth, showing the ability to tear flesh (as flint can). Flint was frequently personified as blades in Aztec iconography.

Both the Mayans (with the God Chac) and the Central Mexicans (with the God Tlalog) had Gods who were hurlers of thunderbolts. Where the lightning struck from these Gods, flint (and sometimes obsidian) was believed to be formed.

Geodes

Geodes (also known as "thunder eggs") resemble nothing so much as a small crystal cave, which is basically what they are. Geodes usually contain either agate, amethyst (these are the most valuable), quartz or topaz, and may have bands of crystals such as agate or jasper surrounding the centre. Geodes have been considered a gift of the gods since ancient times, and have been used in divination and prophecy for thousands of years, acting as the focus in the same manner as a crystal sphere or magick mirror.

There are a number of uses for geodes, which are highly versatile pieces of stone. If possible obtain a geode that has been broken in two, so that the pieces can be re-bound together to make a whole again. The two halves of a geode can provide a nice magickal link between partners when they are apart, acting like a "magickal telephone", particularly if doing the same ritual in different locations. The same principle can be applied to a member of a group unable to attend a ritual using a piece of geode to tune in.
Geodes are also good for storing sigils, talismans, spells, etc in, binding them together with red or black thread afterwards and then storing appropriately (or burying them or disposing of them in water or whatever is desired). If an offering is being made to a site you are building up a rapport with, a small offering of a personal item such as a piece of (preferably gold) jewelry or a crystal, placed in a complete geode and buried there can be a good way to do so (assuming it feels appropriate, the site might prefer offerings like apples or milk and honey).

Be sure that it feels right before "planting" any crystals at sites, you do not want to be guilty of degrading the energies at the site, as some people are wont to do by planting quartz crystals with reckless abandon. I have seen people placing crystals (especially quartz) at sacred sites, both in the ground and in rocks, with no apparent thought for the energy of the place. These people are most indignant if you confront them and challenge their belief structures about such matters, grace and right action are definitely called for in these situations (whatever the temptations might be!).

The funniest way to deal with them I have ever seen was the stoned hippy who when he realised there was a quartz crystal planted in the ground, followed at a distance and collected all the crystals the perpetrators had seeded.

As has already been mentioned, geodes can be used for skrying and divination, acting as the focus and being concentrated on in the same manner as you would a ball or mirror. A half geode if large enough makes a good place for storing other power objects such as crystals, it can be wrapped with silk afterwards to provide a double layer of magickal insulation as well as acting as a "battery" for the stored objects.

Glass

Glass has long been used by man, and has the same chemical makeup as the most common mineral family - the quartzes, i.e. they are both silicon dioxide (SiO_2). Even in ancient times glass was used as well as or instead of gemstones. The name of aventurine comes from the Italian avventura, meaning "by chance", referring to the colour of green glass a glassblower made by chance, and which was then applied to the stone. As will be seen from the different uses given below, items made of glass were especially popular amongst European witches in the Middle Ages.

Glass turns up in a number of folk and fairy tales, usually as the mountain of glass at the end of the world, near the otherworld (underworld). The glass mountain or castle was usually the abode of supernatural creatures, again indicating the otherworldly connection.

In Christianity glass was used to represent purity, and has been especially linked to the Virgin Mary and the immaculate conception. Some paintings show God holding a crystal ball, symbolizing the divine world of light before the creation of the earth. St Benedict, who was poisoned, has been depicted with a crystal glass containing a serpent or a broken crystal glass.

A curious old British custom was that if you looked at someone through a piece of broken glass you would have an argument with them. Breaking red glass was said to indicate trouble was coming, and breaking green glass to indicate a future disappointment. When it comes to breaking glass the worst example has to be the old saying that breaking a mirror brings seven years bad luck, whereas breaking a glass or crystal vase was supposed to be seven years happiness.

Witch Balls

The first recorded witch ball comes from 1690, though their use may be earlier. Also known as wish balls or watch balls, they were large heavy glass balls coated with a silver or gold reflective gloss or brightly coloured paint. 18th century witch balls tended to be smaller and be decorated with swirling multi-coloured patterns. A witch ball would be hung in the window of a cottage or house to attract and neutralise the "evil eye" of any passing witch, by its reflection or by puzzling the witch with its pattern.

Another type of witch ball was made of plain glass filled with brightly coloured tangled threads, which was believed to have the same effect. Witch balls were known as watch balls due to the belief that they would go dull if there was infection in the air, so they needed to be watched regularly.

Witch Bottles

Witch bottles were a common charm used in the Middle Ages. A witch bottle was a bottle filled with certain ingredients and sealed with a spell, that was used a protection for a place or person from magickal attack. Although they were sometimes earthenware, witch bottles were usually made of blue, green or colourless glass, and would have a narrow neck.

They were usually sealed with red or black wax. The bottles were filled with sand or quartz crystals, which was sometimes layered with coloured sand from different sites (which served to trap negative spells or spirits in the interfaces between the layers), and to which were added any or all of the following: salt, urine, rosemary, semen and menstrual blood.

The witch bottle was usually buried under the threshold or hidden somewhere near a door or window. Witch bottles used for personal protection were carried on the person, so this kind were usually small and had to be carried somewhere where they would not get easily broken (thereby releasing the negative energies stored within).

There were variants on the theme with contents, e.g. larger bottles were used, which were packed with needles, pins, nails and other pointed or edged metal objects (note the use of sharp iron inimical to many spirits), as well as broken glass, urine and rosemary, and if desired, semen and/or menstrual blood.

The combination of ingredients and the edges of the metal objects were supposed to serve as a series of psychic boundaries or baffles. These bottles were also sealed with red or black wax and buried under the threshold.

The "Cambridgeshire" witch bottle also employed cord magick in its construction. A small blue bottle was packed with sort red threads (less than 3" long), individually placed in the bottle repeating this spell:

"Thread, tie up this sprite; free us from its spite,
Tangle up the bane; let not a piece remain."

The idea of the threads seems to have been to entangle any negativity, and the use of the red threads is perhaps a remnant from the old ideas of spirit lines being depicted as red cords/threads. It is worth noting the repetition of the spell to build up the magickal charge of the item.

Spirit Houses
In many ways similar to the witch bottle is the spirit house, another device used by witches in the past. A spirit house

was a re-sealable bottle or tube (glass or pottery), which was filled with appropriate items to make a suitable environment for a familiar spirit to dwell in, such as sand, feathers, shells, eggshells, sulphur, mercury, pieces of other metals. A major difference was that a spirit house would have an entrance/exit for the spirit rather than being permanently sealed like a witch bottle.

Glass Heads and Fishing Floats

Two old skrying devices which may still be obtained for skrying work are glass fishing floats, which make a cheap crystal ball, and glass heads for reading smoke patterns in. Fishing floats are sealed hollow coloured glass spheres measuring from 3" - 10" ($7^1/_2$cm - 30cm) across (green and blue seem to be the most common colours, though I have also seen and possess red and yellow fishing floats as well).

Fishing floats may be picked up in antique shops, particularly seaside antique shops, and are usually quite cheap. Glass heads are exactly what they sound like, hollow glass heads, usually life-size, and generally colourless glass, though in more recent times coloured heads have also been produced.

The head is held over some burning incense of an appropriate divinatory nature and placed on a surface such as a table, trapping the smoke in it. The movements of the smoke inside the head provide the medium to skry in.

The medieval tales of Reynard the Fox tell of his glass globe, which could show any scene and reveal any knowledge. Reynard sent it to a queen as a gift, but it never arrived, existing only in his head. From this story came the expression "Your gift was like the globe of glass of Master Reynard", i.e. a great promise with no delivery.

Devil's Drumsticks and Knitting Needles

Devil's drumsticks were drumsticks, sometimes made of glass, with the shaft end rough and unfinished. They were used for drumming out evil spirits, for summoning the spirit world, and for magick to change the weather.

Knitting needles made of glass were sometimes used for stitch magick, where a spell would be repeated each time a stitch was knitted, sewing the power of the spell into an item of clothing. This type of magick can be very powerful, as the repetition of the spell with each action like a mantra can help create a strong build up of magickal charge to effect a desired result.

Hagstones

Hagstones are stones which have a hole running all the way through them, and are usually found in streams or rivers, and at the seashore, where running water has created the hole in the stone. This may be one of the reasons why they are considered so powerful, as it is a common belief that magick cannot work on running water, and these stones have been holed by running water and so retain that influence of protecting from magick.

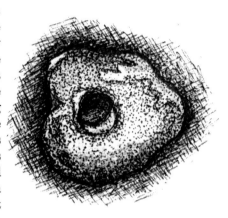

Hagstone

Hagstones are also known as Holy Stones, Holey Stones, Ephialtes Stones, Wish Stones, Nightmare Stones and Witch Riding Stones. They were ascribed with the power of protecting people and animals from the powers of evil spirits and witches, and were often worn around the neck, or hung on the key or door to the cattle stalls or stables. Hagstones were also thought to have the property of preventing milk curdling during a thunderstorm, when evil spirits were most active. This practice continues today in parts of Britain and Europe. In some parts of Europe farmers milked their cows so that the milk passed through a hagstone.

A range of disorders were thought to be cured by hagstones, placing them under the bed was thought to relieve cramp and rheumatism, and they could prevent stomach disorders caused by Hags sitting on the stomach during the night. In Brand's Antiquities, we find the following quote: "A stone with a hole in it hung at the bed's head will prevent the nightmare. It is therefore called a Hag Stone from that disorder which is occasioned by a Hag or Witch sitting on the stomach of the party afflicted. It also prevents witches riding horses, for which purpose it is often tied to a stable key."

As with thunderstones, large quantities of ale poured through a hag stone was given to an expectant mother to ease the birth in parts of Scandinavia. An Arabic custom was to tie a hagstone around the neck of young camels to protect them from evil spirits and the evil eye. In some parts of Britain hagstones were fastened to the bows of boats to keep them safe when at sea. An interesting custom was the use of hagstones as pledge stones, being held to ensure a person was telling the truth.

Perhaps the most interesting properties a hagstone was thought to possess were the ability to enable the bearer to see the faerie folk, and be warded from their enchantments. Hagstones found at mounds or other such sites were considered especially powerful. For a hagstone to keep its full power it was supposed to be found by the bearer or given in love.

Larger hagstones were used for weather magick, having a cord threaded through the hole and tied, and then being swirled vigorously around the head at arms length for dispelling winds and rain clouds.

As wish stones, they were held in the palm of the left hand, and rubbed with the thumb in a deosil (clockwise) manner whilst concentrating on the intent of the wish (this technique was also used with pieces of amber). We can see this as a technique of creative visualisation, using the repetitive rubbing to focus the mind and then concentrating on the desired result (the "wish"). It is interesting to note that although the left hand is used to hold, this was probably not for its "sinister" aspect, but rather so that the rubbing could be done with the dominant (for most people), more "positively aspected" right hand. This is reinforced by the fact that the rubbing is done deosil, i.e. sunwise, in an invoking manner to invoke the desired result.

Holed stones with multiple holes in were used as spell casting stones by medieval witches. The holes would be made in a stone, equidistant and in multiples of three. A cord or pebble would be passed through the holes in patterns of three, whilst the intent of the spell was repeated, usually in multiples of three. This type of spell emphasises a belief in the power of repetition to achieve a desired result.

Influencing the Weather

In New Guinea, shamans brought the rain by placing heavy stones and pieces of quartz in canoes and shaking them vigorously. The loud thunder-like noises made were thought to attract the rain, as rain happens after thunder.

In Northern Queensland rock crystal was mined and pulverised, and then showered over the women to simulate rainfall. The women held troughs over their heads to protect them from the "rain" (and possibly to collect the rain quartz for future use!).

In New South Wales the rainmaker would hold a piece of quartz in his mouth and spit it at the sky to summon rain.

Tribes of the Upper Nile used amethyst, aventurine and quartz as rain stones, plunging one into water and then motioning with a cane which was split at the top at it when the rain was desired.

Jasper is referred to as the "rain bringer" by some Amerindian tribes, this belief was also prevalent in ancient Greece, as can be seen by the reference in the fourth century poem *Lithica*:

> The gods propitious hearken to his prayers,
> Whoe'er the polished grass-green jasper wears;
> His parched glebe they'll satitate with rain,
> And send for showers to soak the thirsty plain.

If these seem like primitive superstitions, bear in mind that larger hagstones were used for weather magick in medieval Britain for dispelling winds and rain clouds.

Meteorites

Meteorites are the remains of extraterrestrial bodies which have fallen onto our planet and survived. The ever-increasing interest in meteorites today is unsurprising when we consider their ability to extend our knowledge, both physical and magickal, to areas beyond our own world.

Types of Meteorites

Meteorites are divided into iron meteorites and stone meteorites, though there are rare intermediary meteorites containing both. The largest iron meteorite recorded weighs about sixty tonnes and lies under guard near Grootfontein in Namibia; the largest stone meteorite weighs over one tonne and fell on 18th February 1948 in Norton County, Nebraska, USA, as one of the stones in a "stone shower" of meteorite fragments.

Iron meteorites are the most common, and were the first recorded; they tend to be exceptionally heavy for their size, and are comprised mainly of iron and nickel. Every iron meteorite examined thus far has contained two alloys, of varying nickel content. The internal structure of these alloys divides into three categories - octahedrons, cube-like and no structure.

The intermediary meteorites are known as pallasites, and contain the same mixture of iron and nickel, with olivine crystals (which are usually rounded in shape) often found in them.

Stone meteorites tend to be smaller than iron meteorites, and are very similar in form to the earth's own igneous rocks. Stone meteorites have a black crusty surface, formed by the intense heat experienced at times during their flight, like when they fall to earth.

The Existence of Meteorites

Even though scientists in the Middle Ages denied stones could fall from the sky, the impact of seeing a meteorite was not something that could easily be denied.

In 1135 the Prague chronicle of the Canon of Vysehrad recorded: "A giant stone as big as a house fell out of the clouds on a plain in Thuringia. People living in the vicinity could hear the noise it was making three days beforehand. As it hit the earth, half of the stone became embedded in the ground and for three days it remained red hot, like steel is when taken out of the fire." Though scientifically inaccurate as a description, this passage does emphasise the occurrence and recording of meteorites.

In 1754 Josef Stepling, a Prague astronomer, observed and recorded a "shower of stones" which fell in the T·bor district of Bohemia; in doing so he became the first person to state with absolute certainty that stones did fall to earth from space.

There was still scepticism about this over the next few decades until 1794, when the German physicist E F Chaladni demonstrated the truth of Stepling's observation with scientific proof.

Tektites

The most famous form of tektite, moldavite, was discovered in 1787 in Bohemia. It was initially thought to be olivine, then volcanic glass, then slag from old glassworks. When more deposits were found in places like south-east Asia and Australia in the late nineteenth century, the conclusion was reached that they were glass meteorites, and they were given the collective name of tektites. Tektites range in colour from dark-green to green-black.

There is still much dispute about the origin of tektites, with theories ranging from stellar to lunar to terrestrial origins put forward. One thing that is certain is that tektites are only found around meteorite craters, which for me lends credence to the theory that they are either stellar, or are created by the effect of a meteorite (which is stellar) on the environment when it impacts. If this is the case, then the transformation created in the rocks to form tektites indicates an imparting of that stellar energy, so they may be used as if they were stellar even if they originally were not.

Many tektites are named after their place of origin, so as well as moldavite (Moravia), there are such names as australite, indochinite, ivorite (Ivory coast), philippinite, thailandite and others such as bediasite and georgianite from North America.

Radioactive dating has indicated that the ages of tektites from differing areas varies: so we know that ivorites are the youngest tektites (around 1.3 million years old) and the North American tektites are the oldest (around 34 million years old); moldavite is in the middle, being around 15 million years old.

Due to their (probable) extra-terrestrial origin, tektites are the obvious choice for people working with extra-terrestrial encounters - if worn they seem to help integrate the experiences into some form of coherence.

Mythical Minerals

Over the centuries there have been described gems and metals which have never been discovered, or to which fantastic origins have been attributed. The fantastic nature of the stones seemed to encourage writers to describe them in great detail and as if there could be no doubt as to their existence. These include:

Abraxas Stone

Actually a real stone but included here for convenience and commonality, Abraxas Stone was usually a form of chalcedony (such as agate, carnelian, heliotrope, jasper, onyx) with a figure of the Gnostic God Abraxas engraved on it. The famous abracadabra triangle was often engraved on the back of these stones. This word is derived from the Chaldean abrada ke dabra which means "to perish like the word" (which abracadabra literally does in the triangle, being reduced to an "a" by the eleventh and final line). Abraxas stones were said to be able to drive away demons and devils, and to protect from the plague.

Adder stone

Adder Stone was thought to be made once a year, when serpents would gather into a writhing mass, producing saliva and shooting it into the air from their hissing jaws. The saliva solidified into Adder Stone. In Cornwall the annual gathering was said to be at the Summer Solstice, and in Wales it was said to be May Eve. If the Adder Stone was holed it was thought one of the serpents had stuck its tail through the stone whilst it was solidifying. Adder Stone was known by a number of names, it was also called Serpents' Egg, Snake Egg, Gleini na Droedh (Magician's Glass), Glaine nan Druidhe (Druid's Glass), and Pliny referred to it as Druid's Egg. In Wales carrying an Adder Stone in the pocket was believed to cure all maladies. A Scottish belief was that an Adder Stone hung around a child's neck would prevent whooping cough. Pliny recorded the British belief that possession of an Adder Stone would bring success in law suits, saying he had seen one (*Historia Naturalis* XXIX.xii) and that "It was round, and about as large as a smallish apple; the shell was cartilaginous, and pocked like the arms of a polypus." To test a stone to see if it was a genuine Adder Stone, it was supposed to be thrown into a stream - if it was genuine it would float against the current, and no weight attached to it could make it sink. Some examples of adder stone have in fact been prehistoric striped glass beads from ancient burial sites, which shows how crystals from a previous time continue to be seen in a magickal light.

Alectorius

Said to be a bean-size bright, transparent crystal-like stone, occasionally veined with pink, alectorius was reputed to be found in the gizzard of a capon (cock). The capon had to be castrated on reaching the age of three, and harvested after the age of seven, when the bird refused to eat and drink at the same time. In Roman time alectorius was thought to bring strength, courage, victory, honour and the power of persuasion to the bearer, and possess the power of making the bearer invisible. It was also believed that an alectorius could help the bearer regain a lost kingdom and acquire a foreign one. When slipped under the tongue it was supposed to bring eloquence. By the Middle Ages a belief had also developed that the bearer of one of these stones would never go thirsty. Finally, it was also thought to restore domestic harmony, and if worn as a pendant or ring by a wife to restore her to favour in her husband's eyes.

Bezoar

Is a real stone recovered from the stomachs of certain animals, especially stags and goats. The name comes from the Persian padzahr meaning "poison expelling". It is also known as Mo-So, Mustika, Guliga (when collected from red monkeys) and Guliga Landak (when collected from feral porcupines). In Malaysia it was believed bezoar could be found inside certain coconuts. A curious oriental belief surrounded the creation of bezoar stones. It was said that stags when old fed on serpents to renew their youth. To counteract the serpents' poison the stags would plunge into a running stream, keeping only the head above water. This caused a viscous liquid to fall from their eyes, which hardened in the sun to from bezoar. Bezoar is usually comprised of mainly lime phosphate, though it may also contain ammonia phosphate or magnesium phosphate. It was thought to be concentrated soul-essence, so contact with an injury or wound would immediately heal the damage. It was also believed bezoar guarded against poisoning, hence scrapings were often included in the handle of a knife. Bezoars were set into rings in China, and licked if the wearer thought they had been poisoned. Bezoar was thought to protect against plague. In the Orient it was believed to bring renewed beauty and youth. The Sioux Indians would blow powdered bezoar into the eyes to strengthen sight and the brain. Powdered bezoar has been widely used as a laxative in places as diverse as India and Persia. In medieval Germany powdered bezoar was taken for toothache. It has been used medicinally for asthma, bladder and kidney complaints, since at least 2000 BCE Persia. In Mongolia bezoar was thought to be a rain stone, able to bring rain.

Cactomite

A mythic stone said to possess magickal properties, including assuring the bearer of victory in battle. It has been suggested that cactomite was actually carnelian.

Cepiodinus

A multi-coloured stone which was said to reflect the likeness of the bearer.

Ceraunis

Also known as cerraclus. Ceraunis was said to be a pyramidal crystalline stone, transparent with a saffron tinge. They were believed to fall from the clouds, and have the virtues of preserving the bearer from drowning and injury by lightning, as well as giving pleasant dreams.

Cobra Stone

Cobra Stone (known as Gemala in Malaysia) was said to possess the same properties as Snake Stone of curing snakebites if applied to the wound, and also to ensure victory in battle. Cobra stone was reputed to shine brightly at night, and was to be found in the head of a cobra under the hood.

Draconius Stone

The draconius was said to be removed from the head of a dragon or great snake, and had to be removed soon after the death of the creature or lose its powers. Sources give differing descriptions - either as a black pyramidal stone or a colourless transparent stone.

As with most mythical stones draconius was supposed to make the bearer immune to poison, though in this case it was all poisons. It was also reputed to make the bearer bold and invincible. It was also believed in the Middle Ages that the eyes of dragons were made of carbuncle (garnet).

Eagle Stone

Also known as Aetites, Aquileus, Ethices, Endes, Gagites and Praegnus, eagle stone was thought to be found in the nests of eagles, or in their stomach's or neck's. Pliny describes four varieties (in Historia Naturalis), and he says they are usually found in pairs, as male and female stones. Eagle stones were said to contain a loose stone (the "callimus"), and the rattling gave rise to the ides of the pregnant stone - "The stone in question is big with another inside it, which rattles, as if in a jar when you shake it." (Pliny *Historia Naturalis* X). The stones were supposed to be kept wrapped in the skins of sacrificed animals and worn as amulets around the neck or on the left arm by pregnant women or other creatures to prevent miscarriage. A British addition to this belief was that an eagle stone tied inside the left thigh of a woman in labour would speed the birth by pulling the child and placenta out, though the stone had to be removed immediately afterwards so it did not cause a prolapse with its attractive powers. It has been suggested Eagle Stones were rounded white quartz pebbles. Because of their rarity and cost, any lucky possessor of such a stone was expected to share it around. This is illustrated in a letter sent by Dr Bargrave, Dean of Christchurch, Canterbury in 1662. He wrote of an eagle stone he had purchased from an Armenian in Rome: "It is so useful that my wife can seldom keep it at home, and therefore she hath sewed the strings to the knitt purse in which the stone is, for the convenience of the tying of it to the patient on occasion, and hath a box to put the purse and stone in. It were fit that the Dean's or Vice-Dean's wife (if they be marryed men) should have this stone in their custody for the public goof, as to neighbourhood; but still, that they have a great care into whose hand it be committed, and that the midwives have a care of it, so that it shall be the cathedral's

141

stone." This letter also illustrates the way the church would turn a blind eye to the use of crystals if they were considered to be being used for good purposes.

Electrum

Electrum was the name given on occasions to amber, and to jet, as well as the silver-gold amalgam it is more usually used to describe. Electrum was also believed to be a legendary metal of magickal properties, Pliny detailing its use in cups made of electrum which would reveal poison. He stated that the liquid would exhibit rainbow-like semi-circles and sparkle and hiss if there was poison present, as if on fire.

Fingitas

A transparent stone said to be as hard as marble. A tale relates of a king who had a temple built of fingitas, which needed no windows, as light was admitted into it through the walls as if it had been open all day.

Fongites

A gem which was said to possess the quality of assuaging anger.

Garatronicus

Alternately described as being multi-coloured or as a red coloured stone, which was believed to be carried by Achilles in battle, making its possessor invincible. From the descriptions this stone was possibly opal or ruby/garnet.

Hyena Stone

A many-coloured stone, which was said to be found in the eye of a hyena. When put under the tongue it enabled the bearer to foretell future events. It was also said to be able to cure gout and quartan ague.

Lapís Monoceros

Also known as Unicorn Stone. This stone was likened to the Philosopher's Stone, and was described as a red stone found at the base of a unicorn's horn. It was credited with the powers of projection attributed to the Philosopher's Stone and also those attributed to Unicorn Horn.

Lígníte

A beautiful glass-like stone. Lignite was said to protect children from witchcraft when hung about their necks. If bound onto the forehead it would stop nosebleeds and restore loss of senses, as well as helping to foretell future events.

Líparea

Also known as Lypparis (Fat Stone). Pliny recorded that liparea was used in fumigation to charm all kinds of wild beasts, that dogs would run to it, and it was found in Libya. It is possible Pliny was describing sulphur from the Lipari Islands.

Lynx Stone

Also known as Lyncurium or Lyncurius. Pliny recorded that lynx stone was said to be formed when lynx urine mixed with a special kind of earth, and that the lynx would cover the spot out of jealousy that man should possess it. It was said to be an amber hue. Lynx stone was said to be able to attach itself to various substances like a magnet, namely leaves, straw, copper and iron. When added to liquid and consumed it was said to dispel urinary problems, and in wine or even just looked at to be able to cure jaundice. It is possible that lynx stone was brown tourmaline. Another version of the origin of lynx stone was that it was a white stone taken from the head of a lynx, and that its possession would remove cataracts.

Memphiticus Stone

Described by the Romans as a round sparkling stone the size and colour of a hazelnut. Its property was that crushing the stone in wine or water was said to produce a very effective local anaesthetic for surgical operations such as cauterising or lancing. When powdered and drunk in vinegar it was said to render men insensible to torture.

Mithril

Although a recent term and one that is used prevalently in fantasy books, the idea of the light, durable and flexible metal which protects better than any other metal as armour has become so widely spread through fiction and the imagination as to be worth including. Mithril is described as being silvery in colour. Mithril is also referred to as "moon silver".

Orichalcum

The legendary metal of Atlantis. Said to float on water, be incredibly strong and more highly prized than gold.

Orphanus

This stone is thought to have been a large opal, and was set in the imperial crown of the Holy Roman Empire. As will be seen from the description given by Albertus Magnus, it seems unlikely to have been anything else: "The orphanus is a stone which is in the crown of the Roman Emperor, and none like it has ever been seen; for this very reason it is called orphanus. It is of a subtle vinous tinge, and its hue is as though pure white snow flashed and sparkled with the colour of bright ruddy wine, and was overcome by this radiance. It is a translucent stone, and there is a tradition that formerly it shone in the night-time; but now, in our age, it does not sparkle in the dark. It is said to guard the regal honour."

The Orphanus Jewel in the German Imperial Crown - "Hortus Sanitatis" of Johannis de Cuba

Pantherus

Also known as pantaura, pantochras and evanthum. Said to be spotted like a panther. Pantherus was supposed to protect against all poisons, and to attract other stones as a lodestone does iron.

Píropholos (or Pyrophilus)

A light, bright red stone said to be found in the heart of a man who has died from poisoning. This stone is reputed to have the virtues of protecting its owner from sudden death, lightning and tempests, and also to bring renown and make the wearer "terrible to his enemies". If the owner caught a disease however, it was said to ensure a lingering death.

Polytrix

A bizarre stone which was said to cause all the hair to fall off the head of anyone unfortunate enough to pick one up.

Pontica

A blue stone with red stars, or drops and lines like blood. Pontica was said to compel the devil to answer questions truthfully, and also to put him to flight.

Quirinus

Also known as quirus. Quirinus was a "juggling stone, found in the nest of the hoopoo". If laid upon the chest of a sleeping person it was said to force them to disclose all their wrong-doings.

Snake Stone

Snake stone was supposed to be a rough black sphere. They were highly prized by magicians as a talisman against evil forces. Removed from the head of a serpent, snake stone was reputedly used as an antidote to snake poison. The snake stone had to be applied to the wound before the venom had spread too far, and would be seen to cling to the wound and then fall off when saturated. A second stone would invariably be required to finish the job. To ready the stones for another use, they would be left soaking in milk, when the milk had thickened and gone a greeny-yellow the stones were cleansed. There were two methods to test snake (and cobra) stones: either they should be placed in the mouth, if genuine they will stick to the palate; or placed in a glass of water, which would seethe and bubble.

Swallow Stone

Also known to the ancients as Chelidonoius, this stone was supposed to be collected from the gaping maws of young swallows, and not permitted to come into contact with other stones, the ground or water to retain their efficacy. There were two varieties, red and white in colour (possibly echoing the red and white symbolism for female and male in alchemy). Swallow stones were supposed to cure a whole range of conditions. They were rolled in a yellow cloth and placed around the throat to cure jaundice and fevers; tied in white linen and placed on the head to cure headache; striking a spark off a swallow stone was said to bring a man out of delusions or hallucinations. Swallow stone was also supposed to be effective for treating melancholy and menstrual problems, and could be used against agues, diseases, eye pains, goblins, incubi, poison, temptation, witchcraft and all manner of evil sorceries.

Toadstone

In form toadstone was supposed to be like a white, brown or black pebble.

As with snakestone, once removed from the head of the toad it was supposed to be an antidote to poison. It was recommended the toadstone be set in a gold ring, with the toadstone actually touching the finger so that if poison came near its burning heat would warn its wearer. One was supposed to be able to test if a toadstone was genuine by holding it in front of a toad, if it leaped towards the stone it was the genuine article. A number of other properties have been ascribed to toadstone, such as the ability to protect houses from burning, and ships from sinking, prev-enting defeat in battle, and keeping children safe from being stolen by fairies (if set in a gold pendant).

As well as these properties it was thought to include in its medicinal properties the ability to protect against plague, ague and falling sickness. A 14th Century Italian ring in

Extraction of Toadstone - "Hortus Sanitatis"

the British Museum (No. 895) was believed to be toadstone, though it is actually a piece of fossilised fish. This ring is a fine example of the use of scripture in a talisman, being made of gold, and with two lines from the Gospels inscribed on the gold in Latin - "Iesus autem transiens per medium illorum ibat" (Luke IV:30 "But Jesus passed through their midst") and "Et verbum caro factum est" (John I:14 "And the word became flesh"). To extract the toadstone from a toad was best done whilst the toad was still alive, one method was to bury the toad in a pot in an anthill, the ants would eat the toad and leave the bones and the stone. An anonymous treatise from the 1660's explained the qualities and colours of toadstone: "It must bee a toade that is very greate and old and hath lived long in hedges or diches or a fenne of reeds because it will be many years or ever the stone can come to any bignesse ... [it]

is of cullar eyther white or a littel darkish browne or blacke haveing in the middest of the stone like unto an eye beeing of a greenish cullar. Especially if the stone bee taken from the toade alive and so is of most vertue off operation ... butt myself had one wch was blacke and spotted with redd spots wch I did set in a ring off gold..."

Unicorn Horn

Another mythical talisman included here is the unicorn horn. These tended to be the tusk of a Narwhale, with its left hand spiral and growing up to two metres long it fitted the description perfectly. Pieces of sliced walrus tusk and rhinoceros horn were sometimes also sold as unicorn horn. Pieces of "unicorn" horn would be placed in pendants, usually gold. These pendants would be touched to food and drink, whereby it was believed any poison would be neutralised. Unicorn horn was also believed to cure diseases, epilepsy, plague, and the bite of a mad dog (rabies). (Supposed) Unicorn horn was greatly prized in medieval times, as is illustrated by the will of Sir Nathaniel Bacon of Stiffkey, made in 1614 when he believed he was dying: "I give to all my daughters the jewel of unicorn's horn, according to their mother's [his first wife's] direction, that each one may challenge the use thereof when needs require, and my wife have the use thereof when she needs, but my daughter [Anne wife of Sir John] Townshend is to have the custody thereof for life." Sir Nathaniel did not actually die until 1622, aged 75, so perhaps the unicorn horn helped him in his time of believed imminent mortality.

Ziazaa

A black and white stone which was said to render it's possessor litigious and to cause terrible visions (thus definitely being a stone to avoid).

Natal Crystals - Crystals and the Months of the Year

The practice of attributing stones to specific months of the year, whose virtues were believed to be transmitted to the bearers of their natal stones can be traced to Josephus in the first century CE. This idea was further developed by St Jerome in the early part of the fifth century CE. Both authors specifically refer to the High Priest's Breastplate, and the twelve stones being attributed to the months of the year and signs of the zodiac.

Curiously the wearing of natal stones for their properties is not recorded until eighteenth century Poland. The influence of Jews who settled in Poland and who were familiar with the High Priest's Breastplate has been suggested by Kunz as the most likely cause for the development of this custom.

As well as the two rhymes given below for the months, there are a number of sets of attributions in Appendix 4.

The gleaming garnet holds within its stay   January
Faith, constancy, and truth to one alway.

Let her an amethyst but cherish well,   February
And strife and care can never with her dwell.

Who wears a jasper, be life short or long,   March
Will meet all dangers brave and wise and strong.

Innocence, repentance - sun and shower -	April
The diamond or the sapphire is her dower.	
No happier wife and mother in the land	May
Than she with emerald shining on her hand.	
Thro' the moss agate's charm, the happy years	June
Ne'er see June's golden sunshine turn to tears.	
No other gem than turquoise on her breast	July
Can to the loving, doubting heart bring rest.	
She, loving once and always, wears, if wise,	August
Carnelian - and her home is paradise.	
If crysolite upon her brow is laid,	September
Follies and dark delusions flee afraid.	
When fair October to her brings the beryl,	October
No longer need she fear misfortune's peril.	
Firm friendship is November's, and she bears	November
True love beneath the topaz that she wears.	
December gives her fortune, love and fame	December
If amulet of rubies bear her name.	

An alternative to the above is:

No gems save garnets should be worn	January
By her who in this month is born;	
They will insure her constancy,	
True friendship and fidelity.	
The February-born may find	February
Sincerity and peace of mind,	

Freedom from passion and from care,
If she an amethyst will wear.

Who on this world of ours her eyes   March
In March first opens may be wise,
In days of peril firm and brave,
Wears she a bloodstone to her grave.

She who from April dates her years   April
Diamonds should wear, lest bitter tears
For vain repentance flow. This stone
Emblem of innocence is known.

Who first beholds the light of day   May
In spring's sweet flow'ry month of May,
And wears an emerald all her life,
Shall be a loved and happy wife.

Who comes with summer to this earth,   June
And owes to June her hour of birth,
With ring of agate on her hand
Can health, long life, and wealth command.

The heav'n-blue turquoise should adorn   July
All those who in July are born;
For those they'll be exempt and free
From love's doubts and anxiety.

Wear a carnelian or for thee   August
No conjugal felicity;
The August-born without this stone,
'Tis said, must live unloved, alone.

A maid born when September leaves   September
Are rustling in the autumn breeze,
A crysolite on brow should bind -
'Twill cure diseases of the mind.

October's child is born for woe,   October
And life's vicissitudes must know;
But lay a beryl on her breast,
And Hope will lull those woes to rest.

Who comes first to this world below   November
With drear November's fog and snow
Should prize the topaz's amber hue -
Emblem of friends and lovers true.

If cold December give you birth -   December
The month of snow and ice and mirth -
Place on your hand a ruby true;
Success will bless whate'er you do.

Zodiacal attributions for gems have flowered to such an extent
that many stones are attributed to a number of the zodiacal
signs, as will be seen in the Gemmology. Rhymes are useful
in that they give complete sets for such attributions, and so I
include one here.

If you would cherish friendship true,   Aquarius
In Aquarius well you'll do
To wear this gem of warmest hue -
              The garnet.

From passion and from care kept free   Pisces
Shall Pisces' children ever be
Who wear so all the world may see
              The amethyst.

Who on this world of ours his eyes   Aries
In Aries opens shall be wise
If always on his hand there lies
              A bloodstone.

If on your hand this stone you bind,   Taurus
You in Taurus born will find
'Twill cure diseases of the mind,
                    The sapphire.

Gemini's children health and wealth command,   Gemini
And all the ills of age withstand,
Who wear their rings on either hand
                    Of agate.

If born in Cancer's sign, they say,   Cancer
Your life will joyful be alway,
If you take with you on your way
                    An emerald.

When youth to manhood shall have grown,   Leo
Under Leo lorn and lone
'Twill have lived but for this stone,
                    The onyx.

Success will bless whate'er you do,   Virgo
Through Virgo's sign, if only you
Place on your hand her own gem true,
                    Carnelian.

Through Libra's sign it is quite well   Libra
To free yourself from evil spell,
For in her gem surcease doth dwell,
                    The chrysolite.

Through Scorpio this gem so fair   Scorpio
Is that which every one should wear,
Or tears of sad repentance bear,
                    The beryl.

Who first comes to this world below   Sagittarius
Under Sagittarius should know
That their true gem should ever show
                    A topaz.

Those who live in Capricorn   Capricorn
No trouble shall their brow adorn
If they this glowing gem have worn,
                    The ruby.

Gemmology

The Gemmology gives the physical information and folklore about popular gems and crystals and some organic substances regarded in a similar way (such as amber, coral, jet and pearl). Where sigils and common alternative names exist for crystals I have included them.

The entries take the form:

Colours: Different colours the mineral occurs in.

Attribution: To fixed stars, planets, zodiacal signs, elements.

Chakras: Which chakras the mineral works well with.

Uses: In healing, magick, etc.

Folklore: Available folklore categorised for convenience.

Used Since: How long we know the mineral has been used by man.

Names: Other names the mineral is known by.

Agate

Agate sigil

"Whilst on that agate which dark Indians praise
The woods arise, the sylvan monster strays."
Marbodius, 11th Century CE

One of the traditional stones of protection, the varieties of agate have a multitude of uses - truly "a gate" which is beneficial to pass through.

Colours: Green, blue, white, red (blood agate), brown, yellow, orange. May have green or brown-black dendritic inclusions (moss agate, mosquito agate or Mocha stone), or regular bands around the edges (fortification agate); with masses of inclusions of turritella shells it is known as turritella agate.

Attribution: Procyon, Mercury, Terra (moss agate), Venus, Virgo, Gemini, Leo, Libra, Taurus, Cancer.

Chakras: Feet, Base, Sacral.

Uses: Protection whilst travelling, massage, healing of the body, general earthing. Agates are good to work with for calming and inducing peaceful atmospheres. Work with for pancreas, lymphatic and circulatory system, balancing and strengthening the colon.

Balancing and giving form. A good stone for using in exorcisms. Can be used to effectively as an astral doorway ("a gate"). Agate eye-stones are good for skrying and work with the third eye chakra. Agates generally make good stone for divination. Moss agate is a good stone for increasing your connection with the land. Fortification agate is a good stone for people who have trouble maintaining clear boundaries, and for loss of self. Lace agate is good for feelings of tranquillity.

Used Since: At least 25,000 BCE.

Names: Achates. Eyed agates are ones where the coloured bands are in a circular form which resembles an eye. Moss agate is also known as Mocha Stone and Tree Agate, and Amberine when it is yellow-green. Agates are often named according to the area they are found in, hence Indian agates, Botswana agates, American agates, etc. Red agate is also known as blood agate. Agates with a red fernlike burst in them are known as plume agates. Agates with two bands, one light and one dark, were known as St James or St Sylvester Stones. Agate where the bands form concentric circles is known as Bull's Eye agate. Iridescent agate is known as Iris or Fire agate. White agate was sometimes known as Milkstone. Agate with two adjacent sets of concentric black circles surrounding a dot are known as Owl's-eye agate.

As an Amulet & Talisman:
In Greek myth a piece of agate was reputedly carried by Orpheus as an amulet during his descent to the Underworld.

158

Banded agate was worn as an amulet by Greek sailors to remove fear of the surging ocean. The Hebrews and Romans wore it as an amulet to prevent falls and accidents, this use spread to being adopted by horsemen as a talisman and being woven into horses manes and mounted in harnesses.

In Qabalah agate is attributed to Hod as a protective stone, as the psychopomp, and also to the Archangel Barbiel. In times gone by Moslems would engrave the names of the grandsons of the Prophet onto agate charms to be worn by children as a protection.

Arrow shaped amulets made of agate were believed to be good for the blood in Arabic countries. It was once believed that wearing agate would turn an enemy's sword against them. Agate has been used as a talisman to ensure a good nights sleep when worn as a ring or pendant.

Protecting Crops:
Moss agate was used in Persia to help crops grow - a good example of sympathetic magick using the Doctrine of Signatures (due to the fern-like patterning resembling plants), and this continued in India where they were thought to protect the crops from drought, flooding and insects when offered to the Gods; in Europe agate was tied to the horns of oxen and harnesses of horses ploughing the fields to ensure a bountiful harvest. .

Pliny described the Persian Magi using agate to avert tempests, and in medieval Europe agate was thought to avert the powers of lightning and tempest. The connection of moss agate with plants is also recorded by Marbodius who said:
"Whilst on that agate which dark Indians praise
The woods arise, the sylvan monster strays."

Axinomancy: Agate Divination:
The Vikings and Saxons had a special use for agate in a form of divination for lost items by axe and stone, known as axinomancy. A double headed axe would be heated to red heat, and then placed in the ground, the haft being pushed into a prepared hole; a round agate pebble was then placed on the axe head. If the agate pebble stayed on the axehead, the querent had to look elsewhere, if it feel off to the ground, the querent had to follow the direction the stone rolled on the floor to find the missing item(s).

Another connection between agate and axe-heads is found in what was Babylon, where a banded agate axehead dating at least 2000 BCE was found, with early cuniform characters inscribed on the blade.

Agate and Health:
Agate was sacred to the Greek God of Healing, Aesclepius. Agate was used in the treatment of lung problems, indigestion, to stem haemorrhages, reduce fever and to prevent diseases, and for strengthening the abdominal organs. A preparation of powdered agate in a (sweet) fruit juice was used to treat insanity, ulcers, boils, kidney and spleen diseases.

Powdered agate on the tongue was also thought to cure poisoning. Placing a piece of agate to the site of a poisonous insect bite was thought to cure it. Agate was thought to promote courage, vigour, strength and boldness, and to protect from poisons. Eye stones were used in Syria to alleviate a nasty condition called Alleppo boils. Agate was sometimes held in the mouth to reduce thirst, like quartz.

Agate in Ancient Babylon
The different types of agate were believed to have different properties in Babylonian times. Red agate was believed to cure insect bites and stings, green to cure eye infections, grey

to cure throat infections, and black or striped agate to protect women from any diseases they were particularly prone to.

Agate in Ancient Greece
Agate was highly prized in Greece. Pliny said of agate: "It makes the wearer victorious, protects the owner against every kind of poisonous reptile, gives a lover favour in the sight of his lady, the sick man who holds it in his hand shall recover. It gives a man riches, health and long life. It also increases a man's intelligence, drives away fevers, epilepsy and madness, stops the flow of rheum in the eye, reduces bleeding and disperses the water in dropsy."

Other Folklore
Agate was the eighth stone on the High Priest's breastplate, representing the tribe of Benjamin. Agate was sacred to the Roman Goddess Minerva. Agate is said to bring good health, longevity, peace and wealth. Wearing agate jewellery is said to endow the wearer with grace, conversation and good manners.

Dreaming of agate is said to suggest a journey by sea, which is interesting considering the use of agate to prevent seasickness; dreaming of moss agate was said to indicate an unsuccessful journey. An old Jewish belief stated that carrying an agate would prevent one stumbling or falling. The Palau Islands use agate cylinders as their third grade of money (they have seven).

People of small stature were called agates due to the custom of carving small figures on agate seals, illustrated by Shakespeare in *Romeo and Juliet*, when Mercutio says of Queen Mab: "She is the fairies' midwife, and she comes in shape no bigger than an agate stone on the forefinger of an alderman." (Act I, Scene 4). Agate is given for the 12th wedding anniversary, moss agate for the 14th.

161

Alexanδʀite

Alexandrite is believed in Russia to bring the bearer good luck, and dreaming of alexandrite is said to indicate a forthcoming time of need.

Stunning for its change from green to red in artificial light, this recently discovered stone is good for eye problems and dealing with stress.

Name: After Prince Alexander II of Russia.

Colours: Emerald green (red in artificial light).

Attribution: Uranus, Air, Aquarius, Gemini.

Chakras: Third Eye.

Uses: Used for eye problems, helps with clarity and insight. Good for dealing with stress and trauma. Works on nervous system, pancreas and spleen. May help with sexual problems resulting from stress and trauma (such as impotence). Also good for work on improving self-esteem.

Used Since: It's discovery in 1830 CE.

Folklore:
Alexandrite is the only crystal discovered so recently to become part of local folklore and custom. Alexandrite is believed in Russia to bring the bearer good luck, and dreaming of alexandrite is said to indicate a forthcoming time of need. In modern Qabalah it has been attributed to Gemini as the 17th path due to its polarization of light.

Amazonite

Amazonite is traditionally known as the "Hope Stone" due to its symbolism of representing the spring sky, and hence the coming light and heat after winter.

The "Hope" stone, symbolising the "Quickening" of Spring, amazonite can help in new ventures, and to reap the rewards of your labours.

Colours: Green, blue-green.

Attribution: Venus, Uranus, Water, Earth.

Chakras: Sacral, Heart.

Uses: Good for dealing with stress and encouraging perseverance and fortitude against adversities. May be used for any new ventures, e.g. romance, business, education, etc. Amazonite is a good stone for helping reach deserved rewards and help you flow in the appropriate direction. Good for unblocking the sacral chakra.

Used Since: At least 3000 BCE Ancient Egypt.

Amazonite and Ancient Egypt
In ancient Egypt the 27th chapter of the *Book of the Dead* was carved on amazonite, and chapters 159 and 160 prescribed its use for amulets. Amazonite was one of the most precious stones to the Egyptians, with lapis lazuli and turquoise.

Other Folklore
Traditionally known as the "Hope Stone" due to its symbolism of representing the spring sky, and hence the coming light and

heat after winter. To the Assyrians amazonite was sacred to
the God Belus, and used in religious rituals.

Amber

$$\underline{2}^3\ 23$$

"Eurymachus received a golden necklace, richly wrought,
and set with amber beads, that glowed as if with sunshine".
"Odyssey", Homer

Like a solidified tear of sunlight from days long past, amber brightens all around it, and has been seen by cultures worldwide since pre-history as radiating protection and healing.

Colours: Yellow, reddish-brown, bluish, greenish (blue and green are caused by fluorescence of light by trapped air bubbles), white, black.

Attribution: Sun, Terra, Spirit, Fire, Leo.

Chakras: Base, Solar Plexus, Heart.

Uses: A wonderful storer of charge and talisman. Used for memory, may help with amnesia; may also be used for past life work. Can help with asthma and breathing and nervous disorders. Works on heart, spleen and endocrine system. Can be worn for courage, and to overcome indecisiveness. Good for general well being, and for enhancing energy levels, being one of the most magnetic of crystals. Good for sorting out blockages of the solar plexus and heart chakras. Amber is

165

good to work with for solar magicks. Amber is pizoelectric, attracting pieces of paper when rubbed.

Used Since: Many thousands of years ago, cannot be specific but at least Paleolithic period.

Names: Lyncurius (after the strange perception of its creation, see above). Some amber has a name based on its place of origin i.e. Bacalite (Mexico), Burmite (Myanmar - formally Burma), Roumanite (Roumania), Simetite (Sicily), Gadenite (Danzig) and Succinite (Baltic) which is the most common form, and is sometimes referred to as "True Amber". Amber with a cloudy appearance due to a lot of bubbles is known as "bastard amber". Amber stained black is unsurprisingly known as "black amber".

Amber Creation Myths:
In Norse myth amber was said to be formed from Freya's tears, either when Odin went to wander the world, or when the hero Svipdag was killed, depending which version of the myth one goes for.

This theme also occurs in Greek myth, where amber was said to be the tears of the Heliades weeping for their brother Phaeton after they had been turned into poplar trees by Zeus; another explanation given was that amber was the fossilized tears of Indian birds.

In ancient Rome amber was said to be formed from lynx urine, the dark ambers being from the male and the light ambers being from the female; however a contemporary writer (Sudines, 240 BCE) refers to a lynx tree from which the amber came.

Other beliefs in ancient times were that amber was congealed rays of the setting sun found on the seashore, solidified brine, the dew of sunbeams, or exuded from warm mud.

Amber and Healing:
Amber has been used extensively by the medical profession over the centuries, the Romans wore pendants and necklaces of reddish amber to protect against asthma, croup, fever, hay fever, and throat infections; amber powdered and mixed with honey and rose oil was used to treat ear infections, and powdered and mixed with Attic honey was used to improve bad vision.

In the Orient amber was used to protect unborn babies, and to sterilize the areas used for childbirth by being burned for its disinfecting properties. Amulets of amber carved into lions, dogs, frogs and fishes were worn to bestow fertility.

Amber beads known as "Lammer beads" were worn in Scotland as a charm to keep away all evil, and their touch was thought to cure many diseases. In the Middle Ages it was used against a whole manner of complaints including arthritic pains, asthma, heart and stomach problems, plague, poisons, diseases and vertigo; a piece of red amber worn on the body being thought to protect against poisons and pestilence. It was also thought to ease birth, bring on periods and provoke urine.

Amber was thought to be good for throat problems and to fasten loosened teeth. Even today amber is still used by the medical profession in most countries, in the form of Oil of Amber, also known as Oil of Succinate, which is used in the preparation of liniments. Amber dissolved in a cordial was used in a number of ways: to prevent epilepsy if placed over the heart, to check paralysis by anointing the spine, and to act as a restorative when inhaled.

In 16th century India powdered amber was mixed with food and used as a general medication. Moslem beliefs about amber included using it is a cure for jaundice (classic colour association) and taken internally in powdered form to strengthen a weak heart or induce sweating. Rubbing the eyes with amber ashes was thought to alleviate soreness. In Louisiana it was used to cure croup.

Amber's protective qualities from infection have led to it being used as the mouthpiece (in carved form) for hookah pipes in Turkey, ornately carved mouthpieces being highly prized as family heirlooms.

Amber in Greek Myth
To the Greeks it was sacred to Apollo and Helios. Amber is referred to in Homer's *Odyssey* in what is probably the first literary allusion to such a stone: "Eurymachus received a golden necklace, richly wrought, and set with amber beads, that glowed as if with sunshine".

Amber in Norse Myth
Freya's necklace Brisingaman was said to be made of amber (some versions of the myths say gold), and she was said to have wept amber tears (see above under Creation Myths). Glaeisvellir was an amber valley paradise, and Glaesir an amber grove at the gates of Valhalla.

Amber in Qabalah
In Qabalah it is attributed to Tiphereth as its colour in the Empress Scale, and Malkuth due to its solidified nature; Cancer as the 18th path due to being its colour in the King Scale, the 30th path as the Sun in the Emperor and Empress scales.

Other Folklore
Amber was known in China as the "Soul of the Tiger". It was said to protect against fire and water. In Rome it was given to

Roman Gladiators before combat to give courage. A phallus carved from amber was believed to protect from the evil eye.

In the Middle Ages it was thought that amber "laid on the breast of a wife when she is asleep makes her confess all evil deeds". Dreaming of amber was said to indicate a voyage.

Amethyst

Amethyst sigil

Amethyst was traditionally thought to prevent intoxication, some sources suggested binding one into the navel to restrain the "vapour of the wine".

The pure purple of amethyst demonstrates its nature as one of the great magickal stones, purifying and protecting as well as helping the spirit grow.

Colours: Purple, Violet-blue.

Attribution: Scorpion 3∞ Sagittarius, Uranus, Neptune, Jupiter, Pluto, Mars, Pisces, Aquarius, Sagittarius, Scorpio.

Chakras: Throat, Third Eye, Crown.

Uses: Used for spiritual growth and protection, purification, mental healing. One of the prime magickal stones. Is a good dreaming stone, placing under the pillow may help with insomnia. Stimulates the third eye chakra, and hence good for inspiration and intuition, as well as sorting out any blocks in that chakra. Amethyst is a good seeing stone, and can help with developing clairvoyance and astral/psychic vision. Works on the immune and endocrinal systems. May influence the pineal and pituitary glands. Can help ease headaches, including migraines. Is used for easing fluid retention. A good stone to work with if trying to overcome addiction.

Used Since: At least 25,000 BCE France.

The Myth of Amethyst
In Greek myth the story was told of how Bacchus was annoyed at having been neglected by mortals, and he swore to have his tigers tear apart the next mortal he came across. The nymph Amethyst was on her way to the temple of Diana to worship and she was the next mortal he met. Amethyst cried out to Diana to save her from being torn apart, and Diana turned her into a pillar of quartz. Bacchus then felt remorse for his actions, and libated wine over the stone in atonement, which absorbed the wine giving it the distinctive colour.

Amethyst and Christianity
Amethyst is one of the most common crystals referred to in Christianity, possibly due to its purple colour (which has long been associated with authority) and purificatory effects. To the early Christians it symbolised the constant thought of the heavenly kingdom in humble souls.

In the Bible amethyst is the twelfth foundation of New Jerusalem. Amethyst was also symbolic of the apostle Matthais, whose attribution replaced Judas. The Pope's Fisherman's ring is made of amethyst, ironic in that amethyst is often attributed to Pisces, whose vice is intoxication (hence "drunk as a fish"), which amethyst is supposed to prevent; a bishop's ring of rank bears an amethyst. St Valentine was said to wear an amethyst ring engraved with a figure of Cupid.

Amethyst Amulets

In ancient times amethyst was frequently used for protective amulets. Amethyst heart shaped amulets were often placed in the mummy wrappings of the Pharaohs. Egyptian ambassadors would carry an amethyst on them when travelling abroad for protection from treachery and surprise attacks.

The Persians believed that two amethysts engraved with the names of the sun and moon together with baboon hairs and swallow feathers worn around the neck would protect against spells; they also believed amethyst would keep away hail and locusts, as well as assist in approaching people of high station (for business or political matters).

To the Romans an amulet of amethyst would protect against spells, hail and locusts. In the Middle Ages an amulet of a bear engraved on an amethyst was thought to put demons to flight, and protect the wearer from drunkenness. Soldiers also carried amethyst into battle to keep them safe and give victory over enemies.

Amethyst and Health

Amethyst was traditionally thought to prevent intoxication, some sources suggested binding one into the navel to restrain the "vapour of the wine".

Amongst the virtues attributed to amethyst in the Middle Ages were the ability to repress negative thoughts and to give good understanding, to help neuralgia and insomnia, to expel poison, to make one vigilant in business, to treat toothache and headache, to treat gout, to protect from poison and plague, and perhaps most curiously to prepare an easy capture of wild beasts and birds.

Amethyst in Qabalah

Amethyst is attributed to Chesed as the traditional stone of episcopal rank, and to Daath for its magickal qualities; as well as the Archangel Adnachiel.

Other Folklore

Amethyst was considered sacred to the Greek deities Hermes and Artemis, and their Roman counterparts Mercury and Diana. It was also sacred to Neptune and worn by Roman sailors to ensure safe journeys. Amethyst was the ninth stone on the High Priests Breastplate, representing the Tribe of Dan, it was placed at the centre of the breastplate.

The tribes of the Upper Nile used amethyst as a rain stone. Dreaming of amethyst is supposed to indicate your next venture will be successful, and/or freedom from harm. Amethyst is given for 17th wedding anniversary.

Ametrine

Ametrine is good as an amplifier of other energies, and for directing energies.

A stone which has become popular in the last twenty years, ametrine combines the virtues (and vices!) of amethyst and citrine quartzes.

Colours: Purple and yellow-brown, sometimes streaked, sometimes with colourless parts as well.

Attribution: Mercury & Uranus, Gemini, Aquarius.

Chakras: Throat, Third Eye

Uses: Good as an amplifier of other energies, and for directing energies. Can be used to open up to inspiration, and to give ideas form. Can help ease the pains of childbirth.

Folklore
I am not aware of any folklore or myths associated with ametrine, they all tend to be for amethyst or citrine, the stones which it is comprised of.

Ammonite

These ancient fragments have a long history of aiding dreamers, and are also good for work reaching back into the past.

Colours: From golden yellow through browns to black.

Attribution: Jupiter, Terra, Sun.

Chakras: Base, Throat.

Uses: Good for dreamwork, and for work with the memory or ancestor work, including past lives work. Good for working with earth energies, and can be good protective stones as well.

Used Since: At least 30000 BCE Europe.

Names: Fairy Loaf, Fairy Stone, Hammonis Cornu, Snakestone.

Early Use
Fossils like ammonites have been found in Neolithic caves in Europe. In ancient Egypt ammonites were sacred to Ammon-Ra (where the name Ammonite comes from) and used in his worship, due to the curved shape suggesting rams horns.

Pliny said that ammonite was "guaranteed to ensure without fail dreams that will come true", referring to its use to aid divination by dream. It was also thought to aid in contemplation of the divine.

Ammonite in India

In parts of Southern India and Nepal a particular amulet, the salagrama is sacred to Vishnu and used in his worship. It is made from concretions of black ammonite and other fossils found in the water of the river Gandaki in Nepal.

St Hilda's Stone

Ammonites are also known as St Hilda's Stones due to the legends of her removal of the poisonous snakes in the area around the River Esk (around 656 CE); she sat in contemplation and prayer to God, and the snakes coiled up and rolled over the cliffs, turning into rock as they fell - these being the ammonites; as a result the ammonites or St Hilda's stones had a reputation for miraculous cures and for being an antidote to poison.

Sir Walter Scott's poem *Marmiom* refers to this -

> Thus the nuns of Whitby told,
> How of thousand snakes, each one
> Was changed into a coil of stone,
> When holy Hilda prayed:
> Themselves within their sacred bound
> Their stony folds had often found.

Other Folklore

It was considered lucky to find an ammonite. On finding the ammonite, one was supposed to spit on it and toss it over the left shoulder to ensure getting its luck. It was said the house of someone who had found an ammonite and kept it there would never lack for bread.

Aqua Aura

Aqua Aura may help against seasonal affectiveness disorder.

A created crystal which has come into prominence in the last five years, aqua aura has a surprisingly natural feel for something man has produced.

Colours: Transparent blue

Attribution: Jupiter, Air, Aquarius.

Chakras: Throat, Third Eye

Uses: Good for alleviating stress, particularly that induced by mundane existence, and may help against seasonal affectiveness disorder.

Folklore

Aqua aura is an artificial crystal, being formed by bonding gold onto the outside of a quartz crystal. This gives a fine transparent blue crystal which is very popular, and has no folklore yet associated with it due to its recent creation.

Aquamaríne

Greek and Roman sailors believed aquamarine provided protection on sea journeys and that an amulet of aquamarine would banish fear, amulets with Poseidon in his chariot carved on were thought to be particularly effective.

The "Sea Stone", aquamarine helps sort out blockages and problems, and allows the unconscious to flow through to the conscious more easily.

Colours: Sea green, sea blue.

Attribution: Neptune, Water, Pisces, Cancer, Aquarius, Scorpio, Gemini.

Chakras: Sacral, Third Eye.

Uses: Good for relieving stress, mental and emotional problems - helps allow the unconscious communicate more effectively with the conscious mind. Is good for soothing the nerves, and may help ease panic attacks. Works well on the sacral chakra and can help with blockages or problems there. Helps with psychism and clairvoyance. Good for dream work and meditation. Works on the liver and the body's water levels, good for reducing fluid retention. Aquamarine is a good cleansing stone when purifying the body and fasting. May help with toothache. Can be used for epilepsy. Makes a good talisman for travelling by water. Can work on the thymus gland.

First Used: At least 2000 BCE Egypt.

178

Aquamarine And The Sea

Unsurprisingly, aquamarine is sacred to Sea Deities such as Mara (Indian), Poseidon (Greek) and Neptune (Roman). Greek and Roman sailors believed aquamarine provided protection on sea journeys and that an amulet of aquamarine would banish fear, amulets with Poseidon in his chariot carved on them were thought to be particularly effective. Roman fishermen thought aquamarine would increase the catch.

Other Folklore

Roman physicians prescribed aquamarine for indigestion and overeating. It was also used for liver complaints. Both Greeks and Romans believed it would bring luck to lovers. Aquamarine was also said to bring youth, hope and health.

In Qabalah it is attributed to Binah as the Great Mother. Christians believed aquamarine symbolised moderation and control of passion. Dreaming of aquamarine was said to indicate new friends.

Aventurine

*The South African Bantu used aventurine as an amulet,
believing it was brought down by lightning and that it*
could be found where the lightning had struck the ground.

The "Gambler's Stone" of luck and fortune, aventurine is also
good for purification, and helps tonify the body when fasting.

Colours: Green, brown, red or yellow with scales of
                  mica.

Attribution: Terra, Mercury, Venus, Earth, Air, Libra.

Chakras: Base, Heart.

Uses: Used for skin complaints such as rashes, sun-
                  burn and eczema. Good for storing energy
                  and purifying the body, using when fasting.
                  Can help with psychosomatic disorders.
                  Helps centre and still the body and mind, a
                  balancing stone. A good stone to gain luck,
                  and break a run of bad luck. If carried may
                  help improve perception and awareness of
                  one's environment. Aventurine is used to aid
                  in gambling.

First Used: At least 300 BCE China and Mediterranean.

Names: Is also referred to as Adventurine. Sometimes
                  known as Indian Jade. Aventurine from
                  Delaware County, Pennsylvania is known as
                  Delawarite.

Folklore

Aventurine has been used extensively in Tibetan statues in the eyes as it was thought to bring increased visionary powers. In Qabalah it is attributed to Malkuth as a stone of balance, and due to its frequent use with skin problems.

Since the Middle Ages it has been believed in Europe to bring luck, this custom is strongest in Italy. The South African Bantu used aventurine as an amulet, believing it was brought down by lightning and that it could be found where the lightning had struck the ground.

Azuríte

In ancient Egypt and Rome azurite was used for its visionary powers and thought to provide insight.

A good stone for dealing with emotional problems, stress and anxiety - azurite is a good stone for getting rid of the "blues".

Name: From the Old French azure meaning "sky blue".

Colours: Green-blue to blue-black.

Attribution: Neptune, Jupiter, Aquarius, Virgo, Taurus.

Chakras: Solar Plexus, Third Eye

Uses: Good for relieving stress and emotional anxiety, should be rubbed to "get rid of the blues" - it works well as a purifying and cleansing stone. A good stone to work with for hypnosis. Works well for divination and general emotional healing. Can help with dreamwork and developing psychic abilities, and to remove blockages to the third eye.

First Used: At least 2000 BCE Egypt.

Names: Blue Malachite, Chessylite, Lapis Linguis, Lapis Lingua.

Folklore
In ancient Egypt and Rome azurite was used for its visionary powers and thought to provide insight. In Qabalah it is attributed to Chesed due to its colour.

Beryl

One who always has beryl with him, who often holds it in his hand and looks at it frequently, is not easily at odds with other people, nor does he dispute, but rather he remains tranquil.
St. Hildegard von Binoen

The beryls are ideal for psychic work of all kinds, and are very positive stones to work with to open up the self to love.

Colours: Grass green (Emerald), yellow to gold (Heliodor - from the Greek meaning "gift of the sun"), sea-blue and sea-green (Aquamarine), pink (Morganite), colourless (Goshenite), blue, violet.

Attribution: Sirius 10^0 Cancer, Sun (Heliodor), Venus, Mars, Water, Cancer, Libra, Capricorn.

Chakras: Sacral, Solar Plexus (Heliodor).

Uses: Good for skrying, and for dreamwork. Beryl can help develop the psychic faculties, for such skills as psychic and astral vision, and makes a good astral doorway. Can help with past life work. A good stone to work with for opening the self up to love, and for attracting love.

Used Since: At least 1000 BCE.
Names: Also known as Ponzoon, meaning "All Life". Greenish-yellow beryl is also called aquamarine crysolite.

Beryl Amulets & Talismans
Having a crow inscribed on the top of a beryl and a crab on the bottom was supposed to bring joy, wealth and conjugal love, all in great measure. Beryl was also thought to reawaken love between a married couple.

An amulet of beryl with a frog engraved on was thought to reconcile enemies and produce friendship where there is discord; an amulet of a hoopoo with a tarragon herb before it engraved on a beryl was thought to confer the power to invoke and converse with water spirits and the dead.

Beryls were thought to aid the bearer in battle and in litigation, the beryl making the wearer amiable and quicker of intellect, as well as unconquerable, able to detect thieves and removing laziness!

Beryl in Christianity
To early Christians beryl was symbolic of the Apostle Thomas, sometimes being referred to as St Thomas' Stone, and was also believed to symbolise the perfect operation of prophecy.

St Hildegard wrote of beryl: "If a person eats or drinks poison, grate a moderate amount of beryl into spring water, or any other kind of water. He should drink this immediately, and do the same thing for five days, drinking once a day on an empty stomach. The poison will either foam out through nausea or pass through his posterior. One who always has beryl with him, who often holds it in his hand and looks at it frequently, is not easily at odds with other people, nor does he dispute, but rather he remains tranquil."

Beryl in Qabalah
Beryl is attributed to the 23rd path due to its colouring and watery symbolism; it is also attributed to the Archangels Humiel and Zadkiel.

Other Folklore
Beryl spheres known as specularii were used for skrying in India around 400 CE. Beryl is sacred to various Sea Deities such as Tiamat (Sumerian), Mara (Hindu), Poseidon (Greek) and Neptune (Roman). Beryl was used to treat jaundice and liver problems in ancient Babylon.

Beryl may have been the tenth stone on the High Priest's breastplate, representing the tribe of Naphtali. In the Middle Ages it was thought to bring the bearer hope, happiness and eternal youth; and to promote marital bliss, reawakening the love of married people if it had gone stale. Beryl was also said to stop sighing and belching!

In ancient China it was worn as a sign of rank by third rank mandarins. Dreaming of beryls was said to indicate happiness in store.

Heliodor
Heliodor was thought to banish laziness. Heliodor was sacred to the Greek Sun God Helios, and could logically be attributed to other solar deities. In Qabalah Heliodor is attributed to Tiphereth and the 30th path (Sun) due to its colouring.

Calcite

Calcite sigil

Iceland Spar is good for vision, both physical and astral.

Soft enough to be worked without too much difficulty, calcite is a good stone for dealing with emotions, and by its adaptability lends itself to creating different forms, a lesson we can all benefit from.

Colours: Blue, Green, Orange, Colourless (good quality colourless calcite is called Iceland Spar).

Attribution: Air (Blue), Fire & Sun (Orange); Mercury, Air, Gemini (Iceland Spar).

Chakras: Heart, Sacral, Solar Plexus, Third Eye (Iceland Spar).

Uses: Used for lung and voice problems, helps develop communication (blue). Can help digestive problems, and to strengthen the emotions (orange). Iceland Spar is good for vision, both physical and astral.

Used Since: At least 1000 BCE.

Names: Silverstone. Oriental Alabaster. Banded calcite is sometimes known as Egyptian

Alabaster and Mexican Onyx. Calcite dyed
green is known as Mexican Jade. Colourless
calcite of quality is known as Iceland Spar.

Folklore

In Qabalah Iceland Spar is attributed to Gemini as the 17th
path due to its polarization of light. I have not found any
other folklore concerning calcite.

Carnelian

Let not the Muse the dull cornelian slight
Although it shine with but a feeble light;
Fate has with virtues great its nature grac'd.
Tied round the neck or on the finger plac'd,
Its friendly influence checks the rising fray
And chases spites and quarrels far away.
Marbodius, 11th century CE

The "Blood of Isis", carnelian has been used for protection and astral travel since Ancient Egypt, and is particularly good for overcoming blocks and obstacles.

Colours: Translucent with red, white, blue or green colour, yellow (Canary Stone).

Attribution: Mars, Sun, Mercury, Venus, Jupiter, Fire, Air, Aries, Taurus, Virgo.

Chakras: Base, Sacral, Solar Plexus.

Uses: Helps with spinal problems, particularly lower spine. Good for clearing blocked sexual energy (works with the kundalini and the base chakra) and may help dealing with sexual dysfunctions. Carnelian can remove shyness/social inhibitions - giving the bearer the courage to speak their mind and act on it. Vitalises blood. Can help gallbladder, kidneys, liver, lungs and pancreas. Carnelian is an activating stone, and can help in realising ideas and making plans manifest - as such it may be used to encourage fertility. Carnelian makes good amulets (particularly protective), and has been used as such since the times of Ancient Egypt. Carnelian has also traditionally been used to aid in astral travel, by placing it in front of a candle and staring into it, using it as an astral doorway.

Used Since: At least 4000 BCE Babylon.

Names: Cornelian (from the Latin cornu meaning "horn"), Carneolus. The stone called "Sardius" is thought to have probably been carnelian. Yellow carnelian is known as Canary Stone.

Carnelian Amulets & Talismans

In the ancient world a talisman of a richly dressed man with a beautiful object in his hand engraved on carnelian was thought to confer honours and staunch the flow of blood; and an amulet bearing a man with a sword in hand was thought to protect the bearer from enchantments and vices, and the place it was in from lightning and tempest.

It was believed that a carnelian bound to the stomach of a pregnant woman would prevent miscarriage. A medieval verse indicates the protective qualities believed to be possessed by carnelian:

Carnelian is a talisman,
It brings good luck to child and man;
If resting on an onyx ground,
A sacred kiss imprint when found.
It drives away all evil things;
To thee and thine protection brings.
The name of Allah, king of kings,
If graven on this stone, indeed,
Will move to love and doughty deed.
From such a gem a woman gains
Sweet hope and comfort in her pains.

Carnelian And The Egyptians

The Egyptians called carnelian "the blood of Isis", carnelian was usually used to make the protective thet (buckle) amulet which was placed on the mummy's neck, and often engraved with the 156th chapter of the Book of the Dead; the tet (representing the mason's table) amulet was also often made of carnelian and placed on the mummy's neck for protection; the ab (heart-shaped) amulet laid over the mummy's heart was also sometimes made of carnelian.

The 29th chapter of the Book of the Dead was only engraved on carnelian. Red carnelian was linked with the god Set, and was known in the Late Period of ancient Egypt as herset meaning "sadness". Carnelian was thought to be a protective stone, and represented nature given form - it was worn by master architects as a badge of rank, and also by soldiers for courage and power to overcome their enemies.

Carnelian and Health

To the Buddhists, Hindus and ancient Greeks carnelian was a symbol of joy and peace, used for promoting good cheer and banishing sorrow. In the Middle Ages it was thought to protect from falling walls and houses, as well as to stem bleeding and protect against poisons.

Carnelian was recommended for those with weak voices or suffering from timidity, as it was thought to give them the courage to speak well and boldly.

In Arab countries carnelian was used as a remedy for loose teeth. Carnelian was considered a potent healing stone in Arab countries, being used against diseases, curing tumours and respiratory diseases, strengthening the voice and stopping bleeding.

Carnelian versus the Evil Eye

Mohammed was said to have worn a carnelian set in silver as a seal on the little finger of his right hand, and carnelian has been widely used in Islam as a protective amulet against the evil eye, being known as the Mecca Stone.

Carnelian has been used all across Asia as a charm against the evil eye, often with an appropriate prayer inscribed on the stone. Carnelian was said to inhibit bad temper, particularly during disputes. Since ancient Egypt an unusual sheen over the surface of a carnelian has been thought to indicate the use of black magick against the bearer. Marbodius wrote of carnelian:

> Let not the Muse the dull cornelian slight
> Although it shine with but a feeble light;
> Fate has with virtues great its nature grac'd.
> Tied round the neck or on the finger plac'd,
> Its friendly influence checks the rising fray
> And chases spites and quarrels far away.

Other Folklore

In alchemy it was used as a "boiling stone" to activate the energy of other quartzes. During their time on the desert the Hebrews were said to have carved figures on carnelian.

Carnelian as the Sardius (see below) was the first stone on the High Priest's Breastplate, representing the Tribe of Reuben. In the Bible it is the sixth foundation of New Jerusalem. Dreaming of carnelian was said to indicate impending misfortune.

Cat's Eye

Cat's Eye was known as Oculus Solis - the "Eye of the Sun".

The "Eye of the Sun", Cat's Eye was used as a protective charm, and is good for enhancing psychic faculties, as well as discrimination and clarity of mind.

Colours: Greenish-yellow with chatoyancy.

Attribution: Sun, Caput Draconis (South Node)

Chakras: Third Eye.

Uses: Work to improve the psychic faculties, and to enhance intuition, discrimination and clarity. May help with eye disorders. Can help overcome hypochondria.

Used Since: At least 500 BCE India.

Names: Was known as Oculus Solis - the "Eye of the Sun". Also known as cymophane.

Cat's Eye and Health
Cat's eye was thought to be able to relieve croup and asthma, to cure chronic diseases and put colour in the cheeks. It could give pleasure to the mind, relieve melancholy and protect the wearer from financial ruin.

Cat's Eye in Arabic Folklore
Cat's eye was thought to make the bearer invisible in battle. It was believed that if a wife drank milk in which cat's eye had been dipped in, it would prevent her from conceiving a child by her lover.

Cat's Eye in Indian Folklore

In Indian myth the uppermost section of the trunk of the Kalpa Tree was made of cat's eye. In Tantra the southern face of Mount Meru is said to be made of cat's eye. Cat's eye has been used as a charm against evil spirits in the Orient. Hindus believed cat's eye preserved the owner's health and also guarded from poverty.

Other Folklore

In the Orient it was believed that placing a cat's eye on the third eye would give foresight. Dreaming of cat's eye was said to indicate treachery. In Ceylon cat's eye was thought to protect against witchcraft, and was believed to be the abode of the genii. The Assyrians recorded a belief that cat's eye could make the bearer invisible.

Chalcedony

But pierced and worn upon the neck or hand
A sure success in lawsuits 'twill command.
Marbodius, 11th century CE

A gentle calming and soothing stone, chalcedony brings to mind the image of a lotus, full of lessons to learn for those who search.

Colours: Translucent with white, grey, lilac, black, yellow, blue or green colour.

Attribution: Deneb Algedi, Tail of Capricorn 15^{0} Aquarius, Moon, Venus, Jupiter, Mercury, Saturn, Air, Aquarius, Cancer, Capricorn.

Chakras: Heart, Third Eye.

Uses: Increases benevolence and reduces irritability. Enhances intuition. Good for emotional and mental purification. Can help with gallstones. Good for inducing calm and banishing fear, may help in dealing with panic attacks. A good protective stone from psychic and negative energies, like jet it protects through absorption, and should be cleaned regularly.

Used Since: At least 3000 BCE Egypt.

Names: White Chalcedony is known as Milkstone. Blue Chalcedony is sometimes known as Blue Moonstone. Lilac Chalcedony is known as Mojave Moonstone. The opalescent yellow variety is also known as Opaline.

194

Chalcedony Amulets
To the Greeks an amulet of chalcedony was believed to protect sailors from drowning, bring victory, joy and intelligence. A talisman of a man with his right hand raised aloft engraved on a chalcedony was thought to give success in lawsuits, keep the wearer healthy, protect during travels and protect from evil chances. Californian Indians used pieces of chalcedony for amulets.

Chalcedony and Healing
The Babylonians used chalcedony as a cure for gallstones. Black chalcedony was used to prevent hoarseness and clear the voice. In the Middle Ages it was thought to aid in the treatment of some forms of insanity; and was supposed to aid with acts of great physical strength.

Chalcedony in Christianity
Chalcedony was symbolic of the Apostle James. In the Bible it is the third foundation of New Jerusalem. In Medieval times chalcedony symbolised chastity, and the flame of inner charity. It was thought to drive away phantoms and night visions.

Other Folklore
In Tibet chalcedony was regarded as the mineral equivalent to the purity of the lotus flower. In Rome blue chalcedony was called leuchachate and was sacred to the goddess Diana.

In Qabalah it is attributed to Aquarius as the 15th path due to its cloudy appearance. Chalcedony was one of the twelve stones on the high priest's breastplate, representing the tribe of Manasseh. Dreaming of chalcedony was said to indicate friends re-joined.

In Italy chalcedony was used to promote lactation in mothers. In ancient times it was believed to bring good fortune in litigation, Marbodius wrote of it:

But pierced and worn upon the neck or hand
A sure success in lawsuits 'twill command.

Chrysocolla

Chrysocolla sigil

In the Orient chrysocolla was thought to bring luck,
prosperity and astuteness in business.

A sphere of chrysocolla looks like the Earth from space, reflecting its value in working with earth energies and providing us with a good grounding foundation.

Colours: Green, or greenish-blue with black or brown.

Attribution: Venus, Terra, Earth, Virgo.

Chakras: Feet, Base, Sacral.

Uses: Good for storing energy, and for working with earth energies. Can help with menstrual problems. Provides inspiration and serenity, whilst being a good balancer of emotions at the same time. Helps with arthritis, digestive problems, lung problems and ulcers. Works with thyroid gland. Good for releasing tension and fear.

First Used: At least 500 BCE Greece.

Names: Green Turquoise.

Folklore
In Qabalah chrysocolla is attributed to Malkuth due to its appearance and its use working with earth energies. In the Orient chrysocolla was thought to bring luck, prosperity and astuteness in business.

Chrysoprase

Alexander the Great was said to have worn a chrysoprase in his girdle, which was bitten off by a snake whilst he bathed in the river Euphrates!

The striking apple green of chrysoprase eases the spirit and engenders positive feelings, it is a stone with secrets to reveal or bring out.

Colours: Translucent apple green.

Attribution: Venus, Mercury, Earth, Water, Cancer, Capricorn.

Chakras: Sacral.

Uses: Produces insight and hope, eases depression and frustration (including sexual). Can help improve finances and is used to attract a better financial situation.

Used Since: At least 500 BCE Middle East.

Names: Crysoprase.

Chrysoprase And Christianity
In the Bible chrysoprase is the tenth foundation of New Jerusalem. It was considered symbolic of the Apostle Jude and Saint Thaddeus. To early Christians it symbolised the work of the blessed martyrs and their reward.

Other Folklore
One of the twelve stones on the high priest's breastplate, representing the tribe of Gad. A bull engraved on a chrysoprase was said to give aid against evil spells and

procure the favour of magistrates. It was said that a thief sentenced to hanging or beheading would immediately escape if he placed a chrysoprase in his mouth.

Alexander the Great was said to have worn one in his girdle, which was bitten off by a snake whilst he bathed in the river Euphrates (better the stone than him!). Chrysoprase shared with opal the supposed property of making its bearer invisible.

Citrine

Let me dip thee in the water,
Thou yellow beautiful gem of power!
In water of purest wave,
Which pure was kept by Bridget.
Old Celtic Christian Blessing

A good stone for healing and self-development, citrine teaches us to trust ourselves and gain the clarity this brings.

Colours:	Yellow or brown.
Attribution:	Mercury, Sun, Air, Fire, Gemini.
Chakras:	Sacral, Solar Plexus, Heart.
Uses:	Helps maintain emotional stability in troubled times, by maintaining and improving self-esteem, and a good stone for emotional healing. May bring abundance. Can help colon, digestive organs, gallbladder, heart, kidneys and liver. A stone to help eliminate toxins from the body. Can help improve psychic abilities and the instincts, or rather the tendency to trust them. A good relaxant, can be used to overcome fear and phobias. May be made by heating amethyst.
Used Since:	At least 1000 BCE Hebrew.
Names:	Brazilian Topaz, False Topaz, Madeira Topaz, Occidental Topaz, Scotch Topaz.

Old Celtic Crystal Blessing
In my research I came across a lovely crystal blessing to be performed at a sacred spring or well, for citrine or ordinary quartz. Though Christian in its imagery, it is also very pagan in its sentiments.

Let me dip thee in the water,
Thou yellow beautiful gem of power!
In water of purest wave,
Which pure was kept by Bridget.
In the name of the Apostles twelve,
In the name of Mary, virgin of virtues,
And in the name of the High Trinity
And all the shining angels.
A blessing on the gem,
A blessing on the water,
And a healing of all bodily ailments
To each suffering creature!

Other Folklore
Citrine was sacred to Hermes. In Qabalah it is attributed to Hod as the Mercurial "Thieves" Stone. Citrine may have been the tenth stone on the High Priest's breastplate, representing the tribe of Naphtali.

Coral

Coral sigils

*"Coral is good to be hanged about the neck of children ...
to preserve them from the falling sickness. It has also some
special sympathy with nature, for the best coral ... will turn
pale and wan if the party that wears it be sick, and it comes to
its former colour again as they recover."*
**"Jewel House of Art and Nature", Sir Hugh Platt,
1594 CE**

Best known for its use protecting sailors and against the evil
eye, coral is very versatile and beneficial to work with, but
remember to check where it came from.

Colours: Red (most valuable), pink, white, black, blue,
golden.

Attribution: Saturn, Neptune, Mars, Moon, Sun, Venus,
Water, Aries, Scorpio.

Chakras: Sacral.

Uses: For work with the bones, and to provide form
to ideas. Can be used for work with fertility
and growth. Coral can be worn as a relaxant.
Good for teething children, and for arthritis.
Can be worn to ease menstrual problems.

Good for emotional strengthening work - "to get some backbone". Coral works well as a protection from negative emotions and thoughts. Good for work with the sea and tidal energies.

Used Since: Has been found in Paleolithic remains around 25,000 BCE. It was depicted on a vase from at least 3000 BCE Mesopotamia.

Names: Gorgeia (after Medusa, a gorgon). Red coral is called Witch Stone in Southern Italy. Black coral is known as Accarbaar or Akabar, or King's coral. The rare grey-blue coral is known as Akori.

The Creation Myth of Coral

Greek myth has it that after slaying Medusa, Perseus was resting on the way home and put the sack with her head in down; the power of the head seeped through the sack into the weed and wood on which it rested and turned them to stone, Sea Nymphs then came and took the fossilised plants into the sea and put them on the seabed where they became the first coral.

Coral and Alchemy

Red and white coral were known as the trees of the sun and the moon respectively. Red coral was also known as the blood-filled sponge, and was believed to represent the union of the four elements, and have strong curative powers - having "the curative power of all herbs together"; it had to be harvested underwater with a sickle carefully, to ensure the blood did not flow out. It has been suggested that the red coral tree/blood filled sponge symbolism also referred to the placenta.

Coral and Amerindian Myth

The four Navaho rain-making gods are depicted with necklaces of coral and turquoise. Red-orange coral is one of the four elemental stones of the Pueblo Indians. Red coral represents the South and the warm energy of the Sun in the Hopi/Zuni Road of Life.

Coral in the Orient

The Chinese used red coral ornaments for the sacrifices made on the Altar of the Sun. In China and India coral was used to adorn statues of deities. In the Orient wearing discoloured or dull coral is said to attract bad luck. In ancient China second rank mandarins wore red coral as a sign of rank.

Coral and the Sea

The ancient Greeks used to nail red coral to the ship's bow to protect it and lead them safely into harbour, strips of seal skin were often used in attaching the amulet to the prow. Bearing red or white coral was said to enable the bearer to still tempests and cross broad rivers safely. Black coral was especially sacred to Poseidon

Coral and Health

Coral, like a number of other stones, had the reputation for fading if its bearer was ill, and returning to colour with their health. It was a common belief in the Mediterranean that coral lost its qualities if it was worked or if it broke, and that it had to be highly visible to work in its protective mode against enchantments and illnesses.

The Romans used to tie twigs of red coral to cradles and make pendants for children, as it was believed to ward off illness and the evil eye and keep the children in good health. Red coral was worn by newlyweds to ensure fertility. In some Mediterranean countries fresh coral is still tied to fruit trees and olive trees to ensure a good crop, and women also wear coral to ensure their fecundity.

Wearing coral was thought to help get rid of black choler and stomach pains in the Middle Ages. Coral has also been thought to staunch the flow of blood, cure madness and give wisdom. Coral twigs boiled in wax were used in the treatment of urinary problems. Eating tiny pieces of coral mixed with plantain was supposed to get rid of itches.

Powdered coral was used to treat haemorrhages, heart problems and infections. Sir Hugh Platt in Jewel House of Art and Nature (1594) detailed the beliefs of the time about coral's healing properties: "Coral is good to be hanged about the neck of children ... to preserve them from the falling sickness. It has also some special sympathy with nature, for the best coral ... will turn pale and wan if the party that wears it be sick, and it comes to its former colour again as they recover."

Sir Thomas Browne said of coral: "Though coral doth properly preserve and fasten the teeth in men, yet it is used in children to make an easier passage for them; and for that intent is worn about their necks." (*Pseudoxica Epidemica* V.xxiii). A curious medieval belief was that coral had to be ground in marble, or it would be dangerous for the patient.

Coral and Protection
In the Middle Ages it was believed red coral would bring wisdom and keep away all evil spirits, but brown coral attracted them. The belief in the ability of coral to protect from witches persists in parts of Italy today, and amulets of red coral shaped into a right hand making the horns (little and index finger raised, others folded) are available and still worn.

Hanging coral in the house is also supposed to banish negative influences such as envy and disharmony. The Torajas of Sulawesi wore pieces of coral on a string around their necks to make them invulnerable in battle. After the fighting, they "fed" pieces of scalps to the coral to ensure its continued co-operation and protection.

Other properties ascribed to coral include protection from lightning, prevention of nightmares and protection from wild animals. A piece of coral and a piece of flint were sewed into dog-collars to cure dogs of rabies in ancient Rome.

Other Folklore
In Indian myth the fresh young leaves of the Kalpa Tree were formed of coral. Giving coral to Krishna was said to bring the ability to "subdue all the three worlds". To the ancient Egyptians coral was sacred to Isis. Dreaming of coral was said to indicate recovery from illness. To the Arabs yellow coral was the gem of everlasting life. Coral is often carried by dancers for luck, especially ballet dancers. A gift made of coral is given for 35th wedding anniversary.

Diamond

Diamond sigils

In Chinese Buddhism the Diamond Throne was said to be the centre of all things, measuring one hundred foot across and made from a single diamond, it is now supposed to be buried in the earth.

The "Ruler" of the mineral kingdom and the most powerful of stones, diamond amplifies all types of energies - so keep positive when using one.

Colours: Colourless, pale tints of yellow, red, pink, green, blue, brown, black. Diamonds may be heat-treated and irradiated to produce blue, golden brown, green, purple, red and yellow colours (this must be disclosed to the purchaser).

Attribution: The Pleaides, Caput Algol 18⁰ Taurus, Spirit, Pluto, Sun, Mars, Venus, Neptune, Saturn, Jupiter, Fire, Aries, Leo, Taurus.

Chakras: Crown. May be used with any chakras.

Uses: Amplifies any energies, purifies. Diamonds will amplify negative energies as easily as positive ones, so if using diamonds, keep them and any other stones clean and well stored. The most powerful of magickal stones.

Diamond is a good stone for works of balance. May be used to help remove any blocks in the crown chakra. Good for works requiring strength - physical and spiritual. Works on the pineal and pituitary glands. Can be used to help treat brain disorders. Diamond is pizoelectric.

Used Since: At least 2000 BCE India.

Names: King of the Stones. Vajra meaning "thunderbolt", aÁira meaning "fire" or "the Sun", and indr.judha meaning "Indra's weapon" (Sanskrit).

Diamond and Qabalah

In Qabalah diamond is attributed to Kether as the ruler of minerals, yellow diamond is attributed to Tiphereth as the reflection of Kether there (other attributions have been made on this principle - blue diamond for Chesed, red diamond for Geburah and green diamond for Netzach), and black diamond to 31-bis as symbolising the blackness of akasa (spirit).

The attribution of diamond to Kether combined with that of coal (from which diamond is formed) to Malkuth emphasises one of the qabalistic axioms - "That which is in Kether is like unto that which is in Malkuth, and that which is in Malkuth is like unto that which is in Kether", or to put it in a less long-winded form - "As above, so below". It is also attributed to the Archangel Humatiel.

Diamond and Christianity

St Hildegard said that diamond was hated by the Devil because it resisted his power day and night. In the Bible the great white throne of judgment is said to be made of Diamond (Apoc xx.11). Wearing diamonds was thought to bring protection against evil.

Diamond and Hebrew Myth

Diamond may have been the sixth stone on the High Priest's breastplate, representing the tribe of Zebulon. The diamond in the High Priest's Breastplate was said in the Talmud to dim in the presence of the guilty, but shine more brilliantly in the presence of the innocent.

Diamond and Indian Myth

Hindus classify diamonds according to the four castes, i.e. Brahmins (which should be as white as shell or quartz), which give power, riches, friends and good luck; Kshariyas (the brown of a hare's eye) which give endurance and stave off the coming of old age; Vaisyas (the shade of the petal of the kadali flower) which give success; and Sudras (the sheen of a polished blade), which bring all sorts of good fortune; additionally red and yellow diamonds were reserved for kings.

The bottom section of the trunk of the jewelled Kalpa Tree was made of diamond. A fifth century Sanskrit document lists the powers of diamond as protection from evil spirits, fire, floods, poison, sickness, snakes and thieves.

Diamond in the Orient

Tibetan Buddhists depict Vajravarahi the Queen of Heaven as a diamond sow. In Chinese Buddhism the Diamond Throne was said to be the centre of all things, was one hundred foot across and made from a single diamond, it is now supposed to be buried in the earth. To retain their powers, it was believed in the Orient that diamonds should be given, buying one immediately disempowered the stone.

Diamond for Healing and Protection

Romans wore uncut diamonds in gold rings as protective talismans. Diamond was the knight's talisman, being set into armour and weaponry to bring courage, strength, protection and victory. In the Middle Ages possession of a diamond was thought to bring many benefits, such as immunity to poisons

210

and diseases (including the plague), and protection from nightmares, demons and devils, being able to tame incubi and succubi; from this power to ward off evil came the custom of giving diamond rings to ones fiancÈe.

Set in gold and worn on the left arm, diamond was thought to drive away evils of the night. Powdered diamond dust in liquid was used to treat bladder conditions and the plague (for the rich). In India it was believed that powdered diamond dust from flawless stones ingested would bring longevity, beauty, energy, happiness, clear skin, strength and a sense of well being; if the diamond was flawed they would bring all manner of illnesses. In Mesopotamia, Rome and India, water in which a diamond had been dipped was believed to cure all illnesses.

Curious Beliefs about Diamond
In his writings Pliny the Elder stated that diamonds had an antipathy for lodestone, which would not work in its presence. Theophrastus (c. 372-287 BCE) divided the stones into male (dark stones) and female (light stones). In 1566 FranÁois Ruet described two diamonds producing offspring, showing how long this belief remained in fashion.

Diamond was once thought to be formed from solidified thunderbolt, a curious contrast to the later medieval Italian belief that diamonds sometimes melted in thunderstorms. Until the Middle Ages a belief persisted that to be softened diamond had to be immersed in goat's blood. It was believed that diamonds could only be found at night.

In ancient times it was thought that small diamonds left buried in soil would grow a cubit every two to three years. By the time of Aristotle there was already a belief that swallowing a diamond would rupture the insides and kill the unfortunate person who had swallowed it (and indeed it would not bepleasant!), this belief persisted until recent times in some parts of the world. Sir John Mandeville recorded the belief that diamonds watered in May dew would grow bigger.

Other Diamond Folklore
Diamond is regarded as the stone of Winter. The chariot of Dahzbog the Slavic Sun God is made of Diamond. In Greek myth Cronos' sickle was made of diamond.

In Persia diamond was viewed as a source of sin and sorrow, and an invention of evil. Diamonds such as the Hope Diamond are infamous for having a history of misfortune and bloodshed attached to them, in which we can see the negative energies of avarice and greed being amplified by the diamond to produce negative results such as bloodshed.

Diamonds were also thought to be able to turn the bearer invisible. Dreaming of diamonds was said to indicate victory over enemies. An item with a diamond in it is given for a 60th wedding anniversary.

Dinosaur Bone

Dinosaur bones have often been thought to be dragon bone in days gone by.

Pulling us back into the distant past, dinosaur bones help the memory and take us deeper into ourselves.

Colours: Browns, reds, yellows.

Attribution: Terra, Saturn, Earth.

Chakras: Base.

Uses: Good for working with memory and recall, for contacting the reptilian brain and working with the deep unconscious. May be used in cases of amnesia. Can also be used for past life work.

Used Since: At least 1000 BCE China, possibly much earlier.

Names: Dragon Bone. Dinny Bone.

Folklore

Dinosaur bones have often been thought to be dragon bones. Dinosaur ("dragon") bones were used powdered as a cure-all in ancient China.

Emerald

The gem which fell from Lucifer's forehead when he was
thrown out of paradise and from which the Holy Grail
was subsequently formed was said to be an emerald.

A powerful stone of great love and purity, emerald helps with vision, including the ability to see through falsehoods and illusions.

Colours: Grass green.

Attribution: Spica Virginis 17∞ Libra, Venus, Terra,
Mercury, Jupiter, Taurus, Virgo, Cancer,
Sagittarius.

Chakras: Heart, Throat.

Uses: Good for healing and love, and for deter-
mining purity (including magickal purity);
may be used for purifying the blood. A good
stone for magickal charge and seeing things
clearly, can improve memory and be used for
mental illness. Promotes self-confidence and
balance. Works on eyes, heart, immune
system, kidneys and liver. Good for
unblocking the heart chakra or any associated
problems. Emerald may also be used to
sharpen the ability to detect lies (and
illusions). Can be used to aid neurological
problems.

Used Since: At least 4500 BCE Egypt.

Names: Another of the stones referred to as chrysolith.

Emerald and Ancient Egypt

Emerald was given by Thoth to the Ancient Egyptians, representing Spring and dedicated to eternal youth. Emerald was also sacred to Horus, Who was known as the Prince of the Emerald Stone.

The uat (papyrus sceptre) amulet was usually cut from matrix-emerald (called Mother-of-Emerald) and placed in the throat of mummies during embalming for protection and youthful vigour on the journey to the underworld - a matrix-emerald uat is referred to in chapter 159 of the *Book of the Dead* as the gift of Thoth and serving as a protection for the limbs.

Emeralds were engraved with a figure of Isis standing, with a scarab beetle above Her head to be used as talismans to attract good fortune.

Emerald and Christianity - The Holy Grail

The gem which fell from Lucifer's forehead (very suggestive of the Third Eye chakra) when he was thrown out of paradise and from which the Holy Grail was subsequently formed was said to be an emerald. Emerald was also likened to God's aura - "and there was a rainbow about the throne, in sight like unto an emerald" (Rev iv.3).

To early Christians emerald symbolised the strength of faith in adversity. It was considered symbolic of St John, and in the Bible is the fourth foundation of New Jerusalem. The Pope's ring of rank bears an emerald.

Emerald and Greek/Roman Myth

Emerald was considered sacred to Mercury and Hermes, especially as the Smagdarene or Emerald Tablet of Hermes Trimigestus on which the laws of magick were written. Emerald was sacred to Ceres, Diana and Artemis and used as a talisman to ensure the safety of pregnant women and an easy birth; it was also sacred to Aphrodite and Venus as ensuring security in love. An emerald ring was placed on the index finger of someone who had died in the flower of youth to signify hope spent (assuming their family was wealthy!).

Emerald and Hebrew Myth
Emerald was thought to be the third (or possibly fourth) stone on the High Priest's breastplate, bearing the name of the tribe of Levi (or Judah). God gave Moses four stones, one of which was an emerald, which were thought to endow him with power over creation.

Emerald and Indian Myth
In Tantra the lingam (phallus) of the Northern quarter is made of emerald. The shoots of the jewelled Kalpa Tree were formed of emerald. When presented to Krishna emerald was said to bring knowledge of the soul and longevity.

Emerald and Peruvian Myth
The Goddess Esmerelda was an Emerald the size of an ostrich egg which was presented with Her daughters (small Emeralds) by the congregation (a novel and interesting way for the Peruvian priests to gain wealth!); the Emerald was hidden from the Conquistadors and never recovered.

The colour of Emeralds was once thought to vary with the phase of the moon and the seasons, and the Peruvians believed the colour ripened as does a fruit, from colourless to its distinctive green, the sun's rays imparting colour (this is highly reminiscent of chlorophyll, the green pigment in plants, and its part in the process of photosynthesis).

Emerald in the Orient
In Islam the first heaven is made of emerald, Moslems have frequently made amulets of emerald with verse from the Koran engraved on. Emeralds were beloved of the Queen of Sheba. In the Orient they were believed to strengthen

memory and increase intelligence, bringing precognition.

Emerald and Qabalah

In Qabalah emerald is attributed to Netzach and the 14th path (traditionally Venus, and also where the Third Eye would be if the chakras were superimposed on the human body as the Tree of Life in microcosm, which is interesting bearing in mind the myth of the emerald falling from Lucifer's forehead); also attributed to Libra as the 22nd path due to being its colour in the King Scale. It is also attributed to the Archangels Muriel and Ophaniel.

Emerald and Healing

Emerald was thought to provide protection against snakes, antidote to wasps, bees and scorpion poison; it was also believed that holding an emerald in front of a snake would temporarily blind it (or even liquefy it's eyes), and that emeralds would burn to the touch at the approach of poison.

It was thought to be usable to treat leprosy when finely ground, and to restore sight to the blind. Emerald was used as a remedy for epilepsy, diabetes, dysentery and jaundice, and for treating liver problems. Emerald was said to remove pain, both bodily and mental.

Having an emerald suspended touching the abdomen and another in the mouth was said to cure dysentery, and this method was also recorded as having been used successfully against poison. Emerald amulets were also given to children to ward off epilepsy, though if the epilepsy was too strong it would break the stone. Emerald was thought to soothe the eyes when gazed at, giving rise to the custom of gem engravers keeping emeralds on their work surfaces.

St Hildegard on Emerald & Healing

St Hildegard recorded a number of healing uses for emerald. For an epileptic, she wrote that an emerald should be placed in the mouth whilst s/he is lying prone to revive her/his spirits; upon standing again the person should look at the stone intently and say "Just as the breath of the Lord filled the whole earth, so may His grace fill the house of my body, so that it can never be moved." Repeating this for nine consecutive mornings was supposed to cure the epilepsy.

For very bad head pains she recorded the cure of breathing on the emerald until it was warm and damp, and rub it to the temples and forehead; the stone was then placed into the mouth, and after a short time the head pains would go. For excess phlegm and saliva, good wine was to be heated and poured into a metallic vessel, through a linen cloth with an emerald in. This process was repeated frequently, and the wine drunk, and eaten mixed with broad beans, to purge the head and reduce the phlegm and saliva.

For being eaten by worms she records placing an emerald wrapped in a linen cloth over the wound, tying it over with other small pieces of cloth to warm the stone, and leaving it for three days, whereupon the worms die.

Other Folklore

Emerald is considered the stone of Spring, which is easy to see with its verdant green colour. It has been considered symbolic of psychic powers, purity and immortality. Emerald was known as a revealer of truth, and illusions and enchantments were thought to be ineffective or dispersed around it, which may be why they were often used in exorcism to banish demons.

It was once believed that light coloured emeralds were brought from the nests of griffins. Emerald were often carried by sailors due to the belief that they could calm seas and ensure safe travels, bringing good fortune. A lover's stone, emerald was thought to lose its colour or turn brown if a partner was unfaithful, and was used as a preventative against lust and lustful thoughts.

Dreaming of emeralds is said to indicate a positive future and contact with old friends, and/or much to look forward to. A gift with emerald in is given for 55th wedding anniversary. Flawless emeralds are very rare, and most stones have an inclusion, known as the jardin (garden) of the emerald.

Fluorite

Fluorite is a good stone of clarity for seeing things in a discriminating light.

A stone of the emotions and love, fluorite helps them flow smoothly, living up to its name.

Colours: Violet, green, yellow, orange, blue, red, pink, brown, black, colourless.

Attribution: Uranus, can vary with colour.

Chakras: Solar Plexus, Heart, Third Eye.

Uses: Concerned with love, both physical and spiritual, and strongly connected with the heart chakra; a good stone for working with this chakra. Good for work with the emotions, e.g. to counteract depression or deal with heartache - in this respect it is also a good stone of clarity for seeing things in a discriminating light. Can be used to help treat bone disorders.

First Used: I have found no uses recorded historically.

Names: Fluorspar. Green fluorite is sometimes known as African Emerald. Blue John is a form of Fluorite.

Folklore

In Qabalah attributed to Mercury as the 12th path due to the yellow and purple colours in the King and Queen Scales. I have not been able to find any other folklore relating to fluorite.

Garnet
(Almandine Garnet & Pyrope Garnet)

Garnet sigil

"If thou wilt make a carbuncle stone, or a thing shining in the night - take very many of the little beasts shining by night [glow worms and fireflies, and put them beaten small in a bottle of glass, and close it, and bury it in hot horses' dung, and let it tarry fifteen days. Afterward thou shalt distil water of them per alembicum,which thou shalt put in a vessel of crystal or glass. It giveth so great clearness, that every man may read and write in a dark place, where it is."
Albertus Magnus, 16thCentury CE

Garnet brings energy and helps with healing, a good stone to wear and work with if you are at low ebb or run down, or working in a high stress environment.

Colours: Red (Pyrope Garnet), brownish-red (Essonite/ Hessonite), colourless, mauve-red to rose- purple (Rhodolite), violet to purple (Almandine Garnet), orange, amber yellow (Succinite), pale green (Grossularite), green (Transvaal Jade), brown to black (Uvarovite).

Attribution: The Hyades, Aldebaran 3∞ Gemini, Heart of the Lion 23^{0} Leo, Mars, Sun, Jupiter, Venus, Fire, Aries, Aquarius, Scorpio, Capricorn.

221

Chakras:	Base, Heart.

Uses: A good energising stone, for when you are at low ebb or need an extra boost. Helps stimulate and strengthen the will. For heart and circulatory problems, and any problems with the blood. A good stimulatory stone, good for sorting out blockages (particularly for the heart chakra) and to produce resolve and determination to attain goals and complete cycles. Can be used to help to increase a low sex drive. A good protective stone. Can be used to help treat hormonal problems. May have four-rayed asterisms (stars).

Used Since: At least 3100 BCE Egypt.

Names: Rhodolite. Known as Carbuncle when cut en cabochon. The brownish-red form is known as Cinnamon Stone. Red garnet is sometimes known as Adelaide Ruby, American Ruby, Arizona Ruby, Bohemian Ruby, Cape Ruby, Colorado Ruby, Mountain Ruby, Montana Ruby. Almandine Garnet is also known as Almandite. Andradite, with the following names Demantoid (green), Melanite (black) and Topazolite (yellow).

Garnet Amulets
The Greeks believed an amulet of garnet would protect sailors from drowning. The well-formed image of a lion on a garnet was said to protect and preserve honours and health, cure the wearer of all diseases, bring honours and guard from all perils while travelling. Garnet was said to provide protection against demons, injury and death in battle, and against airy and vaporous poisons.

Garnet and Christianity
Garnet (or carbuncle as it was known) symbolised blood and suffering, Christ's passion on the cross and martyrdom. Crosses were sometimes made with five garnets on to symbolise the five wounds Christ received on the cross. Some sources say a large Garnet carbuncle was placed on a pedestal on the centre of Noah's Ark for illumination, as they were thought to shine by night. It was also said to symbolise the Apostle Andrew.

Garnet and Healing
In the Middle Ages garnet was believed to be a heart stimulant of great power, the bearer being advised not to get too excited! Keeping a garnet under the pillow was thought to prevent bad dreams, and it has been used in the past in treating mental depression.

Unusual Folklore
There was a medieval myth that dragon's eyes were made from garnet (carbuncle). In the Orient and Far East it was believed to staunch the flow of blood, and also to be able to inflict mortal wounds, when used as a missile.

Making Carbuncle
Albertus Magnus in the 16th century recorded a method for making carbuncle (garnet):
"If thou wilt make a carbuncle stone, or a thing shining in the night - take very many of the little beasts shining by night [glow worms and fireflies], and put them beaten small in a bottle of glass, and close it, and bury it in hot horses' dung, and let it tarry fifteen days. Afterward thou shalt distil water of them per alembicum, which thou shalt put in a vessel of crystal or glass. It giveth so great clearness, that every man may read and write in a dark place, where it is."

Other Folklore
In Qabalah it is attributed to Geburah due to colour, and also to the Archangels Ambriel and Zaphkiel. Garnet was thought to have been the fourth (or possibly third) stone on the High Priest's breastplate, representing the tribe of Judah (or Levi). In Islam the fourth heaven in said to be made of garnet (carbuncle) in the Koran. In China garnet was worn as a sign of rank by second rank mandarins.

Garnet symbolised the sun in early Spanish astrology. Dreaming of garnet was said to indicate the solution to a problem or mystery was at hand, and/or the acquisition of wisdom. When given as a gift garnet is said to confer loyalty and constant affection. Garnet losing its luster was said to herald imminent disaster or danger. Green garnet is said to confer success, especially in business. A gift with garnet in is given for 18th wedding anniversary.

Gypsum

Gypsum sigil

Selenite was known in Greece and Egypt as "Foam of the Moon".

The softness of gypsum belies its strength for helping deal with problems and take matters in hand; a practical stone for doing.

Colours: Colourless to opaque white (Selenite), white (Satin Stone), whitish-green, brown (Desert Rose).

Attribution: Moon, Terra, Earth.

Chakras: Base, Sacral.

Uses: Can relieve stress and enhance willpower. Helps with skin disorders such as eczema and rashes. Can help with fertility. Can help improve a run of bad luck. Steatite is easy to carve and is sometimes used to make figures such as animals which may be used in totemic work.

Used Since: At least 1000 BCE Egypt.

Names: Satin Spar, Satin Stone. Selenite (named after the Greek Moon Goddess Selene) is a form of gypsum. Brown gypsum which forms in a particular flower type pattern is known as Desert Rose. Steatite (soapstone) is also a form of gypsum.

Folklore
Gypsum was believed to bring protection and good fortune. In ancient Egypt when cut in an egg shape they were known as Pharaoh's Eggs. Selenite was known in Greece and Egypt as "Foam of the Moon".

Halíte (Salt)

Salt sigils

The value of salt can be seen in the old medieval custom
of being "Above" or "Below" the salt,
those above the salt being of higher prestige
and actually being allowed to partake of the salt.

Essential to life and one of the great purifiers, salt reminds us that nature is full of purity, it is only when we look to ourselves and our works that we see otherwise.

Colours: Colourless, white, grey, rarely reddish or blue.

Attribution: Terra, Earth.

Chakras: Base.

Uses: Purification. Circle casting. Exorcism.

Used Since: At least early Stone Age, probably earlier.

Names: Rock Salt.

The Sacred Salt

To the Mexicans it was sacred to Uixtochihuatl, Goddess of Salt. The Romans made offerings of salt to the lares (house spirits). Both Greek and Roman priests sprinkled salt on the heads of sacrificial animals to consecrate them. Due to its sacred nature and the association with luck (both good and bad), salt was always the first item laid on the table, and the last removed. An early German custom was to dip the forefinger in salt and then swear an oath.

Salt in Christianity
Due to it's cleansing and purifying properties salt was considered to represent strength and superiority. In the Sermon on the Mount, Jesus calls his disciples "the salt of the earth". Salt has been used by the Christian Church in exorcisms, and is used in the preparation of holy water.

Salt and the Christian Magick Mirror Invocation
An old German manuscript (1658) gives a description of the use by Christians of the magick mirror, which I feel is worth reproducing here. The magick mirror would be set 2" (5cm) above a board, and the questions placed beneath it. The skryer should then place 3 grains of salt on his tongue, repeat a prayer and cross himself. He then takes the mirror with his right hand and breathes upon it three times, repeating the words "In the name of the Father, of the Son, and of the Holy Spirit. Amen.".

This is then followed by the prayer/invocation:

"O thou holy Archangel N(ame), I pray to thee most fervently through the great and unsearchable name of the Lord of all Lords and King of all Kings, Jod, He, Vau, He, Tetragrammaton, Adonay, Schaday, receive my greeting and give ear to the humble partition which I offer in the name of the great and highest God, Elohim, Zebaoth, that thou shalt appear to me in the world-mirror, and give me knowledge and instruction in answer to my questions."

Salt against Evil Spirits
The Moors used to carry salt in the dark to ward off evil spirits. In Morocco salt was put on the wheat sacks to protect them from spirits. A British custom which persisted into the

early 20th century was the placing of a plate of salt on the chest of a corpse until the funeral, possibly to ensure the body did not rise or evil spirits enter the body.

Salt and Witches

A handful of salt thrown into the fire was believed to torment witches and drive them away. In Lancastershire it was believed this should be done to break bewitchments, for nine successive mornings with the words: "Salt, salt, put thee into the fire, and may the person who has bewitched me neither eat, drink, nor sleep, till the spell is broken."

In some parts of Eastern Europe offering a witch salt, bread and wine was thought to give them power over you, a clear derivation of the Christian symbols of communion.

Salt and Babies

Giving a small pinch of salt to newborn babies was thought to ensure they would want for nothing in life, and also to protect them from witches and evil spirits. Note - Never give salt to newborn babies, it is highly detrimental to their health. A modern Jewish belief for dealing with the evil eye when a child has been afflicted is to take a handful of salt around the head of the child, throwing a little in each corner, and the rest over the threshold.

Salt Blessings

I give the benediction of the salt from The Key of Solomon and also the one used in modern Wicca, to demonstrate the obvious derivation of material, the latter being largely identical.

"The blessing of the Father almighty be upon this Creature of Salt, and let all malignity and hindrance be cast forth hencefrom, and let all good enter herein, for without Thee man cannot live, wherefore I bless thee and invoke thee, that thou mayest aid me."

This is spoken over the bowl of salt and followed by the recitation of Psalm CIII.

"Blessings be upon this creature of salt; let all malignity and hindrance be cast forth hencefrom, and let all good enter therein. Wherefore I bless thee and invoke thee, that thou mayest aid me, in the names of Cernunnos and Aradia."

This is usually spoken with the point of the athame (witch's black-handled knife) in the bowl of salt, inscribing a pentagram as the words are spoken.

Salt and Divination
Divination with salt, known as Alomancy, was performed by emptying the salt from a bowl, and interpreting the random patterns left by the salt which had stuck to the inside of the bowl. A simple method of divining with salt was to leave a small pile on the kitchen table on Christmas Eve, if it was unchanged the next day the future would be positive, though if some had melted it was an omen that someone close would die.

Salt Expressions
The value of salt can be seen in the old medieval custom of being "Above" or "Below" the salt, those above the salt being of higher prestige and actually being allowed to partake of the salt. The term "Covenant of Salt" referred to a holy obligation. The word salary comes from the Roman "salarium", being the Legionnaire's allowance for salt, demonstrating the value of salt. From this comes the expression "not worth his salt".

Salt Sellars
Knocking over a salt sellar is said to be an omen of a friendship breaking. A curious German custom was that if a girl forgets to put the salt sellar on the table when laying it she was no longer a virgin.

Spilling Salt

Throwing a pinch of salt over the right shoulder with the left hand is a common superstition to alleviate bad luck or misfortune after an accident. Two different reasons are suggested for this, the first being that Judas spilt salt at the last supper, and the second that evil spirits lurk on the left side of the body behind a person, and the salt blinds them.

In Denmark it is only unlucky to spill salt if it is damp, spilling dry salt is considered lucky. In America it was said that if salt was spilt every grain represented a day of sorrow, hence the expression "Pass me salt, pass me sorrow" (the British version of the same expression is "Help to salt, help to sorrow"); though if the salt was collected and thrown over the kitchen stove the sorrow could be averted.

Salt & Taboos

Amongst Africans and Hindus mourners do not partake of salt. Egyptian priests and various Central and South American medicine men never eat salt. In parts of Central Africa it was taboo to eat salt when travelling. The Yuchi Indians of California would not partake of salt during the ceremonies of the Firstfruits.

The Huichol Indians would not have salt after they had communed with their deities. Salt was not permitted in cooking during the Gilyak Bear Festival. After taking a head the Dayaks may not take salt or touch iron. Baganda fishermen would not touch salt after a catch. In some parts of India salt is not eaten for three days after marriage. In some cultures menstrual women are not allowed to handle salt.

Salt Tracks and Ley Lines

In his classic work *"The Old Straight Track"*, Alfred Watkins put forward the theory that some of the old leys or straight tracks were in fact trading paths for salt. His reasoning for this was based around the place names along these tracks being so focused around certain words connected with salt, these being sal/salt, whites/whits (a whitman or whiteman was a salt carrier) and wicks/weeks/wiches/wyches (a wick marsh or saltern is a salt marsh producing salt by evaporation). Such place names include Sale, Salt Moor, Salt Way, Satley, Salford, Salcot, Saltley, Saltash; White Houses, White Wells, White Stones, White Rocks, White Crosses, Whiteway Hill, Whitley Ridge; West Week, East Week, Great Week, Wick Lane, Wick Moor, Lee Wick, and others

Other Folklore
In alchemy salt is one of the three base elements along with mercury and sulphur. In Greece it was sacred to Aphrodite. In Qabalah it is attributed to Malkuth and the path 32-bis as being of the Earth and due to its purificatory qualities.

Many traditions including Wicca work with salt for its purificatory qualities. It is considered bad luck to put salt on another person's plate. To eat of a man's salt meant to partake of his hospitality, and was considered binding in doing no ill to the person who had given the salt.

Heliotrope

Heliotrope sigil

*"Nor hope had they of crevice where to hide,
or heliotrope to charm them out of view"*
"Vision, Hell, xxiv", Dante

Another good stone for gaining strength and for healing, heliotrope is valuable for its aid in overcoming inertia and replacing inactivity with action.

Colours: Dark green with red spots.

Attribution: Mars, Sun, Earth, Aries, Pisces.

Chakras: Base, Heart.

Uses: Strengthens the will and used with blood problems and protection from poison. Good grounding stone. Strengthens bone marrow, spleen and heart - particularly recommended for anyone who has or has had a heart condition. A good stone to work with for initiating projects and getting things going, giving the vigour to overcome inertia and also emotional blockages. Good for activities requiring physical stamina. Can be used to help give protection from deception.

Used Since: Pre 1000 BCE India, Ethiopia and Cyprus.

Names: Bloodstone. Lapis Sanguinarius. St. Stephen's Stone.

Heliotrope and Healing:
The Egyptians used ground up heliotrope in honey as a cure for tumours, and to stop hemorrhaging. Heliotrope was thought to staunch the flow of bleeding, clear bloodshot eyes and help cure hemorrhoids; it was also believed it could protect the bearer from poison. Dipping a heliotrope in cold water and placing it on the body was thought to help circulation, an interesting example of sympathetic magick.

A Babylonian use of heliotrope was to hang from a necklace so it lay over the chest to prevent or cure internal bleeding. Once the stone had been so used it should never be discarded, as a permanent link had been made.

Heliotrope and Invisibility
In the Middle Ages it was said to bestow the power of invisibility on the bearer when rubbed with the juice of the heliotrope plant - "Nor hope had they of crevice where to hide, or heliotrope to charm them out of view" (Dante: Vision, Hell, xxiv).

Heliotrope and Christianity
The blood of Christ on the cross was said to have splashed on a piece of jasper on the ground, forming bloodstone. Because of this belief it was associated with the old celebrations of Easter. An alternative version of this myth replaces Christ with Saint Stephen, giving rise to the name of St. Stephen's Stone for heliotrope.

Heliotrope in Qabalah
In Qabalah heliotrope is attributed to the 21st path as connecting Tiphereth (Sun) and Geburah (Mars), and it having both martial (bloodstone) and solar (heliotrope) names.

Other Folklore

According to the ancient Egyptian Leyden Papyrus bearing an amulet of heliotrope would ensure the bearer was believed and given whatever he asked for. It was also considered able to make the bearer renowned and famous, and was worn for safety and long life. Heliotrope was used to protect from deception.

In ancient Greece and China heliotrope was thought to detect solar eclipses, indicating the presence of the moon as it approached the sun. An amulet of a bat engraved on heliotrope was said to give the wearer power over demons and help incantations. Dreaming of heliotrope was said to indicate distressing news or long life!

Hematite

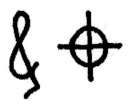

Hematite sigils

"The haematite, named by the Greeks from blood,
Benignant Nature formed for mortals' good."
Marbodius, 11th Century CE

High in iron, a strong stone and very magnetic, hematite can pass the benefits of these qualities onto those who work with it.

Colours: Black, dark grey or either with brown stripes; brown (Limonite).

Attribution: Mars, Mercury, Earth, Aries.

Chakras: Base.

Uses: Gives courage and endurance, used with blood problems, inflammation and ulcers. Enhances aura and courage, increasing personal magnetism. A good grounding stone, can also help provide stability in your life when things are fragmenting. Can help with back problems, particularly of the lower back. A good stone to work with in legal matters. May be used to help ensure balance of the physical, mental and spiritual energies in life.

Used Since: At least 3000 BCE Egypt.

Names: Haematite. "Volcano Spit". Alaska Black
Diamond. Dutch Bloodstone. Brown
hematite is also known as Limonite.

Hematite in Ancient Babylon
In Babylon hematite was believed to procure the favour of
Kings when petitioning and bring good results in lawsuits and
judgments. A seal of hematite was thought to enable a man
to destroy his enemies.

Hematite in Ancient Egypt
The urs (pillow) amulet placed under the mummy's head in
ancient Egypt was often made of hematite, and sometimes
engraved with the 166th chapter of the Book of the Dead. The
neha amulet of protection was usually made of hematite, and
placed on the breast of the deceased. It was also used in
Ancient Egypt to treat inflammation and hysteria.

Hematite in Voodoo
In Voodoo hematite is used for a variety of purposes, including
influencing lovers, gambling charms and to ward off
dangerous illnesses. The charm for warding off illnesses uses
a pair of hematite pieces, one to attract good fortune and the
other to repel evil influences.

Hematite and Healing
Hematite was believed to be good for curing backache in
ancient times, almost all amulets for backache were made of
it. Hematite was sometimes known as "stench stone" due to
its accredited virtue of being able to stop the flow of bleeding.

Galen prescribed hematite for inflamed eyes and headaches.
The methods of application were either to mix the powdered
stone in honey and apply to the eyelids, the other was to rub
the smoothed stone over the eyelids. It was also used for

kidney conditions, the smoothed stone being rubbed over the kidney region of the body.

Other Folklore
In Qabalah hematite is attributed to Geburah due to its high iron content. It was thought that rubbing the body with hematite would confer strength and invincibility on a warrior, ensuring victory. Highly polished mirrors of hematite have been found in Olmec tombs as burial gifts, generally with female bodies.

The 17th century writer Andreas Balvacensis put forward the theory that hematite was made from "dragon's blood". Marbodius wrote of hematite:

"The haematite, named by the Greeks from blood,
Benignant Nature formed for mortals' good."

Ivory

In Greek myth the gate of "false sleep" of Hypnos was made of ivory, which may correspond to astral travel or lucid dreaming.

A beautiful substance which has long been used for decoration and protection, ivory like fur looks best on its natural owner, but may be used if treated with the correct respect.

Colours: White.

Attribution: Moon.

Chakras: Base.

Uses: Traditionally used for spiritual protection in the East, and for rosaries in both East and West. Obviously new ivory should not be purchased as it is propagating the slaughter of elephants, but old ivory goes brown and may be purchased, if you feel uncomfortable about this (or even if you don't), you should perform a simple ceremony calling to the elephant spirit (or Ganesha would be appropriate) and explain why you are using it and ask for their blessing.

First Used: At least 75,000 BCE

Ivory in Christianity
Due to its white colour and smooth texture, ivory was considered to represent purity and moral fortitude. It was also a symbol of Christ as his incorruptibility in the tomb, and this may be the origin of ivory crucifixes.

Ivory in Greek Myth

In Greek myth the gate of "false sleep" of Hypnos was made of ivory, which may correspond to astral travel or lucid dreaming.

The expression "Shoulder of Pelops" used to refer to a distinguishing mark comes from the story of the unfortunate Pelops, who was killed and served in a stew to the Gods. Demeter ate his shoulder, and when he was reconstituted in Her cauldron, the shoulder was not, so she replaced it with one made of ivory.

Folklore

In Qabalah it is attributed to Yesod as the "Gate of the Moon", and due to its connection with the astral. King Solomon's wisdom, contained in the Key of Solomon were placed in an ivory casket which was stored in his tomb with him. In Indian myth ivory is sacred to Ganesha as his tusk.

Haida magicians used pendants of ivory as protection from disease, selling them to tribesfolk when they had been magickally charged. Ivory symbolises the feminine principle, and has long been valued for its beauty and ease of working. It was thought to heal and protect the bearer, and to honour the gods and the ancestors.

Jaðe

With a sky-blue Pi worship is paid to Heaven
With a yellow Ts'ung to Earth
With a green Kuei to the East
With a red Ch'ang to the South
With a white Hu to the West
With a black Huang to the North
***"Book of Rites"*, Chou Kung, 1100 BCE**

Jade is one of the most fascinating and enduring stones in the eyes of man, precious, virtuous, noble and mysterious, it draws our gaze between heaven and earth and reminds us that the path, like beauty, is its own reward.

Although many people do not realise it, there are two stones commonly known as jade - jadeite (from the Spanish *piedra de ijada* meaning "loin stone", referring to its use by the South American peoples for treating kidney disorders) and nephrite (from the Greek *nephros* meaning "kidney", again due to the belief it helped with renal disorders).

There is also a misconception that jade is green only. Although shades of green are the commonest colours for both jadeite and nephrite, jadeite can also be black, blue, pink, lilac, white, mauve, brown, orange, red or yellow; and nephrite can also be white, black, brown, grey or purple.

Colours: Green, black, blue, pink, lilac, white, mauve, brown, orange, red, yellow, grey, purple.

Attribution: Pluto, Terra, Moon, Venus, Earth, Water, Libra, Virgo.

Chakras: Base, Sacral, Heart, Crown.

Uses: Used for earthing and protection, good for eye, heart, kidney and immune system problems and "keeping your feet on the ground". Gives an appreciation of beauty, and brings clarity and virtue. May help reduce swelling. Good for working with earth energies. A good stone for promoting balanced growth - of mind, spirit and emotion. Jadeite is good for promoting projects such as business ventures and worthy causes, and can be used for magick to attract wealth.

Used Since: Neolithic times in China.

Names:

Jadeite: A matrix of jadeite and albite is known as Snowflake Jade. Also known as Kidney Stone. Jade was known as the "Emperor's Stone", the apple or emerald green varieties of jade were the most valuable, and were known as Imperial Jade; though the ancient Chinese called it fei-ts'ui, meaning "kingfisher". The Chinese also called it Yu, though this term was used to signify any precious stone. The same is true of the Japanese use of the words Giyuku and Tama. Deep emerald green jadeite has large amounts of the mineral kosmochlor in it, and is known as Mawsitsit or Tawmawite. Dark green to black jadeite is known as chloromelanite. (from chloros - green and melas - black).

Nephrite: Axe Stone, Kidney Stone, Maori Stone, New Zealand Greenstone or Jade, Greenstone, Honan or Hunan Jade, Wyoming Jade. Grey nephrite is known to the Maori's as Inanga.

White nephrite is sometimes called Mutton
Fat Jade, deep green nephrite from Siberia is
also called Spinach Green Jade. The creamy
brown variety was known as Tomb Jade, due
to the reaction between the fluids used in
mummies and the jade. Jade which has been
buried in soil and lost it's outer colouration is
referred to as "chicken-bone jade".

Jade and the Chinese

There was a belief that jade was solidified dragon semen. It
was known as the "Emperor's Stone" and always connected
with power and authority, the apple or emerald green
varieties of jade were the most valuable, and were known as
Imperial Jade; though the ancient Chinese called it fei-ts'ui,
meaning "kingfisher".

The Chinese also called it Yu, though this term can be used to
signify any precious stone - a good indicator of the supreme
value placed on jade. Jade is considered to be more of a yang
stone, and some believed it to be the solidified essence of pure
mountain water. There were legends of a fountain of jade
wine flowing over jade rocks on the Isles of the Blest, which
bestowed miraculous qualities on any individual fortunate
enough to find it and drink some.

Jade was considered to be a stone demonstrating the five
cardinal virtues of chastity, courage, justice, modesty and
wisdom, and to this end was considered sacred to the Goddess
Kwan Yin, and to Buddha. The philosopher Khwan Ghung
said that the nine qualities of Jade reflected the best attain-
ments of humanity, these were:

1. benevolence suggested by its smoothness,
2. knowledge suggested by the polish,
3. righteousness suggested by its firmness,
4. virtuous action suggested by its harmlessness,

5. purity suggested by its spotlessness,
6. endurance suggested by its imperishable character,
7. ingenuousness suggested by the visibility of any flaw,
8. morality suggested by the ability to be passed between hands unsullied,
9. music suggested by the note it makes when struck.

Indeed, due to its melodic note when struck jade was known as the "concentrated essence of love", and wind chimes and bells were sometimes made from jade, the chimes being carefully shaped to produce unusual sounds. Pieces of jade were placed in the foundations of houses as they were built, as it was believed to protect the house from being struck by lightning.

There is evidence of the ancient Chinese using jade in magick, with different shapes and colours of jade representing different elements, etc. These are given below:

Heaven (Above)	Round Dark Green or Blue Tablet
Earth (Below)	Yellow Octagonal Tablet
Heaven & Earth Conjoined	White Tablet with Yellow Streaks
North	Black Semi-Circle
East	Green Pointed Tablet
South	Red Tablet
West	White Tiger-shaped Tablet

Reference to different colour shaped pieces of jade is also made in The Book of Rites (Chou Kung, 1100 BCE) to the Six Ritual Jades, which are:

• Kuei - a flat green oblong tapering to triangle like a primitive knife blade, symbolising Spring, the East, Imperial Power, Male, Lingam.

- Chang - a flat red tablet symbolising Summer, the South, Fire, Sun.
- Hu - a flat primitive stylised green tiger symbolising Autumn, the West, Military Power, Female, Yoni.
- Huan - a centrally holed black or green tablet broken so as to be like half a Pi, symbolising Winter, the North, Necromancy, Water, Moon. With the passing of time they became stylised in shape to form dragons or fish.
- Ts'ung - a yellow hollowed cylinder carved to appear to have been inserted into a rectangular box of square cross-section, symbolising Earth.
- Pi - a centrally holed blue disk symbolising Heaven, Wind, Void, Creation.

A translation of the accompanying text in *The Book of Rites* says:

> With a sky-blue Pi worship is paid to Heaven
> With a yellow Ts'ung to Earth
> With a green Kuei to the East
> With a red Ch'ang to the South
> With a white Hu to the West
> With a black Huang to the North

After death, the Tsung would be placed on the chest and the Pi at the back, so the departed was firmly between heaven and earth and in no danger of becoming lost or taken to any of the hells. The Chinese also placed jade pieces in the mouths of the dead as a protection for them, these were known as han-y͵ (mouth-jade). At this time the temples favoured yellow jade ornaments for sacrifices on the Altar of the Earth, and white jade for the Altar of the Moon.

Jade has always been believed to have many medicinal virtues, and ancient Chinese medical texts give a variety of uses for jade - as a general tonic if powdered and consumed in fruit juice: calming the nerves, soothing anxieties, making hair glossy and strengthening the voice; it was also recommended in this form for asthma, diabetes and heartburn. Finely powdered in water it was believed to strengthen the heart, lungs and voice.

The Chinese also adapted the idea that contact with the crystal over a period of time could impart its qualities (the principle of contagion or sympathetic magick). The "divine liquor of jade" was made by taking equal parts jade, rice and dew, boiling them in a copper pot and filtering. The resultant divine liquor was believed to strengthen the muscles and make them supple, harden the bones, calm the mind, enrich the flesh and purify the blood. Consistent consumption over a prolonged period was believed to increase tolerance to heat and cold, and reduce the need for other food or drink.

Unsurprisingly considering its value, there is a strong tradition of giving gifts made of jade in China. Jade butter-flies are still exchanged as a token between lovers, a jade phoenix was often given to young girls on their coming of age, and an amulet called "Two brothers of heavenly love" depicting two men was given between friends.

On marriage the bride and groom were given a jade figure of a man riding a unicorn holding castanets, signifying the birth of an heir at the appropriate time! On a more serious note, babies were sometimes given a jade padlock to bind them to life and protect them from diseases.

Jade and South American Myth
Jade was sacred to the Mexican deity Chalchihuitlicue "the precious Green Lady", Goddess of Storms. The Aztecs believed that where lightning struck blocks of green or blue jadeite would be found - a sort of "solid rain". It was strongly connected with death in the minds of the Aztecs and Mayans, being used in funerary masks.

Only royalty and high officials could wear the rare and precious jade whilst alive, though after death all could benefit from its properties - a piece of chalchihuitl (jade) called the heart was placed in the mouth of nobles, commoners had a smaller piece called a texaxoctli used for them.

Jade was identified with maize, water, the sky, vegetation and even life. The Olmecs preferred the blue-green variety, and were the first Mesoamericans to use jade. Votive offerings of small carved rattlesnakes, jaguar masks and carved axes (shaped to depict jaguar faces) made from jadeite have been found in Olmec tombs.

Jade and Other Cultures
The Babylonian Goddess Ishtar's girdle, removed at the fifth gate in Her descent through the underworld, was said to be made of jade (aban al,di in Babylonian), and this may be why jade has been considered the "midwives stone" over the centuries.

The ancient Greeks used jade for eye ailments, placing it on the eyelids, and red jade was considered to stop bleeding. Purple nephrite was thought to help with spleen disorders. Ground jade has been used as a cure for snake and rodent bites, and for stomach complaints.

Jade amulets are still carried today by some Moslems as a protection from injury and annoyance.

The Maori Tikki
The Maori Tikki's (abbreviated form of hei-tikki, meaning "carved image for the neck"), which are curiously contorted human figures usually with the head slanted to 45∫ and large eyes, are often made of nephrite, and are passed down as family heirlooms. Shamans would lead hunting parties to gather punamu (green stone - nephrite) to make Tikki's from, and the spirits they contacted to locate the stone were some-

times thought to resemble the tikki's. Every Tikki has it's own name.

In more recent times a Neolithic jade axehead carved in Switzerland was found in Britain, indicating the extent of trade such a precious and magickal item experienced in such early times.

Jasper

Jasper sigil

"The gods propitious hearken to his prayers,
Whoe'er the polished grass-green jasper wears;
His parched glebe they'll satitate with rain,
And send for showers to soak the thirsty plain."
Lithica, 4th Century CE Greece

The ideal stone for bringing people's heads out of the clouds or earthing after ritual, jasper also has value in healing and has long been used for talismans and amulets.

Colours: Reds, browns, leek-green (Plasma), greens, greyish-blue, black.

Attribution: Arcturus, Spica Virginis 17^0 Libra, Mars, Venus (green), Mercury, Fire, Earth, Virgo, Libra, Scorpio, Leo, Aries.

Chakras: Base, Sacral.

Uses: Helps with bladder, gallbladder, liver and kidney problems, used to strengthen the physical senses. Good for grounding, particularly for people who tend to daydream or live in the clouds, and for after rituals. Can help reduce insecurity and anxiety. May be used to help ease skin complaints.

Used Since: At least 3000 BCE Egypt.

Names: Iaspar, Iaspere, Jasp, Jaspre, Silex. Leek-green Jasper is also known as Plasma, and Mother-of-Emerald. Green Jasper from Vancouver Island is known as Dallasite. When the colour runs in bands it is known as Egyptian Jasper; in stripes it is known as Ribbon Jasper. Black jasper was known as Touchstone, and Lapis Lydius. Jasper with a high percentage of inclusions usually of clay and iron oxide, is known as orbicular jasper.

Jasper Amulets
An amulet of a lion or archer engraved on a jasper was said to give help against poisons and cure from fever; an amulet with a huntsman, stag or dog engraved on jasper was thought to enable the wearer to cure possession and insanity. A jasper arrowhead was said to bring the bearer good luck. A talisman of a man's head facing a bird holding a leaf in its beak cut on jasper was held to bring riches and favour. An amulet of a hare cut onto a jasper was used as a protection from evil spirits and forces.

The symbol for Aquarius ($\approx$) engraved on a green jasper was thought to bring good luck in buying and selling, and was used by traders. Californian Indians sometimes carried pieces of jasper found on the beaches as protective amulets. Black jasper amulets were thought to aid in the capture of cities and fleets in ancient times.

The famous Roman physician Claudius Galenus (Galen) carried a jasper engraved with a man carrying a bundle of herbs, which he believed to aid in his diagnosis of diseases. The same talisman is described by the ancient Jewish Rabbi

250

Chael: "A man with broad shoulders and thick loins, standing and holding in his right hand a bundle of herbs engraved on a green jasper is good against fevers, and if a physician carries it about with him it will give him skill in distinguishing diseases and knowing the proper remedies. It is also good for hemorrhoids and quickly stops the flow of blood." Mottled jasper was worn as an amulet to prevent death by drowning or on/near water.

Jasper as Rain Bringer

Jasper is referred to as the "rain bringer" by some Amerindian tribes, this belief was also prevalent in ancient Greece, as can be seen by the reference in the fourth century poem Lithica:

> The gods propitious hearken to his prayers,
> Whoe'er the polished grass-green jasper wears;
> His parched glebe they'll satitate with rain,
> And send for showers to soak the thirsty plain.

Jasper and Ancient Egypt

Chapter 156 of the Book of the Dead refers specifically to red jasper, as the material the thet buckle amulet was made of. The text reads "Chapter of the buckle of red jasper placed on the neck of the deceased. The blood of Isis, the incantations of Isis, the power of Isis, a charm for the protection of mighty one this, protecting [him from] the doing of what to him is hateful." When two or more thet's were placed on the neck this chapter was often inscribed onto the amulet.

Chapter 34, the Chapter of not allowing a person to be bitten in the underworld by a serpent, was sometimes inscribed on red jasper Serpent's Head amulets placed on the chest or neck. The ab (heart-shaped) amulet laid over the mummy's heart was sometimes made from green jasper, it was considered to possess exceptional powers when used as an amulet. Khenmet, the ancient Egyptian word for jasper, means "delight" and indicates the positive qualities of the colour red like energy, power and life being applied to the stone.

Jasper was used to strengthen the stomach and digestive organs, being considered a powerful astringent. It was often worn in healers rings - a practice which continued in Greece and Rome.

Jasper and Christianity
Jasper symbolised the truth of faith. Reference is made twice in Revelations to jasper: God in comparison to jasper - "And he that sat was to look upon like a jasper" (Rev iv.3), and "And her light was like unto a stone most precious, even like a jasper stone, clear as crystal" (Rev. xxi.11). The Bible also refers to jasper as the walls and the first foundation of New Jerusalem. It was considered symbolic of St Peter and the Apostle Andrew. In medieval times a piece of jasper with the cross engraved on it was thought to protect the wearer from drowning.

St. Hildegard of Bingen in her Subtleties of Diverse Creatures advised women to hold a piece of jasper in the hand during childbirth to guard both mother and child from the evils of demons of the air. Swedenborg said of this stone: "Jasper stone signifies the divine truth of the Word in its literal sense, translucent from the divine truth in its spiritual sense."

Jasper and Healing
An ancient Greek belief was that jasper protected against venomous creatures, a belief which persisted into the Middle Ages. Jasper is said to help ease pregnancy when worn on the body; it was used as a cure for epilepsy and supposed to cure wasting diseases. Jasper was believed to cure blood flux and prevent "offensive imaginations".

Green jasper was widely used in Elizabethan England by the medical profession, being known as "spleen stone". It was worn by physicians to aid in diagnosis, and was thought to drive away evil spirits, cure fevers, dropsy, epilepsy and snakebite. In some instances it was inserted under the skin of epileptics, as it was believed it would stop seizures for three years, and then fall out.

Galen wrote in the 2nd century CE: "That a virtue such as is possessed by the green jasper which benefits the chest and mouth of the stomach if tied upon it, is inherent in precious stones."

Touchstone
Black Jasper was also known as touchstone, lapis lydius (the Lydian Stone) and basanite. When rubbed with a gold alloy or sample, the streak enables calculation of gold purity to 1%.

Other Folklore
Red jasper was a symbol of the God Ganesha in parts of Southern India. Jasper was the twelfth stone on the High Priest's breastplate, representing the tribe of Asher. In Qabalah it is attributed to the Archangels Haniel and Barchiel. In the Middle Ages it was thought to protect against phantasms and witchcraft. In Italy it was thought red jasper could confer the power of invisibility on the bearer, and that black jasper could protect the bearer from lightning.

Mottled jasper was thought to prevent drowning or death on or near water. Green jasper was sometimes used by the Chinese in place of jade as "mouth-jade" (see the entry for Jade). To the Rosicrucians jasper was the centre stone of the vibrations of light. The Palau Islands have jasper as the second of their seven grades of money. Dreaming of jasper was said to indicate love returned.

Jet

"In burning, the perfume thereof chaseth away serpents.
It betrayeth whether a young damsel be a maiden or no.
Wine in which jet hath been boiled cureth the tooth ache.
When tempered with wax it cureth the swellings known as the
King's Evil."
Venerable Bede, 8th Century CE

The best absorber of negative energies, jet has been used to protect from nightmares and whilst travelling; a good stone for improving the psychic abilities - but clean it regularly!

Colours: Black.

Attribution: Saturn, Terra, Earth, Capricorn.

Chakras: Throat, Third Eye.

Uses: Absorbs negative energies like a sponge!
                   Clean regularly or you will pick up the negat-
                   ivity from it. Good to wear as a protective
                   charm, particularly for travelling abroad and
                   to protect from bad dreams and nightmares;
                   also helps protect psychically open people
                   from possession. A truly lovely and magickal
                   stone to work with which can increase the
                   passive psychic faculties like precognition and
                   psychic vision. Can help ease lower back
                   pain. Jet is often worked with to help ease
                   emotional problems and menstrual problems.
                   Much of what is sold as jet is French jet,
                   which is a black glass, so be careful when
                   buying it secondhand.

Used Since: Found in pre-historic burial mounds, one of the first "crystals" used by man.

Names: Black Amber, Witches Amber. Gagates, Gate, Geate, Geet, Geitt, Get, Gete, Gett, Gette, Geyte, Geytt, Giette, Ieate, Ieet, Iet, Iete, Jeat, Jeetstone, Jesstone, Jett, Jette. So-called "French Jet" is a black glass often sold as jet.

Jet Amulets
Jet was thought to overcome spells, illusions and enchantments and hence used to make talismans and charms (jet beetles were very popular in the Middle Ages). In Rome jet was worn by travellers for protection on long journeys. It was also believed jet would protect the bearer from thunderstorms. The Pueblo Indians used jet to make talismans from, sometimes setting turquoise in it.

Bede on Jet
The Venerable Bede (who lived in the 8th century CE) wrote on the properties of jet: "In burning, the perfume thereof chaseth away serpents. It betrayeth whether a young damsel be a maiden or no. Wine in which jet hath been boiled cureth the tooth ache. When tempered with wax it cureth the swellings known as the King's Evil."

Jet and Healing
Roman healers believed jet boiled in wine produced an elixir used to cure toothache, and when added to soft wax was thought to remove scrofulous tumours on contact. Jet was also used as a cure for chills, colds, dropsy, and loss of hair. Powdered jet mixed with the powdered marrow of a stag was used to protect from the bites of serpents.

Other Folklore

Jet was sacred to Pan and to Cybele, whose followers wore it. In Qabalah it is attributed to Binah as the Dark Mother. Jet has a long history of being worn as a mourning stone. In medieval times burning jet was thought to banish serpents. Jet cast on a red hot axe was thought to burn and be consumed, granting a desired wish made at the time.

The Romans thought jet confirmed the state of a woman's virginity, and they also thought that it relieved "suffocation of the uterus". They also believed it drove off snakes. Jet was used in axinomancy, like agate (see entry on Agate for details of this means of divination).

Jet was believed to attract straws, as recorded by Ben Jonson: "Your lustre too'll draw courtship to you as a jet doth straws." Dreaming of jet was said to indicate sorrow.

Jet identified as being mined in Whitby, England, has been found in what was Mesopotamia, showing the way crystals could travel vast distances if they were considered valuable or useful enough.

Kunzite

A lovely stone discovered very recently,
the uses of kunzite are largely in dealing with the rigours
of modern living - a new stone for changing times.

Colours: Pink.

Attribution: Sun, Pluto, Venus, Earth, Fire, Leo.

Chakras: Solar Plexus, Heart.

Uses: Raises self-esteem and tolerance, calms mania
                  and soothes depression. Helps strengthen the
                  cardiovascular system. Can help promote
                  relaxation and better use of energy. May help
                  self-discipline and hence help with overcoming
                  addiction. Can work on the thyroid gland.

Used Since: 1902 when it was identified.

Folklore
Being such a recently discovered crystal, there are no myths
or folklore associated with kunzite.

Kyanite

Kyanite is a good stone for voice work, and for people wishing to work with the element of ice (as in Norse myth) with which it seems to have a strong sympathy.

Colours: Blue, green to grey-green, brown, white (Rhoetizite), black, colourless.

Attribution: Jupiter, Water (Ice), Aquarius.

Chakras: Throat.

Uses: Enhances voice work. Encourages truth, reliability and loyalty, as well as pragmatism. Good for throat disorders.

First Used: I have not found any historical references to this stone.

Names: Cianite, Cyanite, Disthene, Rhoetizite (white form).

Folklore

I have not been able to find any folklore relating to Kyanite, though the Isa Rune as Ice would seem appropriate.

Labradorite

"A man is like a bit of labrador spar, which has no lustre as you turn it in your hand until you come to a particular angle; then it shows deep and beautiful colours."
Ralph Waldo Emerson

A stone of magickal growth, the play of colours in labradorite shows why it may be used as the "rainbow bridge" between conscious and unconscious mind, travelling towards potential.

Colours: Blue and grey, sometimes white, with play of colour.

Attribution: Spirit, Uranus, Jupiter, Sagittarius.

Chakras: Throat, Third Eye, Crown.

Uses: A stone for magickal growth and protection; and both strengthening and healing the subtle body and mind. Good for dream work. The "rainbow bridge" between the conscious and unconscious mind - it is a good stone for working on the higher self and spiritual development. May be used for stellar magicks with good effect.

Used Since: Possibly at least 500 BCE Greece.

Names: White labradorite is known as Rainbow Moonstone, transparent labradorite is known as Black Moonstone. Labradorite is also known as Labrador and Labrador Spar. Labradorite found in Finland with very good sheen is known as Spectrolite.

Folklore

Myths which contain the rainbow motif could be connected with labradorite - e.g. the Norse God Heimdallr and the Bifrost Bridge, the Aboriginal Great Rainbow Serpent, Iris the Greek Rainbow Goddess etc. In Qabalah it is attributed to Daath due to colouring and use with the subtle and spiritual. Labradorite is one of the few crystals which has been found in meteorites.

Ralph Waldo Emerson said of labradorite "A man is like a bit of labrador spar, which has no lustre as you turn it in your hand until you come to a particular angle; then it shows deep and beautiful colours." The beauty of labradorite has been written of since it's "discovery" in 1770, Pinkerton commenting of it: "The beautiful opalised kind of felspar called Labrador stone."

Lapis Lazuli

Lapis Lazuli sigils

His long flowing beard, bright as Lapis Lazuli
Sumerian Hymn to Sin, the Moon God, circa 3000 BCE

The "Stone of Heaven", this Cosmic Goddess stone has been highly prized for millennia, and is particularly good for powerful magicks and voicework.

Colours: Deep blue, often with golden specks of pyrites.

Attribution: The Heavens, Jupiter, Venus, Uranus, Aquarius, Taurus.

Chakras: Heart, Throat, Third Eye.

Uses: For eye, heart and spleen problems, symbolic of the Cosmic Goddess, and a good stone for magickal power, particularly psychic work and voicework, as well as stellar magicks. A good relaxing stone, can help meditation and with insomnia. Helps strengthen bones and works on the thyroid and pituitary glands. Lapis lazuli is a stone of truth and wisdom. The colour Ultramarine was made from powdered lapis lazuli.

Used Since:	At least 4000 BCE Sumeria and Ancient Egypt.
Names:	Lazurite. Zumemo Lazuli, Zemech Lazarilli, Stellatus, Lapis Lazary, Lapis Coelestus, The Azure Gem, The Armenian Stone, Lapis Lazari. The miners of Budukhshan called blue lapis lazuli "Nili", sky-blue coloured "Asmani" and the blue-green tints as "Sabzi". The ancient Greeks referred to "sapphire sprinkled with gold dust", indicating that references to sapphire could be lapis lazuli.

Lapis Lazuli in Ancient Egypt

Lapis lazuli was sacred to Nuit as the night sky. Ra was said to have lapis lazuli hair. Lapis lazuli was also sacred to Mayat, judges wore small lapis lazuli pendants of Her on gold chains. Talismans and amulets were often made from this stone, the 26th chapter of *The Book of the Dead* was often inscribed on lapis lazuli hearts (the ab) bound in with the mummy; also the 140th chapter of the Book of the Dead concerning the utchat eye was only engraved on lapis lazuli.

In the Late Period lapis lazuli was called kheshed a term synonymous with "joy" or "delight". It was believed to be able to cure cataracts (when mixed with milk and Nile slime), and relieve head pains and neuralgia. The Egyptians valued lapis lazuli as highly as gold, and the Pharaoh wore a lapis lazuli eye.

The pigment ultramarine was made from crushed lapis lazuli, and this was used as the world's first eyeshadow - it has been suggested there were magickal aspects to this use as well as cosmetic, providing clear vision (and I consider it possible that it was used to gain magickal night vision with the Nuit association).

262

Lapis Lazuli in Babylonian/Sumerian Myth

The Sumerian Goddess Ishtar's necklace was made of lapis lazuli, which was sacred to Her. The cauldron of Siris was made of lapis lazuli, the Babylonian name for lapis lazuli being ukn°. The flute of Tammuz, able to resurrect the dead, was said to be made of lapis lazuli.

A hymn to Sin, the Moon God, refers to his "long flowing beard, bright as lapis lazuli", demonstrating the association of lapis lazuli with the sacred. A cylinder seal of lapis lazuli was said to give it's owner the power of his God.

Lapis Lazuli in China

In China ornaments of lapis lazuli (Liu-Li) were used when sacrifices were made on the Altar of the Temple of Heaven; records show the priest-kings bore lapis lazuli as an offering to the Gods. Lapis lazuli was one of the eight precious things in Chinese Buddhism. It was worn by third rank Chinese mandarins as a sign of rank.

Lapis Lazuli in Christianity

Epiphanus, Bishop of Constantia in Cyprus wrote in the latter part of the fourth century CE, quoting older sources that the tablets of the Laws of Moses were written on two blocks of lapis lazuli. Lapis lazuli was used to symbolise the purity and chastity of the Virgin Mary.

Lapis Lazuli and Healing

Lapis lazuli was used in the Middle Ages to improve sight, prevent miscarriage and fainting; and cure epilepsy, spleen conditions, melancholy, and forms of dementia. Ultramarine pigment added to a syrup called Alkermes Syrup was given to women experiencing difficult labours in the seventeenth century. Warm lapis lazuli pieces were placed on swellings to help them go down.

In Greece lapis lazuli was known as "Stop Stone" due to its use to prevent miscarriages. An ancient Greek cure for eye problems advised placing a piece of lapis lazuli in a bowl of warm pure water for a few minutes, then for the eye to be bathed with the water. In ancient Egypt placing lapis lazuli on the neck of a sick child was believed to reduce fever.

Other Folklore
In Greece it was sacred to Aphrodite. Lapis lazuli may have been the fifth stone on the High Priest's breastplate, representing the Tribe of Issachar. In Qabalah it is attributed to the 21st path and Chesed due to its Jupiterian associations and colouring being that of Chesed in the Empress Scale.

In ancient times it was thought that lapis lazuli was the stone the City of the Gods is made from. Dreaming of lapis lazuli is supposed to indicate successful affairs of the heart, and fidelity. Lapis lazuli was given to friends as a sign of loyalty.

Lepidolite

Lepidolite may be used to deal with anger, stress and emotional distress.

The "Dream Stone", lepidolite's use in soothing nightmares is typical of its ability to soothe stress and negative emotions.

Colours: Pink to violet.

Attribution: Uranus.

Chakras: Throat, Third Eye, Crown.

Uses: Can help alleviate nightmares. A soothing stone, may be used to deal with anger, stress and emotional distress. Can transform energies from negative into appropriate positive ones, e.g. anger (fiery) is a motivating force (and is usually not a negative force though some people may see it that way), and will not be transformed into love (a watery force) but could be transformed into passion or determination (which are fiery qualities).

First Used: I have not found any historical reference to this stone.

Names: Peace Stone, "the Dream Stone".

Folklore
I have not found any folklore relating to lepidolite.

Magnetite

Magnetite sigils

"The magnet weds the steel, the secret rites
Nature attends and th'heavenly pair unites."
Claudianus of Alexandria

The stone to work with for attracting what you need, magnetite is good for the energies of Mars, a "warrior stone".

Colours: Black.

Attribution: The Pole Star, Tail of the Great Bear 8∞ Scorpio, Mars, Fire, Aries, Virgo.

Chakras: Solar Plexus.

Uses: Problems with the blood and circulatory system. Personal magnetism (it is highly magnetic). Good for courage and strength. May be used in wealth magicks to improve personal circumstances.

Used Since: At least 1100 BCE.

Names: Heraclion or Hercules Stone. Lodestone, from the Old English L·d meaning way or journey, so literally Way-Stone. Magnesium Stone. Siderit.

Hercules and Magnetite

In Greek myth it was said that Hercules, admiring the daring and skill of the Phoenician mariners, wished to help them in their science of navigation. To this end he obtained a cup of heraclion (magnetite) from the Sun God Helios, which always turned to the North.

Pausanius, writing Helbados Periegesis in the second century CE recorded a magnetite image of Hercules at the temple of Hyettos which people came to touch and be healed by.

Magnetite Amulets & Talismans

Magnetite was thought to protect against evil spirits and enchantments, Alexander the Great being said to have given all his troops a piece. An amulet of a man in armour engraved on magnetite was thought to aid in incantations and make the wearer victorious in war. Magnetite was worn in silver to sharpen sight and the senses, and in gold to strengthen the heart.

Marbodius recorded that people believed a talisman of magnetite would enable a thief to burgle any home, however he qualifies this by saying if magnetite was thrown into the hearth fire the fumes would cause all the occupants of a building to leave, thus leaving it empty for the thief to plunder. Bearing an amulet of magnetite was believed to enable the bearer to safely walk through reptiles.

Magnetite and Attraction

The Chinese called magnetite t' su shi meaning "the loving-stone", and in Sanskrit it was known as chumbaka meaning "the kisser", indicating the widespread belief that magnetite attracted iron in the same way as lovers attract. Claudianus of Alexandria said of magnetite:

"The magnet weds the steel, the secret rites
Nature attends and th'heavenly pair unites."

There was a belief about magnetite that it possessed a spirit and this attracted wealth to the bearer. Lucretius recorded the notion that magnetite worked by creating a vacuum: "In the first place, many atoms, or effluvia, must necessarily fly off from the stone, which, by their impact, disperse the air that is situated betwixt the stone and the iron. When this space is emptied, and a large void is made betwixt them, atoms of the iron, immediately darting forward, rush in a body into the vacuum; and the whole [iron] ring of necessity follows, and passes onward with its whole body."

Magnetite and Fidelity
The Greeks believed it could determine the fidelity of a wife when placed under the pillow - if she embraced her husband in her sleep she was faithful, but if she got out of bed she was not - this belief persisted into the Middle Ages.

Magnetite in Healing
St Hildegard of Bingen recorded that magnetite would cure insanity if moistened with the patient's saliva and drawn across the forehead as prayers were spoken. In medieval times magnetite was bound to the feet to "pull out" gout, or carried to remove rheumatism and sciatica. In Italy it was thought to assist in childbirth when worn in a necklace with coral. In the 17th century powdered magnetite was used to treat burns.

Magnetite and Spirits
Magnetite was used in necromancy to attract the spirits of the dead in the ancient world. The Greeks believed that if held close to the eyes magnetite would inspire with a divine spirit, Orpheus recording in the Lithica: "With this stone you can hear the voices of the Gods and learn many wonderful things." In Voodoo magnetite is used as a conjuring stone.

Feeding Magnetite

A Mexican Indian belief was that on Fridays magnetite should be given iron filings to eat, and put in water to drink. The Greeks thought magnetite was antipathetic to diamond and garlic and would not work in their presence. Its powers could be restored by anointing it with linseed oil, wrapping it in goatskin and burying it in the earth for three days. Other methods of restoring its powers were "feeding" it on iron filings, or dipping it in "oil of iron" or goat's blood.

Other Folklore

In Qabalah magnetite is attributed to Geburah due to its highly magnetic nature and high iron content. It has been recorded that Aristotle believed magnetite could set fire to water. In India magnetite was prized as it was believed to preserve the bearer's virility. Dreaming of magnetite was said to warn of subtle dealings and contentions.

Malachite

In Rosicrucian philosophy malachite symbolises
the Spring Equinox and the arising of the spiritual man.

Malachite is a beautiful Goddess stone of protection and healing, which may be well used to overcome barriers and obstacles of all manners.

Colours: Green - light (shallow) and dark (deep).

Attribution: Venus, Terra, Earth, Libra, Sagittarius.

Chakras: Base, Solar Plexus.

Uses: Helps emotional problems (including hysteria) and menstruation difficulties. Can help with insomnia or easing nightmares. Provides protection of the emotions when feeling sensitive or under pressure or threat. A good stone for dealing with emotional blocks, especially from past traumas. Can also help with blocks in visualisation, and enhance psychic vision. Works on circulatory system, pancreas and spleen. May be used to enhance business situations.

Used Since: At least 4000 BCE Egypt.

Names: Satin or Velvet Ore. Some malachite is referred to as Peacock Stone due to the patterns resembling a peacock's tail.

Malachite in Ancient Egypt
The Egyptians used powdered malachite in eye shadow, it has been suggested that this was also used ritually to grant clear

vision and insight. Malachite with the sun engraved on it was thought to be a powerful protection against enchantments, evil spirits and venomous creatures.

Malachite and Healing
Malachite was used to help teething babies. It was thought to stop bleeding if powdered and mixed with honey and applied to the wound. When added powdered to milk and drunk it was thought to cure colic and reduce heart pains; mixed with wine it was said to cure bad ulcers. Malachite was also thought to prevent hernias and avert faintness.

It has been claimed to stop vertigo, rheumatism and asthma, help with ruptures, cure cholera and work on the stomach, kidneys and head. The Greeks and Romans believed it could ward off disease, illness and misfortune, especially from children. Malachite was also believed to be a powerful local anesthetic.

Malachite and Protection
Malachite is known as the "Sleep Stone" due to the tendency to fall asleep if one gazes at it continuously, and the belief that it provided protection from bad dreams (especially for children). In Italy it was used to ward off the evil eye, Peacock Stone (see below) is especially prized for this, and is often set in silver in triangular pieces. Malachite was worn as a stone of protection, and it was believed that it broke in two to warn its owner of impending danger. It was also said to protect the bearer from seduction, accidents, falls and evil magicks.

Other Folklore
In Qabalah it is attributed to Netzach due to its colour and its use in connection with pregnancy and childbirth. In Islam malachite is used in decorating mosques. In Rosicrucian philosophy malachite symbolises the Spring Equinox and the arising of the spiritual man.

Marble

"And the cold marble leapt to life, a god."
Milman

Used to decorate the great buildings of the world, marble reminds us how beautiful stones can be irrespective of size.

Colours: Colourless, white, grey with yellow, blue, red, brown or black tints.

Attribution: Terra, Earth, Gemini.

Chakras: Base.

Uses: General earthing stone, helps maintain emotional stability. Encourages perseverance and dedication.

Used Since: At least 3000 BCE Egypt.

Names: Nicoma. Egyptian Marble is a marble with yellow veins of dolomite and stained black with bitumen. Pure white marble is known as Parian Marble. Portor is a deep black Genoes marble with yellow veinings. Nero Antico is old deep black marble. Rosso Antico is deep blood-red marble with white speckling. Verde Antico is a misty green colour. Giallo Antico is deep yellow with black or yellow rings. Carrara Marble, often used in statues, is fine-grained pure white with grey veins. Marbre, Marbyr, Marbal, Marboll, Marbell, Marbelle, Marbill, Marbull, Marbyll, Merbyl.

Folklore

Marble was used in India to protect against witchcraft. Marbles has long been used in statues and buildings, as illustrated by Milman - "And the cold marble leapt to life, a god." Marble symbolises immortality through its durability, this may give rise to the custom found in many countries of placing a piece of marble in the grave with the corpse. The purity and durability of marble has also made it an ideal stone to use in the headstone to mark and honour the graves of family.

Moldavite

Moldavite is good for works involving travelling
between planes and states, such as astral travel and psychic
work, as well as meditation and pathworking.

A beautiful glass green of possible non-terrestrial origin, moldavite works well on the higher self, and any work involving changing consciousness.

Colours: Green.

Attribution: Pluto, Uranus

Chakras: Throat, Crown.

Uses: Integration and work with the higher self.
                  Good for works involving travelling between
                  planes and states, such as astral travel and
                  psychic work, as well as meditation and path-
                  working. Can be powerful protective stones.
                  Formed 15 million years ago, geologists are
                  still uncertain whether they came to the
                  earth via meteorite or were formed by volcanic
                  activity, but however they were formed, they
                  are good for stellar magicks. A good stone for
                  people dealing with unexplained encounters
                  such as UFO experiences.

Used Since: 1787 CE when it was identified.

Names: Vltavine, Bottle Stone, Water Chrysolite.

Folklore
Due to its recent discovery, there is no folklore for moldavite, though it could be attributed to Stellar and Sky Deities.

274

Moonstone

*A Christian spell to ask for God's guidance for the future
involved holding a moonstone in the mouth when out
alone under a waning moon, sending a prayer to Gabriel.*

A beautiful Goddess stone, moonstone may exert subtle
influence in a similar way to the moon itself, so be sure to
keep one handy.

Colours: Yellow or colourless with opalescence.

Attribution: Moon, Water, Cancer.

Chakras: Sacral, Third Eye.

Uses: Another powerful Goddess stone, and one that
is unmatched for moon magick. Good for
psychic problems, and for developing the
psychic senses, may be used to aid astral
projection. Good for dreamwork and divination. Can help with fertility and balance,
including womb problems; moonstones should
be worn during pregnancy and childbirth to
add their energy and ease the pain levels.
Good for fluid problems such as water
retention. May help treat epilepsy. A good
lovers stone for resolving emotional conflicts,
and may also be used to engender harmony in
an environment. A good stone to wear for
gardening as it can help enhance the lunar
influences which benefit the plants.

Used Since: At least 2000 BCE.

Names: Known as the Travellers Stone. Known to Pliny as Astrion, Astriotes and Ceraunia (Thunder Stone). Was known as Selenites in the Middle Ages. The Indians call moonstone Candra Kanta. Particularly fine specimens are known as Adularia. Also called Ceylon Opal due to their abundance. Blue stones are known as Blue Moonstones. Other names include Mione, Mon, Mone, Moona, Moone, Mowne, Moyne, Mune and Muni.

Moonstone Amulets & Talismans

Christians believed that an amulet of the names of God engraved on a moonstone was thought to protect the place it was kept in from tempests, and give the wearer victory over his/her enemies. Moonstone was thought to protect people travelling by night, and became known as Travellers Stone. Moonstones were hung in fruit trees to ensure good harvests.

Moonstone and the Lunar Cycle

The colour of a moonstone was thought to increase and decrease with the cycles of the moon. Moonstone was used in the Middle Ages for consumption (on a waxing moon), for divination (on a waning moon), and to reconcile lovers (on a full moon). An Indian belief was that Candra Kanta (moonstone) grew under the rays of the moon and absorbed its mystical qualities.

Moonstone in the Mouth

There was a tradition in the Middle Ages that placing a moonstone in your mouth after having rinsed it out with water, if you then thought about your affairs, the important ones would be fixed in your mind and the ones not to be undertaken slipped out of your mind; this is similar to the Indian belief that placing a moonstone in the mouth during a full moon would enable lovers to divine what the future held for them.

A Christian spell to ask for God's guidance for the future involved holding a moonstone in the mouth when out alone under a waning moon, sending a prayer to Gabriel (the lunar Archangel).

Other Folklore

Moonstone is sacred to Lunar Deities such as Selene, Hekate and Artemis/Diana. In Qabalah it is attributed to Yesod and the 13th path by its nature. In ancient Egypt it was sacred to Anup. In India moonstone is a sacred stone. Moonstone was believed to aid in treating lunacy. Moonstone was also thought to keep head and heart in contact with each other.

The Romans believed moonstone could reunite loved ones who had parted in anger, and to endow love, wealth, victory and wisdom. There is a curious Ceylonese belief that every thirty-seven years waves influenced by the moon hurl opalescent blue moonstones on the shores. Dreaming of moonstones was said to indicate travel and health if the stone is bright, but impending danger if the stone is dark. Moonstones are given for 13th (note the lunar 13) wedding anniversary.

Obsidian

In the nine levels of the Aztec underworld,
the Codex Vaticanus lists the fourth level as "the obsidian hill",
the fifth level as "the place of obsidian-knife winds"
and the eighth level as the "obsidian place of the dead".

Obsidian is a stone of balance - it is a "warrior stone" yet is good for healing; it is good for active energy directing and also for passive skrying.

Colours: Black, red and brown, sometimes grey, may have speckles (snowflake obsidian), or bands of colour with sheen (rainbow obsidian).

Attribution: Spirit, Saturn, Terra, Capricorn, Aquarius.

Chakras: Sacral, Heart, Throat, Third Eye.

Uses: Perhaps the most efficient director of energy. Good for skrying and developing psychic powers. Good for high level magicks, and for developing the warrior aspect, especially for unassertive people. Works on stomach, liver and intestines particularly - the "gut" feeling. Obsidian tends to be very sharp so be careful not to cut yourself if using blades, arrow-heads, etc. An egg made of obsidian makes a very good protection, and a good focus for meditation and growth, symbolising as it does the (tattvic) black egg of spirit. May be used to help protect from pollution.

Used Since: At least 3000 BCE Egypt and South America, probably considerably earlier.

278

| **Names:** | Apache Tears, Mountain Jet, Nevada Black Diamond or Topaz. Snowflake Obsidian (speckled), Rainbow Obsidian (bands of colour or golden sheen); brown or grey is known as Iceland Agate. Porous grey obsidian is also known as Perlite. |

Obsidian in South American Myth

The Aztecs called obsidian the source of life, bringer of life and death; the sacrificial knife was made of obsidian. To the Mayans obsidian was sacred to Tezcatlipoca (meaning "mirror that smokes"), God of Magicians, and often used to make magick mirrors. To the Aztecs it was sacred to Itzpapalotl, Goddess of Souls, whose name means "the obsidian butterfly"; and to Itzcoliuhqui, God of Darkness, whose name means "twisted obsidian one".

In the nine levels of the Aztec underworld, the Codex Vaticanus lists the fourth level as "the obsidian hill", the fifth level as "the place of obsidian-knife winds" and the eighth level as the "obsidian place of the dead". The second of the nine Aztec Lords of Night was called Itzti or Tecpatl meaning "obsidian" or "flint". The Aztecs used obsidian powder to heal wounds.

Obsidian in Amerindian Folklore

Bear shamans in south-Central California wore bear hides with sharp pieces of obsidian attached to the sleeves as claws to slash people with during ceremonies. The Wailuki and Yuki tribes of North-Central California held an obsidian ceremony, a strenuous initiation for boys and girls which included being stabbed with obsidian knives.

It has been suggested that the Metal Old Man of the White Mountain Apache was actually obsidian encased. The name Apache Tears comes from the belief that the earth cried each time an apache warrior was killed.

Other Folklore
In Hawaii obsidian is sacred to Pele, the Volcano Goddess. In Qabalah it is attributed to Binah as the Dark Mother. The Greeks believed an obsidian amulet would keep sailors safe on seas and rivers.

Onyx

Onyx sigil

There is a myth that Cupid was paring Venus' nails one day and threw the parings into the Indus River, where they became onyx.

A very good earthing and healing stone, onyx is very common and affordable, and is a good all-purpose stone to work with.

Colours: Green, blue, white, black, red, brown, yellow, orange.

Attribution: Gienah - Left Wing of Raven 8^0 Libra (Onyx), Antares (Sardonyx), Saturn, Terra, Mars, Earth, Capricorn, Aries & Leo (Sardonyx).

Chakras: Base.

Uses: General healing and stress relief, also circulatory problems, hearing difficulties and for strengthening bone marrow and nails. May be used for heart and kidney problems. Used as a protection and grounding stone, also good for balancing polarities. Can help overcome apathy.

Used Since: At least 3000 BCE Egypt.

Names:	Red onyx is known as Sard or Sardonyx. Onyx with a white circle in is known as Lynx Eye Onyx. White or grey banded onyx is also known as Chalcedonyx. Onyx with a thin blue-white layer over a thick black layer is known as Nicolo or Niccolo.

Onyx Amulets

The Indians and Persians believed onyx could protect against the evil eye. An amulet of a camel's head or two goats among myrtles engraved on onyx was thought to enable the wearer to conjure, assemble and constrain demons, however it was cautioned that wearing the amulet at night would produce nightmarish visions. The Persians believed a sardonyx with a quail carved on the top and a sea tench carved on the bottom would make its bearer invisible.

Onyx and Sleep

Onyx was not worn during sleep as it was thought to produce bad dreams, though curiously dreaming of onyx was said to indicate a happy marriage. Onyx is known in Arabic as el jaza meaning "sadness", perhaps due to the bad reputation it had amongst Arabs for giving bad dreams, draining energy, bringing misfortune and other woes.

Dreaming of sardonyx was said to indicate love of friends. It was believed that sardonyx would neutralise any bad dreams brought by onyx, and dispel melancholy.

Onyx in Christianity

Sardonyx was thought to be symbolic of candour and sincerity. It also symbolised the Apostles James and Philip. Sardonyx symbolised the humility of the saints in spite of their virtues. In the Bible sardonyx is the fifth foundation of New Jerusalem.

Onyx in Judaism

There were two Onyx pillars on either side of the Ephod in the Tabernacle, each with the names of six of the tribes on. Onyx was the eleventh stone on the High Priest's breastplate, representing the tribe of Gad. Sardonyx may have been the first stone on the High Priest's Breastplate, representing the Tribe of Reuben.

Onyx in Qabalah

In Qabalah the black onyx is attributed to The Pillar of Severity (Feminine) and to Malkuth as being a very earthy stone; also it is attributed to Saturn as the 32nd path due to its dull colour. Onyx was attributed to the Archangel Camael, sardonyx to the Archangel Gabriel.

Onyx in Roman Myth

There is a myth that Cupid was paring Venus' nails one day and threw the parings into the Indus River, where they became onyx. Onyx and sardonyx were both sacred to the God Mars.

Other Folklore

The Egyptians and Indians believed that onyx worn around the neck cooled the ardors of love, and if worn for too long could even cause lovers to split. Prester John's palace was described as having a courtyard paved with onyx set aside for judicial ordeal combats, the onyx being there to boost the courage of combatants.

In 10th Century C.E. the Abbey of St. Albans possessed an onyx so large it could not be held in the hand, which had a reputation for aiding in childbirth. Another medieval belief about onyx was that it could heal animal bites when applied to them.

St Hildegard on Onyx & Healing

St Hildegard had much to say about the virtues of onyx. For "one whose eyes are foggy" she recommended pouring good, pure wine into a bronze, copper or steel vessel.

An onyx was placed in the vessel and left to soak for fifteen or thirty days. The stone was then removed and the wine touched to the eyes each night to ensure they became clear and healthy. For an ailment of the heart and skin she advises warming an onyx in the hands or against the skin, taking wine from a metallic vessel in the fire and hold the stone over the steaming wine. The onyx is then placed in the wine which is drunk right away. The pains of heart and side would then disappear. (It is interesting to note how many of St Hildegard's cures involved putting stones in good wine and drinking it!).

For stomach pain, wine prepared as above (!), added to a broth with flour and hen's eggs and eaten often. For spleen problems cooked goat meat or young sheep was recommended, dipping it in the wine as described above. For one oppressed with sadness, she recommended looking intently at an onyx, and then placing it in the mouth. For strong fevers, an onyx was placed in vinegar for five days, and then removed. The vinegar would be used to season all foods eaten thereafter until the fever has gone.

For pestilence infested cattle, heat water in a vessel over the fire. Take it from the fire and hold an onyx over it so the steam mixes with the sweat of the onyx. Place the onyx in the water for three days. Remove the onyx and give the water to the cattle frequently to drink, sprinkle it in their food. Do this often and they will better.

Sardonyx in Myth & Folklore

The gates of Prester John's palace were said to be made of sardonyx mixed with the horn or horned serpents to prevent poison being brought in. In the Middle Ages sardonyx was considered lucky for women to wear, particularly if it had a design of a grape vine and ivy entwined on it (reminiscent of Dionysus and his maenads).

Sardonyx was thought to protect against sorcery and charms, and make the bearer fearless and victorious, bringing happiness and sharpening the wits. Sardonyx was worn in the Middle Ages to banish woe and grief, and to bring confidence.

St Hildegard spoke of the purity of this stone and said of it: "When a person places it (sardonyx) against his bare skin, and even frequently puts it in his mouth, so that his breath touches it as he breathes in and out, he strengthens his understanding, his knowledge, and all the senses of his body. Great wrath, stupidity, and illiterateness are removed from that person. The devil hates this purity and flees.

If a man or woman has a nature strongly burning for the works of the flesh, then he should place sardonyx on his loins and she should place it on her umbilicus, and they will have relief from that lust. After someone has sweated from an acute disease and considers himself better, he should soon place sardonyx on his finger, on a ring. He will not again fall into this sickness."

Opal

Opal sigil

"Opal unites in itself all the colours, white, red, yellow, sky-blue and green." Arabic alchemy

A stone as versatile as its colours suggest, opal has an undeserved reputation for bad luck, and is one of the most beautiful and useful stones known.

Colours: White (cacholong), semi-transparent orange to red (fire), transparent blue-white with red colour (girasol), colourless (hyalite), grey or brown (boulder, menilite or liver), yellowish or colourless with a play of colour (Mexican Water or Iris), yellowish or bluish-white or white (milk), green (prase), yellow (resin). The other forms are amber (brown colour), harlequin (regular size patches of colour), hydrophane (dehydrated, becomes opalescent in water), lechosos (shows green colour), moss (dendritic inclusions), matrix (showing some ironstone matrix), precious (showing good colour), white (pale earth), black (very dark earth).

Attribution: Mercury, Neptune, Sun, Air, Gemini, Libra; Moon (Milk Opal), Fire (Fire Opal), Water (Water Opal).

Chakras: Heart, Throat, Third Eye.

Uses:	A stone of love. As with diamond, opal can magnify energies strongly, and should be used when in a positive state of mind. Can be used to help eye and lung problems, promotes communication and mental growth. Good for astral and dream work. Working with opal can help improve strength of will and intuitive powers. Can enhance vitality, it should not be used by people who tend to be hyper. Acts on thymus, pineal and pituitary glands. A good stone to work with to get things you desire, and also for bringing out the inner beauty. Can also help break a run of bad luck or improve luck generally. Can be helpful if doing past life work. Placing an opal on the third eye may help with oracular and prophetic work. May help with work on sexual dysfunction. Opals require careful looking after - see the entry on Opal in the Caring for Crystals section.
Used Since:	At least 3000 BCE.
Names:	Opalite. Cupid Stone. Patronus Furum (see above). Queen of Gems. Stone of the Gods. Fire Opal is also known as Gold Opal. Opal banded with cinnabar-red bands is known as Opalite.

Opal and Luck

Opals were thought in ancient times to bring good luck. In medieval times ladies gave their knights opals for good fortune before they set off on the crusades. Black opals were considered exceptionally lucky. The idea that opals bring bad luck is a modern one which has come about since the implication was written in one of Sir Walter Scott's novels "Anne of Geierstein" (1828) where the heroine's demonic grandmother died when a drop of holy water touched her enchanted opal, putting out its fire.

Opal and Healing
In ancient Egypt and Babylon opals were considered a powerful healing gem, combining the powers of fire and water. Opal was used in mediaeval times to dispel melancholy (worn as a necklace) and to protect from disease. A loss of colour in the opal was thought to indicate the presence of poison. Opals were placed in the navel of an expectant mother to ease childbirth in the Middle Ages. Amulets of opal were thought to strengthen the mind and help correct bad vision.

Opal in Arab Folklore
There was an Arab belief that opal fell from heaven in lightning flashes. Opal was described in Arabic alchemy as "uniting in itself all the colours, white, red, yellow, sky-blue and green." It was believed to shine brighter prior to the death of the bearer (in the case of fever there could be a basis for this as the stone is affected by heat which would dry the stone out).

Opal in Australian Myth
There is a legend that a huge opal governs the stars, this stone is also supposed to guide human love and control the gold in the ground. An aboriginal myth is far more negative about opal, the myth stated that opal is a devil - half human and half serpent, who lurks in holes in the ground always ready to lure men to their doom with flashes of wicked magick.

Opal in Qabalah
Opal is attributed to Hod and the 12th path due to its flashes of colour like the quicksilver nature of Mercury; fire opal is attributed to the 31st path due to its fiery association.

Other Folklore

To the Greeks opal was sacred to Cupid. It has been suggested that the sacred stone called the yarkstein which Vol^ndr formed from the eyes of children, referred to in the Norse Eddas, was opal. The Romans believed opals brought love and confidence, they were so highly prized that Mark Anthony banished a senator who refused to sell him a particularly fine opal.

The Greeks used opal for prophecy and divination. Opal was once believed to shine at night, as was claimed for the opal thought to be the Orphanus stone set in the imperial crown of the Holy Roman Empire (see the earlier section Mythical Minerals). Opal was thought to be able to render the bearer invisible and was known as Patronus Furum (the Patron of Thieves).

A curious mediaeval belief was that wearing an opal necklace would keep the colour in blonde hair. Opal was known as the "Queen of Gems" and as the "Stone of the Gods". Dreaming of opals was said to indicate great possessions.

Pearl

Pearl sigils

"The kingdom of heaven is like unto a merchant man,
seeking goodly pearls, who, when he had found one pearl of
great price, went and sold all that he had, and bought it."
Matthew 13:45

The beauty of pearls has long been associated with aspects of
the Goddess, they are good for healing and tend to reflect the
wearers emotions, so wear them when you are happy!

Colours: White, tinged with cream, pink, yellow, green,
blue, brown or black; pink, black, bronze,
gunmetal.

Attribution: Umbilicus Andromedæ 20⁰ Aries, Spirit,
Moon, Venus, Mercury, Water, Pisces, Cancer,
Gemini.

Chakras: Sacral, Solar Plexus, Heart.

Uses: Helps with patience and resolution of out-
dated ideas and beliefs which need restruct-
uring. Can help in treatment of problems
with the stomach and spleen, and with ulcers.
Pearls tend to reflect emotional state, and
should not be worn when feeling bad. Good
for self-acceptance and improving self-esteem.
Help with bone and hair disorders. May be

dissolved in red wine and drunk. Pearls need careful looking after - see the entry in the notes on Caring for Crystals regarding Pearl.

Used Since: At least 3000 BCE Egypt.

Names: Margan (Persian).

The Yezidi White Pearl Creation Myth

The Mashaf Res (Black Book) of the Yezidi gives a very interesting creation myth from a white pearl. The Book reads: "In the beginning God created the White Pearl out of his most precious essence. He also created a bird named Angar. He placed the White Pearl on the back of the bird, and dwelt on it for forty thousand years ..... created man and the animals and the birds and beasts.

He put them all in pockets of cloth, and came out of the Pearl accompanied by the Angels. Then he shouted at the Pearl with a loud voice. Thereupon the White Pearl broke up into four pieces, and from its midst came out the water which became an ocean. The world was round and not divided. Then he created Gabriel and the image of the bird. He sent Gabriel to set the four corners. He also made a vessel and descended in it for thirty thousand years. After this he came and dwelt in Mount Lalis.

Then he cried out at the world, and the sea became solidified and the land appeared, but it began to shake. At this time he commanded Gabriel to bring two pieces of the White Pearl; one he placed beneath the earth, the other stayed at the gate of heaven. He then placed in them the sun and the moon; and from the scattered pieces of the White Pearl he created the stars which he hung in heaven as ornaments."

Other Pearl Creation and Breeding Myths

An Indian myth recounts that pearls were dewdrops which fell from heaven and were caught by shellfish under the first rays of the rising sun during the period of full moon. Hebrew legend says pearls were the tears shed by Eve on being banish-ed from Eden.

The Romans believed that pearls were formed by drops of dew falling into open oyster shells during the mating season, this belief was shared by the Arabs, who believed this happened on 16th Nisan (April).

In Borneo every ninth pearl collected by the pearl fishers would be saved and put in a bottle with two grains of rice per pearl; the bottle was sealed with a dead man's finger and hung with great and solemn ceremony from a tree - this was known as the "Breeding of the Pearls", and it was believed this magick ritual would ensure the pearls bred well for the next harvest.

Pearl Divination

An old technique of divination with a pearl was used to determine the guilt of a person accused of a crime. This technique, known as margaritomancy, involved placing a pearl under a vase near a fire. The names of the suspected individuals would be spoken in turn, and when the guilty name was uttered the pearl was supposed to bound upwards and pierce the bottom of the vase.

Pearl in Chinese Myth

Ti-Tsang-Pu-Sa, the Chinese God of Mercy, wanders hell with a giant pearl which shines, its light redeeming any souls it touches. Pearls were thought to come with rain from the spittle of fighting dragons, and hence were considered to be a charm against fire.

Chinese dragons have a fascination for pearls, the bigger the better. Pearls were valued by oriental dragons in the same way as occidental dragons were believed to prize gold. Dissolved pearls were often used in love charms. Another belief was that pearls were formed from teardrops, and that possessing them would bring tears to their possessor.

The Pearl Dealer. From the "Hortus Sanitatis" of Johannis de Cuba

Pearl in Christianity

The pearl was considered the most precious jewel. It is referred to twice in Matthew - "The kingdom of heaven is like unto a merchant man, seeking goodly pearls, who, when he had found one pearl of great price, went and sold all that he had, and bought it." (Matthew 13:45), and the famous "Give not that which is holy unto the dogs, neither cast ye your pearls before swine, lest they trample them under their feet..." (Matthew 7:6). The gates of New Jerusalem are described as being made of pearl.

Pearl in Indian Myth

In Indian myth pearl is known as the Mother Gem of the Sea, and is sacred to Lakshmi, Goddess of Wealth. Indians also saw pearl as symbolic of the Moon and of lovers, and used them powdered in love potions. A curious Indian belief is that pearls were thought to be found occasionally in an elephant's brain, stomach or forehead, and to be a powerful charm against danger.

Pearls were also described as being "borne of the light of lightning from out of the ocean." Pearl shell amulets were worn for longevity, overcoming demons, disease and misery.

Pearl in Qabalah
In Qabalah pearl is attributed to Binah as coming from the great sea, which is a title of Binah, also as being formed from a grain of dust surrounded by accreted layers - the accretions being stripped away to the grain of dust on crossing the abyss to Binah. Pearl is also attributed to the Moon as the 13th path due to its position crossing the abyss and Pisces as the 29th path with its lustre and colour being reminiscent of the astral planes.

Pearl and Healing
The Romans used pearl dissolved in lemon juice to treat epilepsy, and in vinegar for casting out demons. Powdered pearls in water were used to fortify the heart and for consumption. In the Middle Ages pearls were though to cure jaundice and vomiting blood, and relieve haemorrhoids and excessive menstruation; they were also thought to get rid of evil spirits from the minds of men.

Pearls were rubbed over the body to try and cure leprosy, the pearls then being burned with coral. A European belief was that a pearl would dull with sickness of the ownder, death sometimes completely destroying their lustre. Pearl dissolved in lemon juice was known as "Salt of Pearl" and used to treat epilepsy and hysteria. Pearl boiled in meat was thought to heal the quartan ague.

Powdered in milk, pearl was used to treat ulcers and clear the voice. When powdered in water, pearl was used as an antidote for poision as late as the 16th century. 13th century physicians prescribed pearls for heart problems because it was described as being "hard like the heart". In 17th century Denmark milk of pearl was used as a general tonic.

Pearl Types and Values

There are four types of pearl, which are listed in order of value - spherical, pear-shaped, button-shaped and irregular (baroque). Pearls which are found attached to the inside of the oyster shell are known as blister pearls. Pearls are weighed by the grain, one grain being half a gram.

Other Folklore

Pearls traditionally depict chastity and femininity. In ancient Egypt they were sacred to Isis. The Love Goddesses Aphrodite and Venus were both known as "Lady of the Pearls". Pearls were also sacred to the Lunar Goddesses Artemis and Diana. To the Aborigines pearl is sacred to the Great Rainbow Serpent. In Norse myth it is sacred to Freya.

In Islam the third heaven is made of large white pearls. Pearls also symbolise enlightenment and wisdom. Dreaming of pearls was said to indicate faithful friends. Pearls are given for 30th wedding anniversary. Pearl is one of the eight sacred things in Chinese Buddhism. The huge castle inhabited by Emma-O, Japanese Ruler of the Dead, was said to be covered in silver and gold, encrusted with rosy pearls and other jewels.

Aristotle believed the noblest pearls were found in south flowing rivers (!). A piece of pearl shell was carried to ensure a safe journey by Romans. An old wealth spell involved throwing a pearl into a stream, possibly on the principle of giving up something valuable to attract more wealth into one's life (it is also interesting to note that oriental dragons loved pearls and often dwelt in water).

Peridot

An amulet of a vulture engraved on peridot was thought to constrain demons and the winds, demons cannot gather near the wearer and must obey him / her.

A stone which has been used a great deal in making talismans, peridot is a good stone for turning a situation around and taking a new approach.

Colours: Oil green to yellowish green, brown.

Attribution: Vega, Tortoise 8⁰ Capricorn, Venus, Terra, Sun, Mercury, Virgo, Libra, Leo.

Chakras: Sacral, Solar Plexus, Heart.

Uses: Good for the digestive system, a good tonic. Can be used to work with emotional over-sensitivity and to balance negative emotions. Works on the adrenal glands. Helps with powers of analysis. Can help get a new start or fresh angle on a problem. May be used about the person and in the house as a protection from theft and burglary. Peridot is one of the gems sometimes found in meteorites.

Used Since: At least 1580 BCE in Egypt.

Names: Peridot is a form of olivine. Peridot was sometimes mistakenly referred to as emerald in ancient times. The stone probably known as (green) chrysolite in ancient times. Sometimes known as Evening Emerald.

Peridot Amulets

In alchemy peridot was believed to protect against negativity when holed and worn as beads in a collar or necklace. Set in gold, peridot was thought to protect against nightmares. If strung on ass hair and tied to the left arm it was thought to protect from evil spirits.

An amulet of an ass engraved on peridot was thought to give the power to predict the future; an amulet of a vulture engraved on peridot was thought to constrain demons and the winds, demons cannot gather near the wearer and must obey him/her. An amulet of a torchbearer carved onto a peridot was thought to bring wealth to its owner.

Other Folklore

Peridot is sacred to Pele, the Hawaiian Volcano Goddess. In Qabalah it is attributed to Virgo as the 20th path due to being its colour in the King Scale and traditional attribution. Peridot may have been the second stone on the High Priest's breastplate, representing the tribe of Simeon.

To the early Christians it was representative of the Apostle Bartholomew, and symbolised true spiritual preaching accompanied by miracles. The Egyptians believed peridots glowed in the dark; some Egyptian priests wore peridots to keep their minds free of jealousy or envy. In medieval times peridot was thought to help with muscle problems and with liver diseases. Dreaming of peridot was said to indicate a need for necessary caution.

Prase

In ancient times Prase wasa known as "Mother of Emerald",
due to the belief that emerald grew from it.

Considering the meaning of its name, it seems highly appropriate that prase should be good for working with water and fluid problems.

Colours: Green.

Attribution: Water.

Chakras: Sacral.

Uses: Good for work with water, including the sea and rivers/lakes. Used for problems with water retention and urine problems.

Used Since: At least 0 CE Greece and Rome.

Names: Mother of Emerald from the belief that emerald grew from prase.

Folklore
In ancient Rome and Greece an amulet of a bull engraved on prase was said to give aid against evil spells and guard the wearer from enchantments and vices. There was a belief that emerald grew from prase, giving rise to the name "Mother of Emerald".

Pyrite

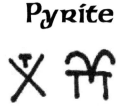

Pyrite sigils

*In Medieval times pieces of pyrite were known as
"Thunderbolts", and thought to protect from lightning.*

If we think of the Fool from the Tarot, then we have a better perspective from which to consider "Fool's Gold", it brings its own rewards.

Colours: Yellow, golden, silver (Marcasite).

Attribution: Sun, Jupiter, Venus, Moon, Saturn, Fire.

Chakras: Solar Plexus.

Uses: Used for blood disorders. A good grounding stone. Pyrite can be used to help treat problems with the digestive system. May help with self-esteem and honest self-evaluation. Can be used to attract prosperity and success.

Used Since: At least 30,000 BCE.

Names: Fire Stone, Fools Gold, Inca Stone, Marcasite (silver variety).

Pyrite Amulets
Amerindian tribes have used pieces of pyrites as amulets and power objects. In Burma pyrites was used as an amulet to protect against crocodiles. In Medieval times pieces of pyrite were known as "Thunderbolts", and thought to protect from lightning.

Other Folklore
Pyrite was a symbol of the Goddess Parvati in parts of Southern India. The Romans believed pyrites could be used for stopping "blood decay". The Incas used polished blocks of pyrite as mirrors. In Italy pyrites was believed to preserve the sight and prevent its deterioration.

Quartz

Quartz sigils

Crystal is ice through countless ages grown
(So teach the wise) to hard transparent stone:
And still the gem retains its native force,
And holds the cold and colour of its source.
Yet some deny, and tell of crystal found
Where never icy winter froze the ground.
Marbodius, 11th Century CE

Quartz is the most widely used and versatile of stones, and has probably been used for longer than any other stone.

Colours: Colourless - may have cracks showing prismatic colours (Rainbow or Iris Quartz), white (Milky Quartz), blue-green (Sapphire Quartz or Siderite), various colours see the entries for Amethyst, Ametrine, Citrine, Prase, Rose Quartz, Smoky Quartz), may have inclusions of rutile (see entry for Rutile Quartz) and tourmaline (tourmalinated quartz).

Attribution: The Pleaides (esp. 24⁰ Taurus), Moon, Uranus, Jupiter, Neptune, Air, Aquarius, Leo, Gemini, Capricorn, Aries.

Chakras: Base, Heart, Throat, Third Eye, Crown. Works on all the chakras.

Uses:	Excellent healing stone, focuses energy for directing well. Good for dreamwork. Amplifies other energies, though not to the same extent as diamond. A good stone for skrying and divination. Works well with earth energies. A good all round stone which may be used for any purpose - the "universal" stone. Tourmalinated quartz combines the properties of tourmaline and quartz (see the entry for Tourmaline). Quartz is pizoelectric. Good quality double terminated faceted quartz crystals are known as Herkimer diamonds, and may be used in place of diamonds for a more affordable alternative, having similar properties but in a slightly lesser degree.
Used Since:	Rock crystal objects have been found from at least 75,000 BCE.
Names:	Colourless quartz with cracks showing prismatic colours is known as Rainbow Quartz or Iris Quartz. Star Stone. Flawless quartz crystals with no inclusions or cracks were known to the Greeks as acenteta meaning "without a core". Herkimer Diamond is a particularly fine clear form of quartz. Other names for Rock Crystal include Arkansas Diamond, Bohemian Diamond, Bristol Diamond, Cornish Diamond, Hot Springs Diamond, Indian Diamond, Isle of Wight Diamond, Lake George Diamond, Mari Diamond, Mexican Diamond, Vallum Diamond.

Quartz Amulets and Power Objects

The Greeks believed an quartz amulet would protect sailors at sea. In the Middle Ages a necklace of beads was thought to ensure lactation in mothers, and an amulet with a griffin engraved on was thought to ensure an abundance of milk. An amulet of a man in armour with bow and arrow engraved on iris (rainbow) quartz was thought to protect the wearer and place from evil.

Amongst Amerindian tribes quartz was considered a powerful divinatory and hunting talisman, the lump of quartz would be rubbed in the blood of the prey and treated as a live creature joining in the consuming of the prey. The Paipai Indians of Northern California called quartz wii ipay - "living rock", and considered it a very potent power object.

The Warao shamans of South America placed pieces of quartz in their medicine rattles, as they believed it helped remove harmful unwanted intrusions from the patient's body; at death the shaman's soul is said to merge with the crystals in the rattle and ascend to the sky in the form of light. In Tantra quartz beads are used for "stopping all action".

Amongst the Aborigines quartz pebbles known as "ultunda stones" are embedded in the body provide magickal power. Stones are also "sung" into the foreheads of shamans so they can "be able to see right into things" (!). Aboriginal shamans also put pieces of quartz in water for apprentices to enable them to see ghosts.

Skulls carved from quartz like the famous "skull of doom" have produced all sorts of curious notions, they are nonetheless amazing and highly impressive objects.

Quartz Creation Myths

The Japanese said small quartz crystals were the congealed breath of the White Dragon, and larger ones the saliva of the

Violet Dragon. Some Aboriginal tribes believed quartz was solidifed light, others believed quartz to be falling stars. Quartz was believed by the ancient Greeks and Chinese to be a permanent form of solidified ice.

Marbodius wrote of it:

> Crystal is ice through countless ages grown
> (So teach the wise) to hard transparent stone:
> And still the gem retains its native force,
> And holds the cold and colour of its source.
> Yet some deny, and tell of crystal found
> Where never icy winter froze the ground.

Quartz and Healing
Pliny wrote that quartz was used in lens and sphere form to cauterise wounds using the suns rays. In the Middle Ages quartz was used on cattle as a charm against disease. A suspension of powdered quartz in wine was used as a treatment for dysentery.

Quartz was also used to reduce fevers and thirst, possibly due to the ice connection of the name. Medicine men of the South American Andoke tribe used quartz disks in healing.

Quartz and Rain-Making
In various parts of the world quartz had a reputation for producing rain. In New Guinea shamans brought the rain by placing heavy stones and pieces of quartz in canoes and shaking them vigorously. The loud thunder-like noises made were thought to attract the rain, as rain happens after thunder.

In Northern Queensland rock crystal was mined and pulverised, and then showered over the women to simulate rainfall. The women held troughs over their heads to protect them from the "rain".

In New South Wales the rainmaker would hold a piece of quartz in his mouth and spit it at the sky to summon rain.

Quartz in Aboriginal Folklore
Amongst the Aborigines pieces of quartz are used to guide and control the Great Rainbow Serpent. Quartz is sacred to Daramulun, the Sky God, being what his throne is made of, or alternatively part of his body is sometimes said to be quartz.

Quartz is said to be found where a rainbow ends in a pool of water. It was believed that pieces of quartz were imbedded in the shaman (in his brain and other organs) during his initiation, so he could call on their powers subsequently. Aboriginal shamans have their quartz power objects buried with them. See also the section above Quartz Amulets & Power Objects.

Quartz in Amerindian Folklore
Ceremonial wands topped with quartz have been found in South California. Quartz stones were used by the Cherokee as divining stones. Quartz pebbles were called "The Raven's Arrows" by the LuiseÒos of South California. The Hopi used quartz for treating disease and in rain-making ceremonies. See also the section above Quartz Amulets & Power Objects.

Quartz in British Folklore
In early Britain quartz pebbles were called star-stones and were believed to have curative powers. Nine star-stones collected from a running brook would impart their curative powers to water, which would be given to the patient for nine successive mornings.

In the Shetland Isles quartz pebbles were believed to cure sterility in women, they would be collected by women and thrown into a pool, where they would wash their feet to gain the curative powers of the stones.

In Ireland pieces of white quartz are often placed at the Saints burial places. Quartz pebbles have been found outside a number of neolithic tombs in Britain, as well as being scattered or buried in some stone circles in Wales and Ireland. It has been suggested that these pebbles could represent a line of demarcation, a spiritual barrier between the living and the dead.

Quartz in Indian Myth
Quartz was symbolic of the Sun God Surya in parts of Southern India, and white quartz of Shiva. The God Maya made a beautiful tank of crystal with pearls encrusted on it and precious stones, it gave off the illusion of water so all who saw it wanted to bathe in it.

Quartz in Japanese Myth
There is a lovely Japnese myth that the Moon is a vast circular palace of white quartz, ruled by thirty princes. Fifteen of the princes wear white robes and fiteen wear black robes, and they each rule a day of the Moon's cycle, thus explaining the Moon's cycle.

Quartz is known as suisho nad it was believed if you looked closely in a piece of quartz the Buddha could be seen riding a white elephant. The Japanese also called quartz tama meaning the "perfect jewel", it is a symbol of purity and the infinite vastness of space, of patience and of perseverance.

Quartz and Shamanism
In shamanism quartz is said to represent celestial power and light. In initiation rites of the Nootka and Kwakiutl tribes a magickal piece of quartz was inserted under the skin by the spirits, which killed the shaman. The spirits would then remove the quartz and restore the shaman to life.

Pieces of quartz called zaztun were used for divining in the Yucatan. Shamans of the South American Carib would send

306

quartz into the body of a person to make them ill. The Melanesians of New Guinea used quartz pieces to cause the death of enemies.

Amongst the medicine man of the Sea Dayaks of Sarawak, quartz is carried to skry the location of a patient's soul if it has become lost. The Mexican Huichol Indians believe a shaman's soul may return as a quartz crystal; a shaman may take a journey to the sky to retrieve such a crystal from behind the sun.

Other Folklore
In Tantra the lingam (phallus) of the Eastern quarter is made of quartz. Quartz was sacred to the Greek Lunar Goddess Selene. In Babylon a quartz cylinder seal was said to extend the possessions of a man.

In Qabalah quartz is attributed to Yesod as the "foundation" stone on which so many others are based, Crowley also notes that "gold is found in quartz, suggesting the concealed glory of the sexual process".

It may have been the sixth stone on the High Priest's breastplate, representing the tribe of Zebulon. Quartz has long been used to make crystal balls for skrying. In Christianity it was believed to encourage purity and faith. A piece of quartz anointed with honey was believed in Persia to encourage lactation in mothers.

The Hottentots used sharp pieces of quartz to sacrificie animals and circumcise young boys, as iron was taboo to the priests. In East Africa hot chunks of quartz were used to heat the drink in the poison ordeal (a test of guilt).

An old folk belief was that holding a piece of quartz in the mouth would quench thirst.

Dreaming of quartz was said to indicate freedom from enemies. Something made of quartz is given for 15th wedding anniversary.

Rhodochrosite

The Incas treasured Rhodocrosite as a precious stone.

This stone reflects the power of Venus, and can bring healing
and balance in a variety of ways.

Colours: Rose red and pink, may have shades of yellow
or brown.

Attribution: Venus, Virgo.

Chakras: Heart.

Uses: Directs energy, and is good for integrating
different types of energy, such as physical,
emotional and mental. Can help with memory
and intellect. Helps the heart, kidneys, spleen
and blood circulation. A good stone for emotional work, both strengthening and dealing
with challenges. Good for stress relief, and
people suffering after the breakdown of a big
relationship; may also help alleviate nightmares. Rhodocrosite is a stone which helps
the bearer appreciate beauty more. Can be
used to help strengthen the astral body. May
help in coping with addiction.

Used Since: At least 1400 CE South America.

Name: Inca Rose, Rosinca.

Folklore

The Incas treasured Rhodocrosite as a precious stone. I have
not found any other folklore relating to it.

Rhodonite

Rhodonite can be used for rapidly closing the chakras if needed.

A little known stone of recent discovery, rhodonite is a good stone for work with the subtle body and for improving low energy.

Colours: Violet.

Attribution: Uranus.

Chakras: Throat, Crown.

Uses: Used for lymph problems, and to strengthen
                 the subtle body. Calms the body and mind,
                 can help reduce high blood pressure. A good
                 energising stone for when you feel down or at
                 low ebb. May be used to increase self-
                 confidence. Can be used for rapidly closing
                 the chakras if needed.

Used Since: 1819 CE when it was identified.

Folklore
Being such a recently discovered crystal, there are no myths or folklore associated with rhodonite.

Rose Quartz

Rose quartz was believed by the Romans and Egyptians to prevent wrinkles and encourage a good complexion.

Rose quartz is an exceptionally positive and useful stone, used to promote the positive qualities and overcome the negative.

Colours: Pink and white.

Attribution: Venus, Sun, Taurus.

Chakras: Solar Plexus, Heart, Crown.

Uses: A stone of beauty, both appreciation and cultivation of. Used for promoting tranquillity, happiness, relaxation and serenity, protection from negative emotions, emotional healing. Rose quartz is a good stone to work with to balance the energies of the chakras and subtle body. Good for purification, may be used in overcoming addiction. A good stone to have a raw chunk of in any living space or temple. Good stone to start dream work with. The stone of unconditional love, and hence also good for work on confidence and self-esteem. Cabochons may show asterisms.

Used Since: At least 2500 BCE Egypt.

Names: Also known as American Ruby, Mont Blanc Ruby.

Folklore

The ancient Egyptians used rose quartz in funerary masks. In Qabalah it is attributed to Tiphereth as its colour in the

311

King Scale. Powdered rose quartz in cosmetics was believed by the Romans and Egyptians to prevent wrinkles and encourage a good complexion.

Ruby

Ruby sigil

"The cowslips tall her pensioners be:
In their gold coats spots you see:
Those be rubies, fairy favours,
In those freckles live their savours."
A *Midsummer Night's Dream,* Act 2, Scene 1,
William Shakespeare.

Burning with its inner fire, ruby is visibly one of the most powerful of stones, being particularly powerful as a protector and healer.

Colours: Red.

Attribution: The Hyades, Aldebaran 3^0 Gemini, Mars, Sun, Venus, Fire, Aries, Leo, Capricorn, Scorpio, Taurus.

Chakras: Base, Heart.

Uses: Good for problems with blood and circulation. One of the best stones for magickal strength and protection. Can bring passion and release of anger and blockages, as well as banishing fear. Can help strengthen the immune system, and work on eye problems (particularly star ruby) and liver disorders. A good stone for ensuring matters are running well -

it promotes success and growth in most manners, and will help focus energy more effectively in ritual. May be worn to help prevent miscarriage. Both ruby and sapphire can have asterisms (six-rayed stars) and are hence known as Star ruby and Star sapphire. Star rubies are particularly good for work on the higher self and integration, and for strengthening the will.

Used Since: Stone Age mines found in Burma.

Names: Known in German as donnerkeil (thunderbolt) and storchstein (stork-stone).

Ruby in Indian Myth

Ruby represented the sun, it was thought to burn with its own inner fire, and to sometimes boil water if placed in it. The fruits of the jewelled Kalpa Tree were rubies. As with diamond, the Hindus divide rubies into four castes: a true ruby is a Brahmin; rubicelle is a Kshatriya; spinel ruby is a Vaisya; balas ruby (garnet) is a Sudra.

The good quality stones, known as padmar,ga (meaning "red as the lotus") were thought to protect from ill fortune and keep the bearer perfectly safe. In Tantra the lingam (phallus) of the Southern Quarter is made of ruby; and the western side of Mount Meru is made of ruby.

In the *Rig-Veda* it is written that he who worships Krishna with rubies will be reborn as a powerful Emperor. Ruby was known as ratnaraj - "Lord of the Precious Stones".

Ruby in Medieval Europe

In interesting medieval British custom was that of touching a ruby (preferably set in gold and normally worn on the left side of the body) to the four corners of your land, then your house, vineyard and orchard - this was considered to protect them from lightning, tempest and bad harvests.

Wearing rubies was thought to attract werewolves, who were drawn by the blood-red colour. In medieval Europe ruby was said to preserve the good physical and mental health of the bearer, control amorous desires and reconcile disputes.

Ruby in Healing

In the Orient ruby was said to stem bleeding in battle, and to purify the blood. Ruby was thought to bring protection in battle, particularly if inserted under the skin; and to protect from poisons. Ruby was thought to protect from plague. It was used to dispel nightmares and banish sadness.

As with some other stones, a change of colour was thought to foretell health problems or misfortunes, with ruby a darkening of colour was the bad omen. An Indian folk belief was that ruby powdered and ingested in solution would dispel fear and excite joyous emotions.

Ruby in Qabalah

Ruby is attributed to Geburah and the 27th path due to its colour and association with martial themes such as blood and battle; Aries as the 28th path due to its colour and hardness. It is also attributed to the Archangel Malchediel.

Star Ruby Folklore

In the Orient the star in star ruby was thought to be formed by three benign spirits whose names translate as Destiny, Faith and Hope; they were imprisoned for some misdemeanour, and are thought to bring good fortune to the bearer of the stone to atone for this.

Pliny suggests star rubies as being conducive to gaining favour with authority. In Qabalah the star ruby is attributed to Chokmah as being the dynamic male creative force.

Other Folklore

Ruby is the gem of Summer. In Buddhism the tears of the Buddha were said to be rubies. Rubies were thought to have flowed from the third egg of the Burmese dragon, Naga. The Tibetans believed rubies could help in problems connected with sperm production. In Islam the fourth heaven is made of ruby, and the angel who supports the world on his shoulders is said to stand on a ruby rock.

Ruby was worn to indicate rank by first rank mandarins. Alchemists used the term "perfect ruby" to refer to the Philosophers Stone.

The Bible refers to rubies in Proverbs - "Who can find a virtuous woman? For her price is far above rubies." (Prov. 31:10). The Egyptians considered the ruby a stone of love and beauty, bringing protection and good fortune, it was considered sacred to the Goddess Sekhmet. In the Orient ruby was said to represent the beauty of the soul. The Greeks believed ruby could melt wax.

Dark rubies and star rubies were thought to be male, lighter rubies to be female. Rubies have also been described as the "fire from heaven", and it was thought they were generated by lightning flashes. A charm of a dragon engraved on a ruby was thought to bring the bearer joy and happiness, and augment worldly goods.

As with some other stones, the darkening of a ruby was believed to indicate forthcoming misfortune, Henry VIII's first wife Catherine of Aragon was said to have foreseen her own doom in the darkening of her ruby. Dreaming of rubies was said to indicate unexpected guests.

Marco Polo talked of ruby in his thirteenth century work Book of Marvels, telling the story of a Sinhalese king who possessed a ruby that measured 4" (10cm), which Kublai Khan offered him a city for, which the king refused.

316

A gift containing ruby is given for 40th wedding anniversary. In Brazil ruby is worn as a professional badge by lawyers.

Rutile

Rutile can help when dealing with emotional blocks,
especially childhood traumas.

Often overlooked, rutile helps deal with traumas and emotional blocks, going to the "heart" of the issue.

Colours: Yellow-brown, blood red, reddish-brown, black (nigrine).

Attribution: Neptune.

Chakras: Sacral.

Uses: Can help when dealing with emotional blocks, especially childhood traumas. May be used for memory and regression work. Try wearing rutile on a pendant or in a pouch by the heart to ensure you receive its benefits. Rutile is often found in twinned crystals, and may be of value to twins.

First Used: I have not found any historical reference to rutile.

Names: The black form is known as Nigrine.

Folklore
I have not been able to find any folklore associated with rutile. Due to the frequency of twinned crystals, it could be used with twin deities, such as Isis and Nephthys.

Rutile Quartz

*Rutile quartz was believed to be a stone of love,
and given to lovers; this is reflected in the names given to it
such as Arrows of Love and Venus' Hair Stone.*

The needle inclusions in rutile quartz remind us that we must at times focus our energy into ourselves to overcome blocks and release that energy into our growth and integration.

Colours: Colourless with inclusions of rutile.

Attribution: Neptune.

Chakras: Third Eye.

Uses: Used for the endocrine glands and bronchitis. A stone for work with the mind and sharpening the psychic abilities. Can help work with aspects of the self such as inner guide, subpersonalities, etc; also work with emotional blockages and past traumas. May have asterisms.

Used Since: At least 1000 BCE.

Names: Hair Stone. Needle Stone. Sagenitic Quartz. Venus' or Thetis' Hair Stone. Arrows of Love.

Folklore

Rutile quartz was believed to be a stone of love, and given to lovers; this is reflected in the names given to it such as Arrows of Love and Venus' Hair Stone. Sacred to the Roman Love Goddess Venus, and also sacred to the Greek Goddess Thetis.

319

Sapphire

Sapphire sigil

In Buddhism sapphire is known as the "Stone of Stones" and is said to promote devotion, tranquillity, happiness, serenity and spiritual enlightenment.

Sapphire is another of the very powerful magickal stones, and is especially helpful for strengthening the will and gaining clarity of vision (psychic as well as physical).

Colours: Blue, colourless (White Sapphire), yellow (Golden Sapphire), brown (Adamantine Spar), orange (Padparadscha), pink, green, purple, violet (Oriental Amethyst).

Attribution: Capella - The Goat 15⁰ Gemini, Jupiter, Saturn, Mercury, Water, Pisces, Aquarius, Virgo, Taurus, Gemini.

Chakras: Throat, Third Eye.

Uses: A spiritual stone. Good for mental problems, and developing self-discipline, clarity and willpower. Good for unblocking the Third Eye chakra or any problems with it, and for work with the eyes. Can enhance psychic abilities and astral work. Can work on the heart and stomach. May stimulate the pituitary gland. Can help dealing with fear and panic attacks. Star sapphires are particularly good for work on the higher self and integration, and for strengthening the will. Sapphire is a stone of inner peace and balance.

Used Since: The Stone Age, mines found in Burma.

Names: Adamantine Spar (Brown), Oriental or Bengal Amethyst (Violet). Green sapphire was often mistaken for emerald until about 100 years ago, and colourless sapphire for diamond.

Sapphire Amulets
In Greek myth Prometheus was said to have worn a sapphire ring when he stole the fire from heaven. Sapphire was worn by kings in jewellery as a protective talisman.

A charm of an astrolabe (an old instrument for measuring altitude) engraved on sapphire was thought to bestow the power to predict the future, and to increase wealth; a ram or bearded man engraved on a sapphire was thought to cure and protect from many illnesses, to free from poison and all demons, it was considered a royal image conferring dignity and honour.

Sapphire in Christianity
The tablets of the Ten Commandments were said to be inscribed on sapphire, and the Holy Throne of Majesty is described as sapphire (Ez i.26 and x.1). In the Bible the second foundation of New Jerusalem is made of sapphire. Sapphire was considered symbolic of the height of celestial hope; it was also symbolic of St Paul and the Apostle Andrew. A cardinal's ring of rank bears a sapphire. Solomon was said to use a sapphire for communion with God.

Sapphire in Greek Myth
Sapphire was sacred to Zeus. Supplicants to the Delphic Oracle (when under the auspices of Apollo) had to wear a

sapphire. Sapphire was reputedly used by witches to bind enchantments and spells, and by necromancers to ensure clear hearing of oracles.

Sapphire in Indian Myth
The roots of the jewelled Kalpa Tree are made of sapphire. In Tantra the lingam (phallus) of the Western Quarter is made of sapphire. Sapphire was thought to bring happiness, wealth, health and the blessings of royalty and deity.

As with diamond and ruby, the Hindus divide sapphires into four castes: light blue is a Brahmin; reddish blue is a Kshatriya; yellowish blue is a Vaisya; dark blue is a Sudra. In Hindu astrology the sapphire corresponds to Saturn and is placed in the West.

Sapphire in Healing
Male Sapphire was said to be the stronger healing stone, and is more of a sky blue, whereas female Sapphire is said to be more sea blue. Sapphire was used for ulcers (powdered and mixed with milk), hot biles, tumours, eye troubles, fevers, agues, the plague, skin disorders and strengthening muscles.

It was believed that sapphire would remove plague if rubbed on the skin early enough. Sapphire was another stone thought to protect the bearer from poison and poisonous bites.

Sapphires into Rubies
There was an Indian belief that colourless sapphires were unripe rubies (which acknowledges the relationship between sapphire and ruby as both being corundum long before it was realised in Europe). Burying the sapphire in the ground would enable it to ripen. If a stone was flawed it was believed this was because it was overripe.

Star Sapphire Folklore
In Qabalah star sapphire is attributed to Binah as representing the great Cosmic Female principle. Star sapphires have the same story of the three imprisoned spirits told about them as star ruby (see the entry for Ruby). Star sapphires were also thought to protect from harm and ensure victory in battle, and were known as siegstein (victory stone) to the Germans. The Cingalese believed star sapphire protected against all forms of witchcraft and enchantment.

Other Folklore
A lot of references to sapphire in the ancient world were probably referring to lapis lazuli. Sapphire is considered the gem of Autumn. Said to induce longevity. Sapphire is traditionally sacred to Sky Gods such as the Indian Indra, the Greek Zeus and the Roman Jupiter.

In Buddhism sapphire is known as the "Stone of Stones" and is said to promote devotion, tranquillity, happiness, serenity and spiritual enlightenment. The Persians believed the earth sat on a giant sapphire which gave the sky its colour, and a sapphire was set into the gold balls they used to skry with (see the earlier section Skrying and Divination).

In Qabalah sapphire is attributed to Chesed due to its colour and its association with wealth and power; it is also attributed to the Archangels Metatron and Hercel. Sapphire may have been the fifth stone on the High Priest's breastplate, representing the tribe of Issachar. Prester John was said to sleep on a bed of sapphire to preserve his chastity.

It was thought to detect liars, frauds and enchantments. Sapphire was said to prevent fear in the bearer, and protect from envy and revenge, and was thought to change colour to violet in the case of infidelity.

Sapphire has been referred to as "The Philosophers Stone", but this is for its properties rather than being likened to the Philosophers Stone of alchemy.

In dreams sapphire was thought to indicate escape from danger. A gift with sapphire in is given for 23rd wedding anni-versary. In Brazil sapphire is worn as a professional badge by engineers.

Serpentine

As the name suggests, serpentine is a good stone for work with the kundalini and with sexual problems.

Colours: Green (when in fine grain plated form known as Lizardite), yellow (Retinalite), black, red.

Attribution: Saturn, Terra, Earth, Scorpio, Capricorn.

Chakras: Base.

Uses: Good for work with the Kundalini and sexual problems or blockages. May be used to help with memory problems (i.e. bad recall, short or long term memory). Good to wear whilst travelling, particularly to new places.

Used Since: At least 3000 BCE Egypt.

Names: Serpentinite. Green Serpentine is known as New or Hunan Jade. A pale-grey to green variety of serpentine, sometimes with lamellar inclusions is known as Antigorite. Green to red-brown serpentine found on the Lizard promonotory of Cornwall, England, is known as Lizardite. A hard pale grey to cream and pale green variety is known as Bowenite, and Korean Jade. The yellow variety is also known as Retinalite. A yellow to dark green variety is known as Williamite.

Serpentine Amulets

Serpentine was often used in amulets, talismans and jewellery in ancient tombs. Some Amerindian tribes wore serpentine with coral to ensure survival in harsh environments. A chalice of serpentine was used to detect poison, it being believed that it would bring to sweat if any poison was put in it. Serpentine amulets were used as a protection whilst travelling, both by land and sea.

The Romans thought serpentine would protect from unseen dangers in the night if worn. A cylinder seal of green serpentine was a highly prized object in ancient Babylon, it being written "heresoever a man carrieth a seal made from green serpentine he shall have blessing upon blessing bestowed upon him."

Serpentine and Healing

In ancient Egypt and Rome it was used as a protection from and as a remedy to snakebite, was thought to be able to draw the venom out from the bite, though it was thought to lose its power if worked (like coral).

In the Middle Ages binding serpentine into rheumatic joints was thought to relieve the pain, and it was used tin ancient times to reduce excess body fluid by sitting in the sun for short periods with a piece of serpentine in each hand.

Other Folklore

In Qabalah serpentine is attributed to Scorpio as the 24th path due to its name and early use as a remedy. The 30th chapter of the Book of the Dead was only engraved on serpentine. Serpentine was used in ancient Africa as trading beads. Voitve axes made from serpentine have been found in Olmec tombs.

Shell

Conch Shell sigils

Shell is universally sacred to Sea Deities such as the Assyrian Dagon, the Haitian Agwe, Loa of the Sea, the Greek Poseidon and Roman Neptune.

When you hold a shell to your ear on the beach, appreciate the beauty of this key you hold, offering to open the key to uncharted depths.

Colours: All colours can be found.

Attribution: Moon, Saturn, Water.

Chakras: Base.

Uses: Work giving form to ideas. Problems with the bones, such as fractures and breaks. As a container or vessel for other precious objects.

First Used: Many thousands of years ago, at least Stone Age if not earlier.

Cowri Shell
The name cowri is possibly derived from the pre-vedic Indian Goddess Kauri. Cowri's have been used to avert the evil eye in a number of cultures. Cowri's have been found at sites going back to 20,000 BCE. They have been used in the Middle East, Egypt and the Mediterranean as a charm for healing, fertility, luck and magickal power.

Romans called the cowri shell "matriculus" ("little matrix/womb") and "porcella" ("little sow" or "vulva"). Sudanese Christians used strips of leather with nine cowri's in a cross on as an amulet.

Cowri's are used in Santerĺa as the main form of divination, usually in sets of eighteen, of which sixteen are thrown by the querent. Gypsy women also used cowri's as a focus for divination.

Folklore
In Chinese Buddhism shell is one of the eight emblems of good luck. Shell is universally sacred to Sea Deities such as the Assyrian Dagon, the Haitian Agwe, Loa of the Sea, the Greek Poseidon and Roman Neptune. Shell is usually considered representative of the feminine.

As the conch shell it is sacred to the Goddess, and to the Indian Shiva. In Tibet the conch shell trumpet (sankha) is a symbol of victory. Shells have been used by many cultures as symbols of wealth, and for trading. The art of cameos revolves around shells.

Smoky Quartz

In Qabalah smoky quartz is attributed to Binah due to its colouring.

Smoky quartz is a good releaser of energy, helping you to overcome negative states and cope with difficult situations and phases of life.

Colours: Transparent amber-brown to black.

Attribution: Saturn.

Chakras: Base.

Uses: Used for problems with kidneys, pancreas and sexual organs, and general abdominal pains. Good protector and transformer of energies. Can help release blocked energies, particularly deep blocks (including kundalini), so good to wear and wrk with during counselling or therapies. Can aid concentration and relaxation. Good for overcoming depression and negative emotional states. A good purifying and grounding stone.

Used Since: At least 3100 BCE Egypt and Sumeria.

Names: The very dark brown form is known as Morion. Sometimes known as Radium Diamond. A brilliant form of smoky quartz found at Alencon in France is known as Pierre d'Alencon (Alencon diamond).

Folklore

In Qabalah smoky quartz is attributed to Binah due to its colouring. I have not found any other folklore associated with it, though it has a long history of use in jewellery.

Sodalite

Sodalite was used by Egyptian priests for dispelling fear and guilt, and to strengthen the mind.

Like the "comrade" it is named for, sodalite helps you keep a clear perspective on your life, and maintain your well-being.

Colours: Blue to deep blue, green to deep green. greenish-grey, grey, white, colourless.

Attribution: Jupiter.

Chakras: Throat, Third Eye.

Uses: General health and well being. Helps bring clear vision and dispel illusions (including those about yourself). Can help deal with oversensitivity.

Used Since: At least 2000 BCE Egypt.

Names: Often confused with lapis lazuli and turquoise in ancient texts.

Folklore

In Qabalah sodalite is attributed to Chesed due to its colouring. Sodalite was used by Egyptian priests for dispelling fear and guilt, and to strengthen the mind. The name of the stone comes from the Latin sodalitas meaning "a comrade".

Spinel (Ruby)

In the Middle Ages spinel was thought to protect
from financial and physical disaster.

Like the ruby, spinel helps protect and provide energy, and
also helps purify and overcome blockages.

Colours: Pink, rose (Balas Ruby) to deep red (Ruby
Spinel), purple red (Almandine Spinel),
orange-yellow (Rubicelle), blue (Sapphire
Spinel, Gahnospinel), grass-green
(Chlorospinel), dark green (Gahnite,
Ceylonite, Pleonaste) to black (Franklinite),
purple.

Attribution: Mars, Neptune, Pluto.

Chakras: Solar Plexus, Third Eye, Crown.

Uses: Good for problems with blood and circulation.
One of the best stones for magickal strength
and protection, provides extra energy. Can
bring passion and release of anger and blockages, as well as banishing fear. A good energising stone for when you are at low ebb and
need more energy. Can be used for purification and detoxification, and hence a good
stone to work with to overcome addiction.
May also be used to help with leg problems.

Used Since: Probably at least 1000 BCE, Ruby Spinel was
often mistaken for Ruby, and was classified as
a female Ruby.

Names:	Balas Ruby (pink, rose), Ruby Spinel (deep red), Almandine Spinel (purple red), Rubicelle (orange-yellow); Sapphire Spinel, Gahnospinel (blue), Chlorospinel (grass-green); Gahnite, Ceylonite, Pleonaste (dark green), Franklinite (black).

Folklore

In Qabalah spinel ruby is attributed to Geburah due to its colouring. In the Middle Ages spinel was thought to protect from financial and physical disaster. Due to its red colouring, spinel was thought to cure hemorrhages and inflammatory diseases, and dispel anger and conflict.

It was also believed to have the powers to control the thoughts, expand the imagination and enlarge the mind; ruby spinel has been associated with the medical profession for these reasons. There was an Indian belief that spinel powdered and consumed in a potion would bring happiness and remove forebodings. Until recent times was often confused with and described as Ruby.

Staurolite

A legend tells of the fairies crying tears which turned to stone crosses when they heard the news of the death of Christ.

The "Fairy Stone", the equal armed cross usually present on staurolite indicates its natural function as a balancer of energies, particularly earth energies and primal (pre-metal) sites; it is also good for increasing luck - a mineral four-leafed clover.

Colours: Brown, reddish-brown to black-brown.

Attribution: Terra, Earth, Taurus, Capricorn.

Chakras: Base, Feet.

Uses: Good for working with earth energies. A good balancing stone, for all sorts of energies, and a good protector stone as well. Staurolite can be used to attract luck, and may help in attracting wealth. It may also be used to help stay earthed when dealing with the Faerie.

Used Since: At least 1000 BCE, probably much earlier.

Names: Twinned crystals are known as Cross Stones and Fairy Stones. Also known as Baseler Taufstein (baptismal stone) or lapis crucifer

Folklore
In Qabalah staurolite is attributed to Malkuth due to its earthy nature and use with earth energies, also the equal armed cross often found on it reminds one of the depiction of Malkuth as being quartered into colours in several of the colour scales.

In France it was believed to have dropped from heaven.

One legend tells of the fairies crying tears which turned to stone crosses when they heard the news of the death of Christ. Staurolite was carried by British sailors as a protection against shipwreck.

Sunstone

Sunstone can be used for works to increase prosperity
and to attract money and the inspirations to make money.

Like the sun it is named after, sunstone brings a light
disposition and sense of well-being into life, and helps with
heart disorders.

Colours: Spangled bronze, spangled black (Black
                  Sunstone).

Attribution: Sun, Leo.

Chakras: Heart, Throat (Black Sunstone).

Uses: Good for general health and well being.
                  Works on the heart and heart disorders.
                  Sunstone is (obviously) good for solar magicks.
                  Black Sunstone is a very magickal stone and
                  good for spiritual development and strength-
                  ening the will, and may be used during
                  eclipses to very powerful effect. Can be used
                  for works to increase prosperity and to attract
                  money and the inspirations to make money.

First Used: I have not found any historical reference to
                  this stone.

Names: Oliglocase. Crushed and reconstituted
                  sunstone is sold under the name of Goldstone.

Folklore

In Qabalah it is attributed to Tiphereth by its nature. I have
found no other folklore associated with this stone, though by
its name we could associate it with the many solar deities.

Tektite

The Greeks carried tektites set in gold as good luck charms,
calling them aerolites.

The origin of tektites is still uncertain, however we can be
certain that they are good stones for development of the self
and for psychic work.

Colours: Olive-green to black-green.

Attribution: Spirit, Aquarius.

Chakras: Crown.

Uses: Works of integration and with the higher self.
                    Good for works involving travelling between
                    planes and states, such as astral travel and
                    psychic work, as well as meditation and path-
                    working. Can be powerful protective stones.
                    It is still not known whether tektites are
                    meteorological and hence non-terrestrial in
                    origin, but they are certainly useful for stellar
                    magicks.

Used Since: At least 1100 BCE.

Names: Aerolite.

Folklore
The Greeks carried tektites set in gold as good luck charms,
calling them aerolites. See also the section on Tektites in the
chapter on Meteorites.

Tiger's Eye

*The Egyptians believed that tiger's eye and the other
associated "Eye" stones enabled the bearer to see everything,
even behind closed doors!*

A powerful stone for improving vision, including the ability to
see goals and find ways to manifest them.

Colours: Yellow or amber-brown chatoyant (cat's eye
effect from refraction of light from fibres in
the crystal), grey-green chatoyant (Cat's Eye),
blue-grey chatoyant (Hawk's or Falcon's Eye
or Crocidolite).

Attribution: Saturn, Sun, Terra, Leo, Gemini.

Chakras: Solar Plexus, Third Eye.

Uses: Promotes clear self-perception and insight if
you are willing to be honest. A good aura
strengthening stone. Can aid visualisation
and astral vision. May aid in materialisation
or giving form to desires, and hence is good for
getting new jobs, relationships, etc. Aids the
digestive system and the eyes. Helps restore
the sense of humour. Can help overcome
hypochondria. A good stone for making
amulets. A good energising and protecting
stone.

Used Since: At least 3000 BCE Egypt.

Names: Tiger's Eye was formerly known as Oculus
Beli. Crocidolite. Hawk's Eye is also known
as Falcon's Eye.

Tiger's Eye in Ancient Egypt

Tiger's eye was used to decorate statues of the deities in Egypt and Assyria, particularly as eyes. It was especially sacred to the Sun God Ra. The Egyptians believed that tiger's eye and the other associated "Eye" stones enabled the bearer to see everything, even behind closed doors! It was also used as a protection against witchcraft and sorcery.

Tiger's Eye in India

In India tiger's eye was thought to bring wealth and prevent the bearer from losing wealth. It was said to help in childbirth if tied in the hair of the expectant mother, and to help heal sores if applied as a powder.

Other Folklore

In Qabalah it is attributed to Leo as the 19th path due to its name.

Topaz

Topaz sigil

Topaz worn in a ring was said to protect against accidental or untimely death due to its supposed tendency to lose colour in situations of danger.

Could be considered the "Buddha Stone", as it engenders and enhances the noble qualities in man, such as wisdom, serenity, purity, selflessness and spiritual growth.

Colours: Yellow (sherry topaz), orange (imperial topaz), green, blue, pink (almost always heat treated), colourless.

Attribution: Alphecca, Right & Left Wing of Raven 8∞ Libra, Sun, Jupiter, Saturn, Mars, Air, Fire, Gemini, Sagittarius, Taurus, Scorpio, Leo.

Chakras: Heart, Solar Plexus.

Uses: Good for working on eye problems. Promotes selflessness and purity of will, benevolence. May be used to help overcome loss of appetite. A good stone for spiritual growth and increasing wisdom. Can help detoxify the body, and is good for overcoming addiction. Helps in regeneration and strengthening the body's system, restoring lost energy and reduces stress. Blue topaz is relaxing and serene in addition to these properties described. Topaz is a good stone to place under your pillow to benefit from its qualities, and it is a good stone to work with for dreamwork. Topaz is pizoelectric.

Used Since: At least 2000 BCE Egypt.

Names: Colourless topaz is known in Brazil as *pingas d'agua* which is Portuguese for "tear drops", and as Saxony Topaz. Blue topaz is also known as Brazilian Aquamarine, and yellow topaz as Brazilian Topaz. Topaz was known to the Romans as Chrysolith.

Topaz Amulets
A topaz strung on a hair taken from an ass's mane it was thought to guard against evil spirits and nightmares. A charm of a topaz with a falcon engraved on it was thought to be good for acquiring the goodwill of kings, princes and magnates. Topaz worn in a ring was said to protect against accidental or untimely death due to its supposed tendency to lose colour in situations of danger.

Topaz in Christianity
Topaz was symbolic of the Apostles Matthew and James the Lesser. In the bible the ninth foundation of New Jerusalem is Topaz. Topaz also symbolised "the ardent contemplation of the prophecies".

Topaz in Healing
The Greeks thought topaz exuded a milky fluid which could be used an antidote for rabies. In the Middle Ages topaz was placed under the pillow for stress relief and to restore energy, wearing topaz was thought to strengthen the mind. It was believed to help calm frenzy, lunacy and anger; and to ease sorrow, fear and melancholy and to be good for lung

complaints and asthma. Topaz worn around the neck was thought to prevent colds and tuberculosis.

Topaz has been used to treat haemmorhoids and gout; and insanity. It is another stone that was thought to staunch the flow of blood, and also prevent haemorrhaging. Marbode recommended topaz as a cure for weak vision.

Other Folklore
In Indian myth the middle section of the trunk of the jewelled Kalpa Tree was made of topaz. Topaz represents Jupiter in Hindu astrology. In Qabalah it is attributed to Tiphereth and the 30th path due to its golden colouring and traditional solar attributions, also to the 11th path as the pure yellow of Air; and to Taurus as the 16th path for reasons I have not been able to determine; topaz is also attributed to the Archangels Michael and Asmodel.

In ancient Egypt topaz was sacred to the Sun God Ra. Topaz may have been the second stone of the High Priests Breastplate representing the tribe of Simeon. The Greeks believed topaz tipped wands could be used to divine the whereabouts of gold and other precious metals. In the Middle Ages topaz was thought to be a stone of purity and wearing one was thought to prevent covetousness, lust and love excesses.

Topaz was thought to make the bearer invisible and to dispel illusion. Dreaming of topaz was thought to indicate that no harm should befall the dreamer. A topaz gift is given for 16th wedding anniversary. Topaz is the professional badge of dentistry in Brazil.

Touαmaline

A dreaming stone, tourmaline is one of the high energy stones
which also works well for protection and healing.

Colours: Colourless (achroite), red and pink (rubelite),
green, blue, yellow-green, honey yellow, pale
coloured (elbaite), violet (siberite), dark blue
(indicolite), brown (dravite), black (schorl).
Tourmaline may have asterisms.

Attribution: Uranus, Neptune, Venus, Terra, Earth,
Gemini.

Chakras: Heart, Throat.

Uses: Good for dreamwork and spiritual growth.
Promotes growth of the throat chakra, and
good for throat disorders. Good protection
stone, dispelling nightmares, negativity and
ignorance. Can enhance sensitivity and help
ease mental distress or disorders. Tourmaline
is a high energy stone and may help give you
a boost when needed, or increase the energy
levels in a ritual. Tourmaline is pizoelectric.

First Used: At least 300 BCE Rome.

Names: Known to the ancients as Lyncunium or
Lychnis. Used to be known as Ashentrekker
until about 1750. When green at one end and

pink at the other it is known as Water-melon tourmaline. The yellow-green form is sometimes known as Brazilian Peridot and Ceylonese Chrysolite or Peridot. The green form is also known as Emeraldite and Brazilian Emerald. Blue Tourmaline is sometimes known as Inicolite or Indigolite, also as Brazilian Sapphire. Black Tourmaline is known as Schorl.

Folklore

In Qabalah it is attributed to Gemini as the 17th path due to its polarization of light. Tourmaline was believed by the Romans to calm the mind and body, and produce relaxed sleep. Red and pink tourmaline were worn by first rank mandarins in China as a sign of rank. Dreaming of tourmaline was said to indicate an accident would happen.

John Ruskin said of tourmaline in his book *The Ethics of Dust* (1866) - "And on the whole, the chemistry of it is more like a mediaeval doctor's prescription than the making of a respectable mineral."

Turquoise

Turquoise sigil

The Egyptian Late Period term for turquoise, mefkat,
was also synonymous with "joy" or "delight".

The "Horseman's Stone", turquoise is one of the first crystals used by man, and has a very long history as a sacred stone with many protective qualities.

Colour: Blue, green.

Attribution: Jupiter, Venus, Mercury, Sagittarius, Libra, Aquarius, Pisces, Cancer.

Chakras: Heart, Throat.

Uses: Used as a protection and charm, to absorb general negative energies. Helps soothe the emotions and enables the bearer to appreciate beauty more readily. Can help protect the body from pollution and the stresses of modern living. If you wear your turquoise and it changes colour it may indicate persistently high stress levels - as the bodies copper levels can rise at such times, causing the stone to change colour - a good demonstrable example of the physical interaction between body and stone.

Used Since: At least 5300 BCE Mesopotamia (Iraq).

Names: Callaite, Callaica, Callaina, Callais, Fayruz (Arabic - "lucky stone"). Blue or green turquoise is known as Chalchuite.

Turquoise and Amerindian Myth

The four Navaho rain-making Gods wore necklaces of turquoise and coral, and the God of Whirlwinds was also depicted wearing turquoise necklace and ear pendants. The Navahos believed throwing a piece of turquoise into a river whilst praying to the Rain God would ensure rain. Apache medicine-men needed turquoise as part of their regalia as a talisman or badge of rank and respect, it was also thought to guide the hunter's arrows and spear to fly true.

Turquoise was used to guard burial sites. Turquoise was seen as being symbolic of the great sky spirit, considered the universal stone, it was believed a turquoise would be found in the ground at the end of a rainbow. Due to its ability to change colour it was used for prophecy and prediction of drought and other natural disasters.

The Pueblo Indians considered turquoise the most sacred stone, the colour turquoise representing male and yellow representing female. Some tribes believed that a turquoise would be found in the damp ground at the end of a rainbow (like the idea of the pot of gold), these stones were believed to be thunder stones which could control the weather.

Turquoise and Ancient Egypt

The ancient Egyptians prized green turquoise very highly, considering it as precious as lapis lazuli. Like lapis lazuli, the Late Period term for turquoise, mefkat, was also synonymous with "joy" or "delight". The green colour of the turquoise symbolised fertility and resurrection.

345

Turquoise and Islam

In Islam turquoise was thought to be one of the best protections against evil spells, and amulets with verses from the Koran inscribed on them were frequently worn. It was said that to escape evil and attain good fortune one must see the reflection of the new moon on the Koran, the face of a friend or a turquoise, demonstrating the high value placed on it.

Turquoise in Medieval Belief

In Medieval Europe turquoise was believed to ease any pains resulting from being exorcised if possessed by a demon, and was thought to protect against snake and scorpion poisons. Turquoise was thought to turn black on infidelity and hence was given to lovers in. It was also thought to fade when the owner was threatened with danger or illness. Turquoise was believed to ease melancholia and used in the treatment of malaria and heart complaints.

Turquoise in South American Myth

Turquoise was believed to give courage in battle. To the Aztecs the Solar Serpent was made of turquoise; they believed it protected against snake and scorpion venoms, and death masks to deities were often inlaid with turquoise. The Mayans considered it sacred to the Gods and humans were not allowed to wear turquoise. In Mexico turquoise was sacred to Xiuhtechuhtli, the God of Fire and Turquoise Lord.

Turquoise and Qabalah

In Qabalah it is attributed to Chesed due to its colour and the 25th path due to its association with horsemanship and Sagittarius; also Venus as the 14th path due to it being the colour of Venus in the Queen Scale, and its tendency to fade to green.

Other Folklore

Turquoise is known as the "Horseman's Stone" due to the belief that it protected from falls, particularly from horseback (hence the connection with Sagittarius). In the Middle East it was thought to protect from the evil eye and bring good luck, often braided into the tails of beasts of burden, in Iran a piece of turquoise would be placed in a sheep's eye for this purpose.

Turquoise is considered to be a symbol of affection, and should be given not bought, to ensure the recipient receives good luck, hence the Oriental proverb "given by a loving hand it brings with it happiness and good fortune". It is also considered to symbolise sincerity and generosity.

There is a Hindu belief that if you look at the New moon and then immediately look at a turquoise it will bring great wealth. In Northern India it was worn in water to protect against serpents and boils. Buddha once destroyed a monster with the aid of a magick turquoise. Dreaming of turquoise is said to indicate coming prosperity.

Zircon

"The jacinth also possesses virtue from the sun against poisons, pestilences, and pestiferous vapours. Likewise it renders the wearer pleasant and acceptable. Being simply held in the mouth it wonderfully cheers the heart and strengthens the mind."
"The Magus, or Celestial Intelligencer", Francis Barrett, 1801

A good stone for meditating with, zircon is in many ways the stone for modern living - good for pepping up and increasing energy, and for dealing with indecision and stress.

Colour: Colourless, gold yellow, blue (all heat treated), honey yellow, light green, brown (jacinth or hyacinth), blue, red (high); leaf green to brown green (low).

Attribution: Shoulder of Equis Major 18∞ Pisces, Sun, Pluto, Mars, Jupiter, Cauda Draconis (North Node), Air, Leo, Sagittarius, Scorpio, Virgo.

Chakras: Third Eye.

Uses: Used for heart and liver problems, and gaining knowledge. Helps against depression and insomnia. Good for people with low energy levels who need "pepping up". Can work on the pineal and pituitary glands. A good stone for people who are indecisive and need to take control of their situation. A meditation stone which can help provide insight and calm the mind. Can be helpful for people doing past life work.

Used Since: At least 1000 BCE.

Names:	Hyacinth or Jacinth (brown zircon). Ligure, Jacant. Blue heat-treated zircon is also known as Siam Aquamarine. Colourless zircon is sometimes known as Ceylon or Matura Diamond. Yellow zircons are also known as Jargons or Jargoons. Brown zircon is also known as Malacon.

Zircon Amulets & Taslismans

Old beliefs attributed protective qualities against bowel disorders, and as a mental tonic and protection against mental temptation. Zircon was used by farmers as a talisman to ensure fruitful harvests. Thomas de Cantempre described zircon as a protective amulet from poison and melancholy.

Francis Barrett recorded "The jacinth also possesses virtue from the sun against posinos, pestilences, and pestiferous vapours. Likewise it renders the wearer pleasant and acceptable. Being simply held in the mouth it wonderfully cheers the heart and strengthens the mind."

Zircon and Christianity

Symbolic of the Apostle Simon. In the Bible the eleventh foundation of New Jerusalem. Zircon was considered a symbol of humility. It was also thought to symbolise "the celestial rapture of the learned in their high thoughts and their humble descent to human things out of regard for the weak".

Zircon and the Christian Bread Blessing Spell

St Hildegard, records a Christian spell for the use of zircon (jacinth), as follows:

If any one is bewitched by phantoms or magical spells, so that he has lost his wits, take a hot loaf of pure rye bread and cut the upper crust in the form of a cross - not, however, cutting it quite through - and then pass the stone along the cutting,

349

reciting these words: "May God, who cast away all precious stones from the devil ... cast away from thee, N., all phantoms and all magic spells, and free thee from the pain of this madness". Drawing the same stone across the bread saying, "Just as the splendour which the devil had in him was taken from him because of his transgression, so also let this madness which torments you, N., by various delusions and magic words, be taken from you, and disappear." The bread from around the area through which you drew the zircon (jacinth) should be given to the afflicted person to eat. If he cannot eat the rye bread because of the debility of his body, then using the jacinth and the same words, bless warm, unleavened bread in the same way, and give it to him to eat.

Zircon in Indian Myth
The foliage of the jewelled Kalpa Tree (except the young leaves) was entirely formed of green zircons. Zircon was known as rhuratna after the dragon which periodically consumed the sun and moon causing eclipses, as a result it was believed to be a good stone to avert malevolent influence by being a more powerful evil which would deter lesser evils.

Zircon and Islam
A large zircon of dazzling whiteness was given by the Archangel Gabriel to Ishmael when he was building the Kaaba; this zircon was the angel who had failed to protect Adam and Eve from the serpent's wiles, it has been turned black by the kisses of the sinful, at the resurrection the angel will be restored to its true form and bear witness to all those who have made the pilgrimage to Mecca. In Islam the sixth heaven is said to be made of zircon.

Zircon and Healing
The ancients thought zircon could cure wasting diseases and drive away insomnia. In medieval times it was thought to be a good traveller's charm, being known as "the protector stone from heaven", and said to protect against bandits, lightning,

350

injury, poisons and pestilence; and was used to assist women in childbirth.

Zircon was thought to lose its colour if the bearer got the plague or went near someone with the plague. A zircon worn over the heart was thought to strengthen it, and having a zircon in the mouth was though to strengthen the mind and cheer the heart.

Aristotle said zircon "prepared a woman for miscarriage". Medically it was used in the treatment of dropsy, indigestion, jaundice, poisons and fevers. When held against the forehead it was said to give a calm mind and clear thoughts.

St Hildegard recommends zircon for the eyes, saying "A person who suffers fogginess in his eyes, or whose eyes are agitated or suppurative, should hold a jacinth in the sun. It immediately remembers that it was born from fire and quickly heats up. He should then dampen it with his saliva and quickly place it on his eyes, so that it warms them. He should do this often, and his eyes will become clear and healthy."

Zircon and the Weather
Zircon was also thought to indicate changes in the weather, brightening before a sunny day, going dull before bad weather, and going the colour of a "burning coal" if there was an impending tempest.

Other Folklore
In Qabalah it represents Sagittarius as the 25th path due to Hyacinth's death from an arrow shot by Apollo; and is also attributed to the Archangel Zuriel. Zircon was the seventh stone of the High Priest's breastplate, representing the tribe of Joseph. Zircon was thought to dispel sadness and vain suspicions.

It was believed in the Middle Ages that zircon could help the bearer get to sleep. Carrying a zircon was said to make the bearer more attractive and energetic, and bring riches and glory. Dreaming of zircon was said to indicate success or a heavy storm. Given for 19th wedding anniversary

Zoïsite

Zoisite can be used to help overcome traumas.

A recently discovered stone which has beneficial effects on the emotions.

Colours: Blue (tanzanite), green, grey, yellow, pink and red (thulite), brown.

Attribution: Venus.

Chakras: Solar Plexus, Heart.

Uses: For emotional problems and emotional growth, including balancing the emotions and facing fear. Can be used to help overcome traumas. May help with menstrual difficulties, and ease problems with the cervix.

Used Since: 1905 CE when it was identified.

Names: Blue zoisite is known as Tanzanite.

Folklore
In Qabalah attributed to Netzach due to its colouring. Due to its recent discovery there is no folklore associated with zoisite.

Appendix 1
Crystals and Deities

The Goddess in Three Phases

Maiden   Amber, Chalcedony, Diamond, Emerald,
              Jadeite, Kunzite, Moonstone, Opal, Pearl,
              Quartz, Zircon.

Mother   Aquamarine, Chrysocolla, Fluorite, Garnet,
              Labradorite, Lapis Lazuli, Malachite,
              Moonstone, Prase, Rose Quartz, Ruby, Rutile
              Quartz, Turquoise, Zoisite.

Crone   Coral, Glass, Hagstone, Jet, Kyanite,
              Moonstone (Black), Nephrite, Obsidian,
              Onyx, Smoky Quartz, Tourmaline.

Specific Goddesses

Aphrodite	Greek	Emerald, Lapis Lazuli, Pearl
Artemis	Greek	Amethyst, Emerald, Moonstone, Pearl
Ceres	Roman	Emerald
Chalchihuitlicue	Mexican	Jadeite
Cybele	Roman	Jet
Diana	Roman	Amethyst, Chalcedony (blue), Emerald, Moonstone, Pearl
Freya	Norse	Amber, Pearl
Hekate	Greek	Moonstone
Ishtar	Sumerian	Lapis Lazuli
Isis	Egyptian	Carnelian, Coral, Jasper, Pearl

Itzpapalotl	Aztec	Obsidian
Kwan Yin	Chinese	Jadeite
Lakshmi	Indian	Pearl
Mayat	Egyptian	Lapis Lazuli
Minerva	Roman	Agate
Nuit	Egyptian	Lapis Lazuli
Parvati	Indian	Pyrite
Pele	Hawaiian	Obsidian, Peridot
Selene	Greek	Moonstone, Quartz, Selenite
Sekhmet	Egyptian	Ruby
Thetis	Greek	Rutile Quartz
Uixtochihuatl	Mexican	Halite
Vajravarahi	Tibetan	Diamond
Venus	Roman	Emerald, Pearl, Rutile Quartz

The God in Three Phases

Horned/Green	Amber, Aventurine, Heliotrope, Nephrite, Peridot, Staurolite, Turquoise, Zoisite.
Solar	Citrine Quartz, Diamond, Orange Calcite, Ruby, Sapphire, Sodalite, Spinel, Topaz.
Underworld	Agate, Haematite, Magnetite, Obsidian, Onyx, Smoky Quartz.

Specific Gods

Agwe	Haitian	Shell
Ammon-Ra	Egyptian	Ammonite
Anubis	Egyptian	Moonstone
Apollo	Greek	Amber
Belus	Assyrian	Amazonite
Cupid	Greek	Opal
Dagon	Assyrian	Shell

Daramulun	Aboriginal	Quartz
Ganesha	Indian	Jasper (red)
Great Rainbow Serpent	Aboriginal	Pearl, Quartz
Helios	Greek	Amber, Heliodor
Hermes	Greek	Amethyst, Citrine Quartz, Emerald
Horus	Egyptian	Emerald
Hypnos	Greek	Horn & Ivory
Indra	Indian	Sapphire
Itzcoliuhqui	Aztec	Obsidian
Jupiter	Roman	Sapphire
Lucifer	Roman	Emerald
Mara	Indian	Aquamarine, Beryl
Mars	Roman	Onyx, Sardonyx
Mercury	Roman	Amethyst, Emerald
Neptune	Roman	Amethyst, Aquamarine, Beryl, Shell
Pan	Greek	Jet
Poseidon	Greek	Aquamarine, Beryl, Coral (black), Shell
Ra	Egyptian	Lapis Lazuli, Tiger's Eye, Topaz
Set	Egyptian	Carnelian (red)
Shiva	Indian	Quartz (white), Shell (conch)
Sin	Sumerian	Lapis Lazuli
Surya	Indian	Quartz
Tezcatlipoca	Mayan	Obsidian
Vishnu	Indian	Ammonite
Xiuhtechuhtli	Mexican	Turquoise
Zeus	Greek	Sapphire

356

Appendix 2
Elemental and Planetary Attributions

Elemental Attributions

Air
Agate, Chalcedony, Citrine Quartz, Ivory, Kunzite, Lapis Lazuli, Opal, Rose Quartz, Sapphire, Sodalite, Turquoise.

Fire
Amber, Calcite (Orange), Citrine Quartz, Garnet, Heliotrope, Obsidian, Ruby, Spinel, Topaz.

Water
Amethyst, Aquamarine, Beryl, Chalcedony, Coral, Kyanite, Lapis Lazuli, Moonstone (white and black), Pearl, Prase, Quartz, Tourmaline, Turquoise.

Earth
Amber, Aventurine, Chrysocolla, Emerald, Fluorite, Jadeite, Jet, Magnetite, Malachite, Nephrite, Obsidian, Onyx, Smoky Quartz, Staurolite, Zoisite.

Spirit
Amethyst, Diamond, Kunzite, Jadeite, Labradorite, Opal, Pearl, Sapphire, Tourmaline, Zircon.

Planetary Attributions

Sun
Amber, Calcite (orange), Diamond, Hematite, Topaz, Zircon.

Moon
Chalcedony, Ivory, Moonstone, Pearl, Quartz.

Terra (Earth)
Amber, Aventurine, Chrysocolla, Emerald, Jadeite, Nephrite, Onyx, Staurolite, Zoisite.

Mercury
Agate, Citrine Quartz, Labradorite, Opal.

Venus
Emerald, Jadeite, Malachite, Nephrite, Peridot, Rose Quartz, Zoisite.

Mars
Garnet, Hematite, Heliotrope, Magnetite, Ruby, Spinel.

Jupiter
Lapis Lazuli, Sapphire, Sodalite, Turquoise.

Saturn
Coral, Jet, Obsidian, Onyx, Smoky Quartz.

Uranus
Amethyst, Kunzite, Labradorite, Opal.

Neptune
Aquamarine, Beryl, Coral, Pearl, Prase.

Pluto
Diamond, Jadeite, Kunzite, Zircon

Appendix 3

Gemsong

I have included this poem I wrote and use to give an example of rhyming verses for some of the stones. Chanting such verses whilst using the stones in spells and/or charms can help empower the spell or charm greatly, it is always worth remembering that sound is transmutable energy, and can add greatly to the power of virtually any ritual or spell. You may prefer to write your own verses if you use this technique.

A gate into darkness And charm for safekeeping Still cannot protect Against folly's sad weeping	Agate
Light changes colour Red turns to green Stresses dispersed By raised self-esteem	Alexandrite
Hope Stone quickening With the vigour of Spring Empowering new ventures Is the gift you bring	Amazonite
Solid sunlight >From times long past Stores our energies And holds them fast	Amber

Purple and pleasure
The mystical stone
Guarding and purifying
The spirit and tone

Amethyst

Banded together
Though an octave apart
The forces of magick
Are balanced to start

Ametrine

Curled like a ram's horn
Black and white stone
Brings dreams and memories
Back to be known

Ammonite

The sea's colour captured
In a translucent green
Through its emotions
The Mother is seen

Aquamarine

Named by chance
The stone of good luck
For healing and purity
The balance is struck

Aventurine

For dreaming and skrying
The doors open wide
Seeing a way
To let love inside

Beryl

The Blood of Isis
Unblocks the way
Lighting the path
It keeps evil at bay

Carnelian

The purity of lotus
Made crystal and found
Protection and serenity   Chalcedony
Radiate and abound

Hawk, cat and tiger
All turn their gaze
To the binding power   Chatoyant Stones
Of a chatoyant maze

From the womb of the Earth
To balance and heal
Inspiring to let go   Chrysocolla
And let yourself feel

Cunning and clever
The Mercurial thief
Brings insight and knowledge   Citrine Quartz
To thought and belief

Trees found growing
Beneath flow of sea
Protect from the water   Coral
And people's envy

Transparent brilliance
Scintillating king
Amplifying energy   Diamond
Is the gift you bring

The green of truth
The loving stone
Shattering illusions
May cut to the bone   Emerald

As above, so below
Purple, green and brown
The emotional stone calms   Fluorite
And brings energies down

Fluorite
The dragon's eye
Of blood red fire
Boosts will and body   Garnet
To goals set higher

Thunder eggs cracked
Reveal crystal treasure
Help casting spells   Geodes
And showing true measure

Strengthening will
And giving protection
This stone of overcoming   Heliotrope
Will cut through deception

Healing and balancing
The strength to be sure
For blood and back problems   Hematite
This stone is the cure

The powers of Earth
Most commonly green
Are clearly touched   Jade
In an Emperor's dream

Grounding to earth
And strengthening the senses
The bringer of rain   Jasper
Helps the subtle defences

In dull blackness
Is purity found
The strength of a tree   Jet
Preserved in wet ground

Flashes of colour
Catching the eye
Inspire the will   Labradorite
To transcend any lie

Voice and body of Goddess
From stars to the earth
With the powers of words   Lapis Lazuli
Our desires find new birth

Womb of the Mother
Within and without
Calms the emotions   Malachite
And helps you shed doubt

A stellar green
Expands the mind
Beyond the void   Moldavite
Secrets to find

Luminescence shining
Reflecting the moon
The dance of emotions   Moonstone
Harmonised to Her tune

Shining blackness
From deep earthy fire
Focuses power   Obsidian
And sends it on higher

Though colours may vary
In shade and in tone
For healing and balance   Onyx
Use this earthy stone

Rainbows caught dancing
Between shades of white
Aids in communication   Opal
Through both day and night

Pried from its shell
Sand turned to treasure
The dragon's hoard   Pearl
Brings wisdom and pleasure

To guard the home
Or make a new start
Such green beauty   Peridot
Goes straight to the heart

Focusing and guiding
The universal stone
Beneath a rainbow serpent   Quartz
You are never alone

Calming and healing
The serenity of pink
Unconditional love   Rose Quartz
The lucky shall drink

The arrows of love
Shine a glistening gold
First love your self   Rutile Quartz
All healers are told

Blood red fire
Hardened to tears
The warrior's courage   Ruby
To face all dark fears

Sky and sea seen
In an astral blue
The third eye opens   Sapphire
To a subtler view

An equal armed cross
Shows the Fairy Stone
From the roots of the Earth   Staurolite
Their powers are known

The smoky colour
Clears with a view
Transforming and cleansing   Smoky Quartz
To reform anew

Three lines join
To form a star
You are the centre   Star Stones
Wherever you are

Sparkling glistening
Sun's bright power
Helps growth of will   Sunstone
From seed to flower

For journeys more subtle
And calls to the higher
These black stellar stones   Tektites
Will protect and inspire

Pure will shining
With bright inner fire
The noblest qualities   Topaz
This stone can inspire

Favoured of dreamers
Black turns to green
Bringing the gifts   Tourmaline
Of the witches' Dark Queen

Sacred and guarding
The Horseman's green-blue
Keeps heart and mind focused   Turquoise
On a holistic view

Healing and energising
The power to take charge
When spirit is centred   Zircon
The past may loom large

Appendix 4

Crystals and Time

Attributions to the Hours of the Day and Night

	Hours of the Day		Hours of the Night
1	Zircon	1	Smoky Quartz
2	Emerald	2	Hematite
3	Beryl	3	Malachite
4	Topaz	4	Lapis Lazuli
5	Ruby	5	Turquoise
6	Opal	6	Tourmaline
7	Peridot	7	Sardonyx
8	Amethyst	8	Chalcedony
9	Kunzite	9	Jade
10	Sapphire	10	Jasper
11	Garnet	11	Lodestone
12	Diamond	12	Onyx

Attributions to the Days of the Week

Monday	Moonstone, Pearl, Quartz
Tuesday	Star Sapphire, Red Coral, Ruby, Emerald, Jasper
Wednesday	Star Ruby, Cat's Eye, Amethyst, Magnetite
Thursday	Cat's Eye, Emerald, Sapphire, Carnelian
Friday	Alexandrite, Amethyst, Diamond, Emerald, Cat's Eye
Saturday	Labradorite, Sapphire, Turquoise, Diamond
Sunday	Sunstone, Ruby, Topaz, Diamond

Attributions to the Months of the Year

	Arabic	Hindu	Jewish
January	Garnet	Serpentine	Garnet
February	Amethyst	Moonstone	Amethyst
March	Heliotrope	Gold Lingam	Jasper
April	Sapphire	Diamond	Sapphire
May	Emerald	Emerald	Chalcedony, Carnelian, Agate
June	Agate, Pearl, Chalcedony	Pearl	Emerald
July	Carnelian	Sapphire	Onyx
August	Sardonyx	Ruby	Carnelian
September	Peridot	Zircon	Peridot
October	Aquamarine	Coral	Aquamarine
November	Topaz	Cat's Eye	Topaz
December	Ruby	Topazq	Ruby

	Italian	Polish	Russian
January	Zircon, Garnet	Garnet	Garnet, Zircon
February	Amethyst	Amethyst	Amethyst
March	Jasper	Heliotrope	Jasper
April	Sapphire	Diamond	Sapphire
May	Agate	Emerald	Emerald
June	Emerald	Agate, Chalcedony	Agate Chalcedony
July	Onyx	Ruby	Ruby, Sardonyx
August	Carnelian	Sardonyx	Alexandrite
September	Peridot	Sardonyx	Peridot
October	Beryl	Aquamarine	Beryl
November	Topaz	Topaz	Topaz
December	Ruby	Turquoise	Chrysoprase, Turquoise

	Roman	Isidore, Bishop of Seville	15th - 20th Century
January	Garnet	Zircon	Garnet
February	Amethyst	Amethyst	Amethyst, Pearl, Zircon
March	Heliotrope	Jasper	Heliotrope, Jasper
April	Sapphire	Sapphire	Diamond, Sapphire
May	Agate	Agate	Agate, Emerald
June	Emerald	Emerald	Agate, Cat's Eye, Turquoise
July	Onyx	Onyx	Onyx, Turquoise
August	Carnelian	Carnelian	Carnelian, Moonstone, Topaz, Sardonyx,
September	Sardonyx	Peridot	Peridot
October	Aquamarine	Aquamarine	Beryl, Opal
November	Topaz	Topaz	Pearl, Topaz
December	Ruby	Ruby	Heliotrope, Ruby

Attributions to the Seasons of the Year

Spring	Summer	Autumn	Winter
Emerald	Ruby	Sapphire	Diamond
Amethyst	Alexandrite	Cairngorm	Labradorite
Chrysoberyl	Garnet	Peridot	Moonstone
Diamond (green)	Opal (fire)	Sapphire (brown)	Pearl
Peridot	Spinel Ruby	Topaz	Quartz
Spinel Ruby	Topaz (pink)	Tourmaline	Sapphire (white)
Topaz (pink)	Zircon	Zircon	Turquoise

Appendix 5

List of Essential Oil Attributions

Essential Oils by Elemental and Planetary Attribution:

Air	Benzoin, Eucalyptus, Lavender, Pine
Fire	Basil, Cinnamon, Frankincense, Ginger, Hyssop, Juniper, Rosemary
Water	Camphor, Eucalyptus, Geranium, Jasmine, Myrrh, Sandalwood, Ylang Ylang
Earth	Cedar, Myrrh, Patchouli, Pine, Vetivert
Spirit	Frankincense, Lotus
Sun	Cedar, Chamomile, Cinnamon, Frankincense, Ginger, Juniper, Rosemary
Mercury	Benzoin, Caraway, Cedar, Eucalyptus, Lavender, Lemon, Sandalwood
Venus	Benzoin, Geranium, Lavender, Lemon, Pennyroyal, Peppermint, Pine, Rose, Sandalwood, Ylang Ylang
Moon	Aniseed, Camphor, Eucalyptus, Jasmine, Lavender, Myrrh, Pennyroyal, Rose, Sandalwood, Ylang Ylang

Terra	Patchouli, Pine, Vetivert
Mars	Basil, Benzoin, Ginger, Hyssop, Juniper, Pine
Jupiter	Cedar, Hyssop, Myrrh, Sandalwood
Saturn	Camphor, Lavender, Myrrh
Uranus	Cinnamon, Clove
Neptune	Lemon
Pluto	Patchouli

Further Information on the Uses of Oils

Aniseed
Moon. Protects against disturbing dreams, harmonises physical and spiritual bodies.

Basil
Mars, Fire. Gives (spiritual) courage and determination, sharpness. Steadies one for initiation and against fears associated with spiritual growth and the unknown. Used to attract money. A funerary scent.

Benzoin
Mars, Mercury, Venus, Air. Spiritual journeys and transitions, removes blockages to growth. Assists concentration and meditation, instils calm. Helps in grounding and curing selfishness. Works well on throat chakra.

Camphor
Moon, Saturn, Water. Good for self-purification. Works on sacral and third eye chakras.

Caraway
Mercury. Consecration, retaining things.

Cedarwood
Jupiter, Mercury, Sun, Earth. Preserves identity, helps in journeys to unknown places. Recommended for consecrating wands. Works well on base chakra

Chamomile
Sun. For success and protection. Encourages dreaming.

Cinnamon
Sun, Uranus, Fire. Increases concentration and aids communication and prophecy. Protects from the jealousy and envy of others. Helps bring an understanding of eternity. Works on solar plexus chakra.

Clove
Uranus. Promotes kinship and amiability. Increases psychic ability and ability to perceive the astral.

Eucalyptus
Mercury, Moon, Air, Water. Used for healing, purification and protection.

Frankincense
Sun, Spirit, Fire. For protection and purification. Teaches discipline - restrains pride and self-indulgence. Heightens awareness and focuses the mind. Works on heart, throat and third eye chakras.

Geranium
Venus, Water. Sexual balance and fulfilment. Used for happiness and control over our lives.

Ginger
Mars, Sun, Fire. Helps with energy, confidence, courage, will. Works well on solar plexus chakra.

Hyssop
Jupiter, Mars, Fire. Protection and purification, cleans the aura.

Jasmine
Moon, Water. Stimulates creativity and fertility, enhances feelings of love and is very uplifting. Works on the heart chakra.

Juniper
Mars, Sun, Fire. Helps give up bad habits and maintain good ones - purificatory works. Said to protect against curses and theft. Used for psychic protection.

Lavender
Mercury, Moon, Saturn, Venus, Air. Stability, promotes inner calm and peace of mind. Dispels depression, helps attract wealth. Used to bless homes. Works on the heart and third eye chakras.

Lemon
Venus, Mercury, Neptune. Mental clarity and decisiveness. Attracts love, good for emotional stress and lack of humour.

Lotus
Spirit. Purity. Spiritual awakening. Works on the crown chakra.

Myrrh
Jupiter, Saturn, Moon, Earth, Water. Promotes spirituality. Brings peace and gives ease to sorrow.

Patchouli
Terra, Pluto, Earth. Attracts love, and releases anxieties over sex. Often used in wealth magick.

Pennyroyal
Moon, Venus. Repels negative thoughts, strengthens astral body, eases mental confusion. Note never work with Pennyroyal when you are pregnant as it is an abortificant.

Peppermint
Venus. Awakens the conscious mind, helps dispel negative thoughts. Good for self-purification. Brings dreams of prophecy.

Pine
Mars, Terra, Venus, Air, Earth. A herb of immortality. Energy, healing and purification.

Rose
Moon, Venus. Attracts love, helps maintain trust, calms strife.

Rosemary
Sun, Fire. Protection against bad dreams, purification, fortification against illness, improves memory.

Sandalwood
Jupiter, Mercury, Moon, Venus, Water. Used to calm the mind and for meditation and divination. Good to attract success. Works on the base chakra.

Vetivert
Terra, Earth. Used for wealth and connecting to the earth. Works on the base chakra.

Ylang Ylang

Moon, Venus, Water. Brings peace. Used for love and as an aphrodisiac. Works on sacral chakra.

Appendix 6

The Abra-Melin Squares Concerning Crystals & Treasures

The following Magic Name Squares relating to locating unguarded metals, jewels and gemstones are to be found in the classic medieval magickal text The Sacred Magic of Abra-Melin the Mage. To use the squares, one needs to have performed the intense six month devotional retreat which is detailed in the book, but I have included them here for their curiosity value. I would strongly discourage people from using them without having worked through all the accompanying practices and devotions.

For Jewels:

B	E	L	I	A	L
E	B	O	R	U	A
L	O	V	A	R	I
I	R	A	V	O	L
A	V	R	O	B	E
L	A	I	L	E	B

For Stolen Jewels:

K	I	X	A	L	I	S
I	R	I	N	E	Q	I
X						
A						
L				M		
I	Q					
S						K

For Balasius Rubies:

H	E	T	I	S	E	R
E						
T						
I						
S						
E	C	I	N	E	S	E
R						H

For Diamonds:

B	I	C	E	L	O	N
I	R	O	L	A	T	O
C	O	R	A	M	A	L
E	L	A	M	A	L	E
L	A	M	A	R	O	C
O	T	A	L	O	R	I
N	O	C	E	L	I	B

For Emeralds:

A	S	T	A	R	O	T
S	A	L	I	S	T	O
T	L	A	N	B	S	R
A	I	N	O	N	I	A
R	S	B	N	A	L	T
O	T	S	I	L	A	S
T	O	R	A	T	S	A

For Pearls:

I	A	N	A
A	M	E	N
N	E	M	A
A	N	A	I

For Rubies:

S	E	G	O	R
E				
G				
O				E
R			B	S

For Great Treasure:

S	E	G	I	L	A	H
E	R	A	L	I	P	A
G						
I	L	E	N	L	I	
L						
A						
H						

For Small Treasure:

N	E	C	O	T
E				
C				
O				
T				N

For Unguarded Treasure:

M	A	G	A	T
A	R	A	T	O
G	A	L	A	G
O	T	A	R	A
T	O	G	A	M

For a Treasure Hidden by a Particular Person:

K	E	R	M	A
E				
R				
M				
A				K

For Diverse Visions in Mirrors of Glass & Crystal:

	I	L	I	O	N	I	N
I							
L							
I							
O							
N							
I							
N							

(Top-left cell: **G**)

For Diverse Visions in Rings & Crystals:

B	E	D	S	E	R
E	L	I	E	L	E
D	I	A	P	I	S
S	E	P	P	E	D
E	L	I	E	L	E
R	E	S	D	E	B

Appendix 7

Christian Consecration of Crystals

Considering the Canon which forbade the use of amulets from the Council of Laodicea in 355 CE, it is interesting to find by the Middle Ages there is a Christian ritual for reconsecrating gems recorded in more than one source (Le Grand Lapidaire by Jean de Mandeville and Buch der Natur by Konrad of Megenburg), which by its nature emphasises the talismanic use of gems by the rich and powerful, and indeed the Church. The gems were wrapped in a perfectly clean linen cloth and placed on the altar. Three masses were said over the gems, and during the third mass the priest said the following benediction:

The Lord be with us. And with thy spirit. Let us pray. Almighty God and Father, who manifested Thy virtue to Elias by certain senseless creatures, who orderest Moses, Thy servant, that, among the sacerdotal vestments, he should adorn the Rational of Judgement with twelve precious stones, and showedst to John, the evangelist, the famous city of Jerusalem, essentially constituted by the same stones, and who hadst the power to raise up sons to Abraham from stones, we humbly beseech Thy majesty since Thou hast elected one of the stones to be a dwelling-place for the majesty of Thy heart, that Thou wilt deign to bless and sanctify these stones by the sanctification and incarnation of Thy name, so that they may be sanctified, blessed, and consecrated, and may receive from Thee the effect of the virtues Thou hast granted to them, according to their kinds, and which the experience of the learned has shown to have been given by Thee; so that whoever may wear them on him may feel the presence of Thy power and may be worthy of Thy grace and the protection of Thy power. Through Jesus Christ, Thy Son, in whom dwells all sanctification, benediction, and consecration; who lives with Thee and reigns as God for all eternity, Amen. Thanks be to God.

The use of this benediction does not seem so curious when we recall the old belief that gems could lose some or all of their powers if they were touched or even looked at by impure sinners. Some even declared that gems had been corrupted by Adam's original sin, so they needed to be blessed and consecrated to make them handleable so they would not continue to transmit this "sin".

Glossary

Alloy: A mixture of metals.

Amorphous: Means "Without form", and refers to materials which have no definite internal structure, i.e. which are not crystals.

Assembled Stone: A stone comprised of two or three pieces (doublet or triplet), usually including glass and done as a means of fraud.

Asterism: Refers to the four, six or twelve rayed star seen in certain stones if cut correctly. Generally in corundum's (i.e. ruby and sapphire), sometimes in rose quartz, and occasionally in garnets and spinels. Stones with an asterism in are generally known as Star Stones, hence Star Ruby and Star Sapphire.

Axis: Direction in a crystal.

Base Metal: A common metal, excluding iron.

Bolide: A bright meteor.

Brass: An alloy of copper and zinc.

Brazil Twin: Name given to a twin quartz crystal.

Brilliance: The reflection of light in a gemstone. The greater the reflection, the greater the brilliance.

Bronze: An alloy of copper, tin and zinc.

Butterfly Twin: Name given to a twin quartz crystal. See also Brazil Twin.

Cabochon: A style of cutting stones, with a dome shaped top.

Cameo: A crystal cut in relief with an image.

Caput Draconis: "Head of the Dragon" - the old term for the Moon's North Node in astrology.

Carat: Refers to the weight of a gemstone, one carat (abbreviation ct) being 200mg (milligrams) = 0.2g. When spelt with a "k", karat refers to the purity of gold. Pure gold is 24 carats.

Carbuncle: Any bright red gem quality stone with a cabochon cut.

Cauda Draconis: "Tail of the Dragon" - the old term for the Moon's South Node in astrology.

Cavestone: A name for stalactites and stalagmites.

Chatoyant: Or "cat's-eye effect", a wavy changeable band of light reflected from the surface of the crystal, at right angles to the direction of the fibres. Best demonstrated when stones are cut en cabochon. Seen in Cat's Eye, Hawk's Eye and Tiger's Eye, also observed in chrysoberyl, quartz and tourmaline.

Cleavage: The breakage of a mineral in definite directions along smooth surfaces, or a rock into rough slabs.

Composite Gem: A gem consisting of several parts put together.

Conchiolin: The organic substance in the shell of the pearl mollusk.

Face: The flat, outer surface of a crystal.

Facet: The flat, outer surface of a cut and polished gemstone.

Fire: The way in which light splits into the rainbow colours when passing through a stone.

Gel: A liquid or solid compound which has fine particles of a substance diffused through another.

Gem: Or gemstone, a mineral that has been fashioned into a specific shape, valued for its rarity and/or beauty.

Geode: A crystal lined cavity found in a rock.

Ghost Crystal: Also known as Phantom, Spectre or Shadow Crystal, this is where one or more crystals appear to be contained within the main crystal, an effect caused by interrupted growth of the crystal.

Group: A collection of minerals sharing the same crystal structure.

Hallmark: The mark put on gold and silver jewellery by a jeweller to indicate the details required by law, such as who made the item, and the purity of the metal. The old system of karats has now been replaced in hallmarks by a three digit number indicating the purity, hence 9 karat gold, which is 37.5% gold, is 375. Likewise 18 karat is 75% gold and indicated by the number 750.

Hardness: The power of a substance to resist abrasion or scratching when another substance is drawn across it (a substance will be scratched by a substance with a higher hardness). Mineral hardness is measured on a decimal scale known as the Mohs Scale, 10 being diamond and 1 being talc. The difference between units on this scale is not equal, diamond being 120 times harder than ruby (hardness 9) but 4 million times harder than talc.

Substance	Hardness
Talc	1
Gypsum	2
Calcite	3
Fluorite	4
Apatite	5
Feldspar	6
Quartz	7
Topaz	8
Corundum	9
Diamond	10

Inclusion: Refers to impurities in a stone. These may be other stones, like rutile in rutile quartz, or liquids or gases trapped in a stone, or dead creatures as may be found in amber.

Iridescence: The prismatic colour effect seen in flaws and cracks in a stone, as in Rainbow Quartz.

Labradorescence: The play of colour seen in labradorite.

Lamellar: Thin layers of plates or scales (laminae) which when catching the light in a certain way, produce a sheen effect, as in labradorescence.

Life: Another name for Brilliance.

Matrix: Also known as Mother Rock. A mass of rocks in which crystals and minerals are found.

Microcrystalline: Crystals so small they are only visible under a microscope.

Mineral: A naturally occurring inorganic material of fixed composition and structure.

Navratna: An Indian amulet with nine gems on, comprising amethyst, cat's eye, coral, diamond, emerald, pearl, ruby, sapphire and topaz.

Opalescence: The reflection of a pearl or milky light from the interior of a stone.

Organic Gem: Any gem originally formed of living animal or plant material.

Pancharatna: An Indian five jewel amulet, comprising amethyst, diamond, emerald, gold and pearl.

Phantom Crystal: See Ghost Crystal.

Pizoelectric: Developing a measurable electric charge when squeezed, and changing shape when a charge is placed on it. This phenomenon is used with quartz and other pizoelectric materials to control the frequency of radio broadcasting and other electronic devices.

Rough: The natural, uncut state of a gemstone or mineral.

Sandwich Stone: Jeweller's term for a doublet or triplet. See Composite.

Sigil: A pictograph usually representing a magickal intent or entity.

Twin: An intergrowth of two crystals forming a visually spectacular twinned crystal.

Variety: A name for a specific quality or colour of a gemstone, such as ruby and sapphire for red and blue corundum.

Bibliography

Agrippa, Henry Cornelius   *Three Books of Occult Philosophy*
Llewellyn, Minnesota, 1998.

Alderman, Clifford Lindsey   *Symbols of Magic: Amulets and Talismans*
Julian Messner, New York, 1977.

Andrews, Carol   *Amulets of Ancient Egypt*
British Museum Press, London, 1994.
Ancient Egyptian Jewellery
British Museum Press, London, 1990.

Anon   *Tracts on Alchemy*
Mss, S1. 836., British Museum, London, 1650

Anon   *Signa Lapidum pretiosorum (et) Elementorum signa*
Mss, S1. 89., British Museum, London, C17th

Ashley, Leonard R.N.   *The Complete Book of Superstition, Prophecy and Luck*
Robson Books, London, 1984

Aveni, Anthony   *Behind the Crystal Ball: Magic and Science from Antiquity to the New Age*
Newleaf, London, 1996

Bannerman-Phillips, E. Iuya   *Amulets and Birthstones: Their Astrological Significance*
Llewellyn, Los Angeles, 1950.

Barrett, F   *The Magus, or Celestial Intelligencer*
The Citadel Press, New Jersey, 1967.

Beard, Charles R.   *Luck and Talismans*
Sampson Low, Marston & Co. Ltd, London, Undated

Becker, Robert O. & Selden, Gary   *The Body Electric*
William Morrow, 1986.

Berthelot, M.P.E.   *Les Origines de L'Alchimie*
1885.

Best, Michael R. & Brightman, Frank H.   *The Book of Secrets of Albertus Magnus*
Oxford University Press, London, 1974.

Borner, R.	*Minerals, Rocks and Gemstones* Oliver and Boyd, Edinburgh, 1966.
Brandon-Jones, David	*Practical Palmistry* Rider & Company, London, 1981.
Briard, Jacques	*The Bronze Age in Barbarian Europe - From the Megaliths to the Celts.* Book Club Associates, London, 1979.
Brusatin, Manlio	*A History of Colors* Shambhala, London, 1991.
Bryant, Page	*Crystals and Their Uses* Sun Books, Sante Fe, USA, 1984.
Budge, E.A. Wallis	*Amulets and Superstitions* Dover, London, 1930. *Amulets and Talismans* University Books, New York, 1968. *The Mummy* Wings Books, New Jersey, 1989.
Campbell, Joseph	*The Masks of God: Primitive Mythology* Viking, New York, 1959
Ed. Carmichael, David L., & Hubert, Jane & Reeves Brian & Schanche, Audhild	*Sacred Sites, Sacred Places* Routledge, Londom, 1994.
Cook, David & Kirk, Wendy	*Field Guide to the Rocks & Minerals of the World* Kingfisher Publications plc, London, 1991.
Cooper, J.C.	*Brewer's Myth and Legend* Cassell Publishers Ltd., London, 1992.
Crollius, O.	*De Signaturis, seu vera et viva Anatomia Majoris et Minoris Mundi* 1612.
Crow, W.B.	*Precious Stones: Their Occult Power & Hidden Signficance* The Aquarian Press, London, 1968.
Crowley, Aleister	*Magick* Routledge & Kegan Paul, London, 1973.
Crowley, Aleister	*777 and Other Qabalistic Writings* Samuel Weiser Inc., Maine, 1983.

Czaja, Michael	*Gods of Myth and Stone: Phallicism in Japanese Folk Religion* John Weatherhill Inc., New York, 1974.
da Cuba, Johannis	*Hortus Sanitatis* Jean Pryss, Strassburg, 1483.
Dake, H.C., Fleener, Frank L. & Ben Hur Wilson	*Quartz Family Members* McGraw Hill, New York, 1938.
Deaver, Korra	*Rock Crystal* Samuel Weiser, Maine, USA, 1985.
DeLys, Claudia	*The Giant Book of Superstitions* Citadel Press, New Jersey, 1979.
Desaulets, Paul E	*The Gem Kingdom* MacDonald & Co, London, 1971.
Devereux, Paul, Steele, John & Kubrin, David	*Earthmind: Communicating with the Living World of Gaia* Destiny Books, Vermont, 1989
Diderot & d'Alembert	*Encyclopedie. Recueil de Planches, sur les Sciences Et les Arts (Chimie)* 1763.
Douglas, Nik	*Tibetan Tantric Charms & Amulets* Dover Publications Inc., New York, 1978.
Eliade, Mercia	*A History of Religious Ideas* Collins, London, 1979 *Shamanism, Archaic Techniques of Ecstasy* Princeton University Press, New Jersey, 1964.
Ellis, Clarence	*The Pebbles On The Beach* Faber & Faber Ltd, London, 1965.
Evans, Joan	*Magical Jewels of the Middle Ages and the Renaissance* Dover Publications, New York, 1977.
Ferguson, George	*Signs & Symbols in Christian Art* Oxford University Press, Oxford, 1954.
Fielding, William T.	*Strange Superstitions & Magical Practices* Blakiston, New York, 1943.
Fortune, Dion	*Moon Magic* Weiser, New York, 1985.

Francklyn, J. (previous owner)	*Explanation of Chymical Signs* Mss., S1. 2792, British Museum, London, 1627.
Fraser, J.T.	*Time - The Familiar Stranger* Tempus, 1987.
Frazer, J.G.	*The Golden Bough* Hazell, Watson & Viney Ltd, Slough, 1922.
Geddes & Grossett	*Dictionary of the Occult* Geddes & Grossett Ltd, New Lanark, 1997.
Gessmann, G.W.	*Die Geheimsymbole der Alchymie, Arzkunde und Astrologie des Mittelalters* 1906.
Gettings, Fred	*Dictionary of Occult, Hermetic and Alchemical Sigils* Routledge & Kegan Paul Ltd, London, 1981.
Griffith, F.L. & Thompson, Herbert	*The Leyden Papyrus: An Egyptian Magical Book* Dover Publications Inc., New York, 1974.
Hadingham, Evan	*Secrets of the Ice Age: The World of the Cave Artists* Book Club Associates, Norfolk, 1980.
Harner, Michael	*The Way of the Shaman* Harper, San Francisco, 1990.
Hastings, James (ed.)	*Encyclopedia of Religion and Ethics* (13 vols.) T & T Clark, Edinburgh, 1937.
Harvey, Anne	*Jewels* Putnam's, New York, 1981.
Hodges, Doris M.	*Healing Stones* Perry: Pyramid Publishers, Iowa, 1961.
Howes, Michael	*Amulets* Robert Hale & Co., London, 1975.
Hughes, J. Donald	*American Indian Ecology* Texas Western Press, Texas, 1983
Hunger, Rosa	*The Magic of Amber* N.A.G.Press Ltd, London, 1977.
Husymans, J.K.	*Là-Bas* Dover, New York, 1972.

Hutton, Ronald	*The Pagan Religions of the Ancient British Isles* Blackwell Publishers Ltd, Oxford, 1991.
Isaacs, Thelma	*Gemstones, Crystals and Healing* Lorien House, New Columbia, No date.
Jobes, Gertrude	*Dictionary of Mythology, Folklore & Symbols* Scarecrow Press, New York, 1962.
Joseph, Isya	*Devil Woirship: The Sacred Books and Traditions of the Yezidiz* The Gorham Press, Boston USA, 1919.
Kapoor, Gouri Shanker	*Gems and Astrology: A Guide to Health, Happiness and Prosperity* Ranjan Publications, New Delhi, 1985.
Kieckhefer, Richard	*Magic in the Middle Ages* University Press, Cambridge, 1989.
King	Natural History of Precious Stones London, 1865.
King, Francis X.	*The Encyclopedia of Fortune-Telling* Octopus Books, London, 1988.
Knappert, Jan	*Pacific Mythology* Aquarian Press, London, 1992.
Koch, R.	*The Book of Signs* 1930.
Kourimsk˝, Dr J.	*The Illustrated Encyclopaedia Of Minerals And Rocks* The Promotional Reprint Co. Ltd, London, 1992.
Kozminsky, Isidore	*The Magic and Science of Jewels and Stones, Vols. I & II* Cassandra Press, California, 1988.
Kunz, George Frederick	*The Curious Lore Of Precious Stones* Dover Publications Inc., London, 1971. *The Magic of Jewels and Charms* Lippincott, Philadelphia, 1915. *Gems & Precious Stones of North America* Dover, New York, 1968.

Kyte, Geoffrey	*The Mystical Crystal* C.W. Daniel Company Limited, Saffron Walden, 1993.
Leach, Maria (ed.)	*Standard Dictionary of Folkore,* *Mythology & Legend* Funk & Wagnalls, New York, 1950.
Leechman, Frank	*The Opal Book* Ure Smith, Sydney, 1978.
LeGrand, Jacques	*Diamonds: Myth, Magic, and Reality* Crown, New York, 1980.
Leland, C.G. M. & D. Pazzaglini (trans)	*Aradia or The Gospel of the Witches* Phoenix Publishing Inc., Washington, 1998.
Leonardi, Camilli	*Speculum Lapidum* Venetia, 1502.
Lucretius (Trans. J.S. Watson)	*On the Nature of Things* George Bell & Sons, London, 1901.
McNeill, F. Marion	*The Silver Bough* Canongate Publishing, London, 1956.
Martin, G.T.	*Scarabs, Cylinders and other Ancient* *Egyptian Seals* Warminster, 1985.
Mathers, S.L. MacGregor (trans)	*The Key of Solomon the King* (Clavicula Salomonis) Samuel Weiser Inc., Maine, 1972
(trans)	*The Sacred Magic of Abra-Melin the* *Mage* Aquarian, Surrey, 1976
Melton, Robert	*Voodoo Charms & Talismans* Original Publications, New York, 1997.
Merrifield, Ralph	*The Archaeology Of Ritual And Magic* Guild Publishing, London, 1987.
Miller, Mary & Taube, Karl	*The Gods & Symbols Of Ancient* *Mexico & The Maya* Thames & Hudson Ltd, London, 1993.
Miller, Richard Alan	*The Magical and Ritual Use of* *Aphrodisiacs* Destiny Books, Vermont, 1985.
Muller, Helen	*Jet* Butterworths, London, 1987.
Newman, Harold	*An Illustrated Dictionary of Jewelry* Thames & Hudson, London, 1987.

Ogden, Jack	*Jewelry of the Ancient World* Rizzoli, New York, 1982.
Onomasticum	*Hermeneia, Das ist ein Onomasticum, Interpretatio odor erklerunge* Thurneyssers zum Thum, 1574.
Pavitt, W. & K.	*Book of Talismans, Amulets & Zodiacal Gems* Hollywood, Wiltshire, 1970.
Pearl, Richard M.	*Rocks and Minerals* Barnes & Noble Inc., New York, 1956.
Petrie, W.M.F.	*Amulets* London, 1914.
Pliny the Elder (Caius Plinius Secundus)	*Natural History (Historia Naturalis)* Harvard University Press, Cambridge, 1956.
Radford, E. & M.A.	*Encyclopaedia of Superstitions* Rider, London, 1947.
Rainbird, Ariadne & Rankine, David	*Magick Without Peers: A Course In Progressive Witchcraft For The Solitary Practitioner* Capall Bann, Chievely, 1997.
Rankine, David	*Magickal Dictionary Of Symbols* Unpublished, Private Papers, 1985-86.
Rankine, David	*On Jade Magick* Unpublished, Monograph, 1986.
Rawson, Philip	*Erotic Art of the East* Putnam, New York, 1968.
Saunders, Nicholas J.	*People of the Jaguar* Souvenir Press, London, 1989
Schumann, Walter	*Gemstones of the World* Sterling, New York, 1977.
Schmidt, Phillip	*Superstition and Magic* Newman Press, Westminster, 1963.
Seidler, N.	*Gems and Jewellery* Odyssey Library, 1964.
Seligmann, Kurt	*Magic, Supernaturalism and Religion* Pantheon, New York, 1948
Shah, Idries	*The Secret Lore of Magic* Citadel, New York, 1970.
Shah, S.T. Ali	*Occultism, It's Theory and Practice* Dorset, New York, 1969

Sheldrake, Rupert	*A New Science of Life* Paladin Books, London, 1987.
Shelton, Robert	*Collection of Medical Observations,* *Tables of Sigils and Alchemical* *Receipts* Mss., S1. 997., British Museum, London, C17th.
Shepherd, W.	*Shepherd's Glossary of Graphic Signs* *and Symbols* 1971.
Simpson, Jacqueline & Roud, Steve	*A Dictionary of English Folklore* Oxford University Press, Oxford, 2000.
Sinkankas, John	*Emerald and Other Beryls* Chilton, Radnor, 1981.
Sofianides, Anna S. & Harlow, George E.	*Gems & Crystals* Parkgate Books Ltd, London, 1990.
Sommerhoff, J.C.S.	*Lexicon Pharmaceutico-Chymicum* 1701.
Spence, Lewis	*The Encylocpedia of the Occult* Bracken Books, London, 1988
Steiner, Stan	*The Vanishing White Man* Harper & Row, London, 1976
Stewart, C. Nelson	*Gem Stones of the Seven Rays* Adyar, Madras, 1939.
Stutley, Margaret	*Ancient Indian Magic and Folklore* Routledge & Kegan Paul Ltd, Henley- on-Thames, 1980.
Sumner, William Graham	*Folkways and Mores* Schocken Books, New York, 1979.
Tait, Hugh	*Jewelry: 7,000 Years* Harry N. Abrams, New York, 1986.
Talent, J.	*Minerals, Rocks and Gems* Tri-Ocean, San Francisco, 1970.
Thompson, R. Campbell	*Semitic Magic: Its Origins and* *Development* Samuel Weiser Inc., New York, 2000.
Thomson, H.A.	*A Legend of Gems and Strange* *Beliefs Which the Astrological* *Birthstones have Collected Through* *the Ages* Graphic Press, Los Angeles, 1937.

Thorndyke, Lynn

Thurneyssers &
Thum

Tortora, Gerard J. &
Anagnostakos, Nicholas
Trigg, Elwood B.

Uyldert, Mellie

Vinci, Leo

Von Bingen, Hildegard
(trans. Priscilla Throop)
Walker, Dael

Walters, Raymond J.L.

Waring, Philippa

Watkins, Alfred

Webster, Robert

Wilkinson, Richard H.

Wright, Mick

Worldige, J.

*Traditional Medieval Texts
Concerning Engraved Astrological
Images*
Mélanges August Pelzer, Louvain
Bibliothèque de L'Universite, 1947.
*Hermeneia, Das ist ein
Onomasticum, Interpretatio
odor erklerunge* 1574.
Principles of Anatomy and Physiology
Harper & Row, New York, 1987.
Gypsy Demons and Divinities
Citadel Press, New Jersey, 1973.
The Magic of Precious Stones
Turnstone Press, Wellingborough,
1981.
*Gmicalzoma - An Enochian
Dictionary*
Neptune Press, London, 1992.
Physica
Healing Arts Press, Vermont, 1998.
The Crystal Book
Sunol, California, USA, 1983.
The Power of Gemstones
Carlton Books Limited, London,
1996.
*A Dictionary of Omens and
Superstitions*
Souvenir Press Ltd, London, 1978.
The Old Straight Track
Abacus, London, 1974.
Gemmologists' Compendium
N.A.G. Press Ltd, London, 1979.
Symbol & Magic in Egyptian Art
Thames & Hudson Ltd, London,
1994.
*Treasures Of The Earth: The
Minerals & Gemstones Collection*
Orbis Publishing Limited, London,
1996-98.
*A Table of Chymical and
Philosophical Characters*,
Dated 1651, bound into 1671 edition
of "Last Will And Testament" by R
Valentine 1651.

Zolar   *Zolar's Encyclopaedia of Omens,*
                                Signs & Superstitions
                                Simon & Schuster Ltd, London, 1989.

If you have enjoyed this book and wish to contact the author, please either write to:

David Rankine, BM Avalonia, London WC1N 3XX

or visit www.avalonia.co.uk

FREE DETAILED CATALOGUE

Capall Bann is owned and run by people actively involved in many of the areas in which we publish. A detailed illustrated catalogue is available on request, SAE or International Postal Coupon appreciated. **Titles can be ordered direct from Capall Bann, post free in the UK** (cheque or PO with order) or from good bookshops and specialist outlets.

Do contact us for details on the latest releases at: **Capall Bann Publishing, Auton Farm, Milverton, Somerset, TA4 1NE.** Titles include:

Angels and Goddesses - Celtic Christianity & Paganism, M. Howard
Arthur - The Legend Unveiled, C Johnson & E Lung
Astrology The Inner Eye - A Guide in Everyday Language, E Smith
Auguries and Omens - The Magical Lore of Birds, Yvonne Aburrow
Asyniur - Womens Mysteries in the Northern Tradition, S McGrath
Beginnings - Geomancy, Builder's Rites & Electional Astrology in the
    European Tradition, Nigel Pennick
Between Earth and Sky, Julia Day
Caer Sidhe - Celtic Astrology and Astronomy, Vol 1, Michael Bayley
Call of the Horned Piper, Nigel Jackson
Cat's Company, Ann Walker
Celtic Faery Shamanism, Catrin James
Celtic Faery Shamanism - The Wisdom of the Otherworld, Catrin James
Celtic Lore & Druidic Ritual, Rhiannon Ryall
Celtic Sacrifice - Pre Christian Ritual & Religion, Marion Pearce
Compleat Vampyre - The Vampyre Shaman, Nigel Jackson
Creating Form From the Mist - The Wisdom of Women in Celtic Myth and
    Culture, Lynne Sinclair-Wood
Crystal Clear - A Guide to Quartz Crystal, Jennifer Dent
Crystal Doorways, Simon & Sue Lilly
Crossing the Borderlines - Guising, Masking & Ritual Animal Disguise in the
    European Tradition, Nigel Pennick
Dragons of the West, Nigel Pennick
Earth Dance - A Year of Pagan Rituals, Jan Brodie
Earth Harmony - Places of Power, Holiness & Healing, Nigel Pennick
Earth Magic, Margaret McArthur
Eildon Tree (The) Romany Language & Lore, Michael Hoadley
Enchanted Forest - The Magical Lore of Trees, Yvonne Aburrow
Eternal Priestess, Sage Weston
Everything You Always Wanted To Know About Your Body, But So Far
    Nobody's Been Able To Tell You, Chris Thomas & D Baker

399

Face of the Deep - Healing Body & Soul, Penny Allen
Fairies in the Irish Tradition, Molly Gowen
Familiars - Animal Powers of Britain, Anna Franklin
Fool's First Steps, (The) Chris Thomas
Forest Paths - Tree Divination, Brian Harrison, Ill. S. Rouse
God Year, The, Nigel Pennick & Helen Field
Goddess on the Cross, Dr George Young
Goddess Year, The, Nigel Pennick & Helen Field
Handbook For Pagan Healers, Liz Joan
Handbook of Fairies, Ronan Coghlan
Healing Book, The, Chris Thomas and Diane Baker
Healing Homes, Jennifer Dent
Healing Journeys, Paul Williamson
Healing Stones, Sue Philips
Herb Craft - Shamanic & Ritual Use of Herbs, Lavender & Franklin
Hidden Heritage - Exploring Ancient Essex, Terry Johnson
Hub of the Wheel, Skytoucher
In Search of Herne the Hunter, Eric Fitch
Inner Celtia, Alan Richardson & David Annwn
Inner Mysteries of the Goths, Nigel Pennick
Legend of Robin Hood, The, Richard Rutherford-Moore
Lid Off the Cauldron, Patricia Crowther
Light From the Shadows - Modern Traditional Witchcraft, Gwyn
Lore of the Sacred Horse, Marion Davies
Lost Lands & Sunken Cities (2nd ed.), Nigel Pennick
Magic of Herbs - A Complete Home Herbal, Rhiannon Ryall
Magical Guardians - Exploring the Spirit and Nature of Trees, Philip Heselton
Magical History of the Horse, Janet Farrar & Virginia Russell
Magical Lore of Animals, Yvonne Aburrow
Magical Lore of Cats, Marion Davies
Magical Lore of Herbs, Marion Davies
Magick Without Peers, Ariadne Rainbird & David Rankine
Masks of Misrule - Horned God & His Cult in Europe, Nigel Jackson
Mirrors of Magic - Evoking the Spirit of the Dewponds, P Heselton
Moon Mysteries, Jan Brodie
Mysteries of the Runes, Michael Howard
Mystic Life of Animals, Ann Walker
New Celtic Oracle The, Nigel Pennick & Nigel Jackson
Oracle of Geomancy, Nigel Pennick
Pagan Feasts - Seasonal Food for the 8 Festivals, Franklin & Phillips
Patchwork of Magic - Living in a Pagan World, Julia Day
Pathworking - A Practical Book of Guided Meditations, Pete Jennings
Personal Power, Anna Franklin
Pickingill Papers - The Origins of Gardnerian Wicca, Bill Liddell
Pillars of Tubal Cain, Nigel Jackson
Places of Pilgrimage and Healing, Adrian Cooper

Practical Divining, Richard Foord
Practical Meditation, Steve Hounsome
Practical Spirituality, Steve Hounsome
Psychic Self Defence - Real Solutions, Jan Brodie
Real Fairies, David Tame
Reality - How It Works & Why It Mostly Doesn't, Rik Dent
Romany Tapestry, Michael Houghton
Sacred Animals, Gordon MacLellan
Sacred Celtic Animals, Marion Davies, Ill. Simon Rouse
Sacred Dorset - On the Path of the Dragon, Peter Knight
Sacred Grove - The Mysteries of the Forest, Yvonne Aburrow
Sacred Geometry, Nigel Pennick
Sacred Nature, Ancient Wisdom & Modern Meanings, A Cooper
Sacred Ring - Pagan Origins of British Folk Festivals, M. Howard
Season of Sorcery - On Becoming a Wisewoman, Poppy Palin
Seasonal Magic - Diary of a Village Witch, Paddy Slade
Secret Places of the Goddess, Philip Heselton
Secret Signs & Sigils, Nigel Pennick
Spirits of the Earth series, Jaq D Hawkins
Stony Gaze, Investigating Celtic Heads John Billingsley
Symbols of Ancient Gods, Rhiannon Ryall
Talking to the Earth, Gordon MacLellan
Taming the Wolf - Full Moon Meditations, Steve Hounsome
Teachings of the Wisewomen, Rhiannon Ryall
The Other Kingdoms Speak, Helena Hawley
Tree: Essence of Healing, Simon & Sue Lilly
Tree: Essence, Spirit & Teacher, Simon & Sue Lilly
Understanding Chaos Magic, Jaq D Hawkins
Water Witches, Tony Steele
Way of the Magus, Michael Howard
Weaving a Web of Magic, Rhiannon Ryall
West Country Wicca, Rhiannon Ryall
Wildwitch - The Craft of the Natural Psychic, Poppy Palin
Wildwood King , Philip Kane
Wondrous Land - The Faery Faith of Ireland by Dr Kay Mullin
Working With the Merlin, Geoff Hughes

FREE detailed catalogue and FREE 'Inspiration' magazine

Contact: Capall Bann Publishing, Auton Farm, Milverton, Somerset, TA4 1NE

Some other titles from Capall Bann Publishing

Crystal Doorways by Sue & Simon Lilly

"Attuning oneself to one's self, and harmonising with the energies that surround one and one's immediate environment is the basis for this innovative book. For those who work with crystals regularly, on an amateur or professional basis, a copy of Sue and Simon's work should be a 'must' for your collection." British Astrological and Psychic Society Newsletter

"Crystal Doorways" focuses on a very particular system of using crystals and colour to bring about changes in your consciousness and an increasing understanding of the energy world around us. The idea of using crystals placed on and around the body has been known for a long time, but most layouts required a vast number of large and expensive crystals or an honours degree in geometry to work them out. Developed as a result of running many courses, 'Crystal Doorways' gives a clear, immediately understandable, system of "energy nets" using small, easily obtainable crystals. These energy nets are simple, usually only requiring small tumbled stones, but they can be extremely powerful. Each net is illustrated and described in full, with what stones to use, where to place them, potential uses and background information.   ISBN 1898307 98 9   £11.95

The Seer's Guide To Crystal and Gem Divination by Gale Hallaran

Gale is in the very pleasant position of being pushed and encouraged by many students of her students to produce this book. It is a fully comprehensive guide to working with crystals and gems for divination purposes, suitable for complete beginners and for competent astrologers, healers and seers alike. Gale lives and works in Glastonbury, where she lectures and writes about her work as a colour and crystal therapist, esoteric astrologer and counsellor. She runs the Inner Brilliance School of Healing, a well-established training school offering diplomas in both Crystal and Colour Therapy, which has students all over the UK and abroad. She also lectures at a local college offering nationally recognised qualifications in holistic crystal and colour therapy. ISBN 186163 2770   £11.95

Working With Crystals - A Practical Guide   Shirley O'Donoghue

An eminently practical book on the uses of crystals for healing. The history and theory of crystal healing is discussed, together with the various approaches to how and why crystal healing works. Attunements and subtle energy systems for the body, meditations and working with guides and working with angelic frequencies are all included here, together with possible barriers to successful healing and potential problems - and fixes - for the healer. In working with crystals you will encounter great wonder and even joy - this book, based as it is on sound, extensive experience and a profound belief in the ethics of working in this way and how it should be carried out will give inspiration and support to those wishing to work with crystals. ISBN 186163 191X   £9.95

Working With Natural Energy - A Beginner's Guide To Accessing and Working With Natural Energy Forces   Shirley o'Donoghue

Shirley is a Crystal Healer who runs courses on Psychic awareness and Crystal Energy. Here she shares her experience with us, giving us a basic guide to getting started. In easy to understand terms, we are given information on Dowsing; Human Energies; Chakras and how they are changing; Meridian and Auric Systems; Protection of the Energy Field; Crystals; Healing Using Light and Colour; Earth Energy, Plant Energies, Working With Plants and Trees; How to make our own essences and vibrational sprays; Solar and Lunar Energy and much more. A book everyone can learn from, whether experienced or not. ISBN 186163 1545   £7.95

402